A Master Class in Children's Literature

NCTE Editorial Board

A Master Class in Children's Literature

Trends and Issues in an Evolving Field

Edited by

April Whatley Bedford
University of New Orleans

Lettie K. Albright
Texas Woman's University

Foreword by
Amy A. McClure

NCTE

NATIONAL COUNCIL OF TEACHERS OF ENGLISH
1111 W. KENYON ROAD, URBANA, ILLINOIS 61801-1096

Manuscript Editor: Theresa L. Kay
Staff Editor: Bonny Graham
Interior Design: Jenny Jensen Greenleaf
Cover Design: Pat Mayer
Cover Image: iStockphoto.com/Andy_R

NCTE Stock Number: 30827

It is the policy of NCTE in its journals and other publications to provide a forum for the open discussion of ideas concerning the content and the teaching of English and the language arts. Publicity accorded to any particular point of view does not imply endorsement by the Executive Committee, the Board of Directors, or the membership at large, except in announcements of policy, where such endorsement is clearly specified.

Every effort has been made to provide current URLs and email addresses, but because of the rapidly changing nature of the Web, some sites and addresses may no longer be accessible.

Library of Congress Cataloging-in-Publication Data

Bedford, April, 1963–
    A master class in children's literature : trends and issues in an evolving field / April Whatley Bedford, Lettie K. Albright.
        p. cm.
    Includes bibliographical references and index.
    ISBN 978-0-8141-3082-7 (pbk)
    1. Children's literature—Study and teaching. 2. Children—Books and reading.
3. Education, Higher. I. Albright, Lettie K., 1961– II. Title.
    PN1008.8B43 2011
    809'.89282071—dc22

                                                                    2011003180

We dedicate this book to our loving and supportive husbands, Blair Bedford and Jon Muckley, and to our parents, who continually fostered our love of literature by making countless trips to bookstores and libraries. We also dedicate the book to the wonderful group that is the Children's Literature Assembly.

Contents

Foreword

A Seed Is Planted
Launching the Master Class

AMY A. MCCLURE, *Ohio Wesleyan University*

Sometimes the best ideas happen by chance—a casual comment, a wondering query, a memory jogged plants a seed that grows into a fully flowering idea. So it was with the Children's Literature Assembly (CLA) Master Class in Teaching Children's Literature. The class was conceived at the 1993 NCTE Annual Convention in Pittsburgh during one of those author dinners so many of us have had the opportunity to enjoy. Several CLA members—Amy Cohn (then CLA president), Carl Tomlinson (professor at Northern Illinois University), and Amy McClure (professor at Ohio Wesleyan University)—were enjoying a delightful dinner with author Steven Kellogg. As always, Steven was an entertaining dinner companion, interested in the worlds of classroom teaching, children's literature academia, and publishing. "How are you doing teaching future teachers about using books, when there is so much demand to teach phonics?" he asked. Conversation turned to the then-current debate about how to use children's books in classrooms when the political climate was demanding more phonics-based teaching.

At that time the debate between whole language and phonics teaching philosophies was raging, with much polarization between the two perspectives. Whole language proponents often felt beleaguered and besieged. Teacher educators, particularly those who taught children's literature courses and often had prepared those whole language teachers to use children's books wisely and effectively, also felt isolated and unsupported. Many of them wanted their children's literature courses to reflect their strong belief in and commitment to showing teachers how to create passionate, lifelong readers. Yet they had little training in how to do this. They typically had to accomplish this goal in a single course or less. Additionally, since many were the only children's literature specialists in their university, there were few opportunities to share teaching strategies, favorite books, or syllabi with colleagues.

We realized there was a need for professors of children's literature to come together to discuss our work. We needed to share how we organized our courses, how we handled the typically crushing workload, what books seemed to work magic in turning college students on to reading and other issues. And we also realized there was no forum for this kind of sharing at NCTE, International Reading Association, or any other conferences typically attended by this constituency.

How to do this? we wondered. Carl had attended an NCTE session when he was a young professor in which Janet Hickman from The Ohio State University and Diane Monson from the University of Minnesota had presented their children's literature course syllabi. He recalled how much help this had been as he started his work in the field. What if we had a "master class," taught each year by expert children's literature professors, to help people share effective teaching strategies for their children's literature courses? The presentations would be followed by opportunities for the audience to discuss the topic that had been presented, sharing insights and ideas with each other. We presented the idea to the CLA board. Their enthusiasm was such that we immediately began work on developing a class for the next Convention.

Our first class occurred at the 1994 NCTE Annual Convention in Orlando, Florida. Our objective was to bring together children's literature professors from departments of education, English, and library science so that we could overcome perceived differences among these departments and build a strong cohort of people who would likely wish to meet on a yearly basis. Speakers included Taimi Ranta from the Illinois State University English Department, John Stewig from the University of Wisconsin–Milwaukee, and Christine Francis from the University of Alberta (filling in for Jon Stott). Each spoke on the challenges and issues involved in teaching children's literature from various disciplinary perspectives. A standing-room-only crowd listened to the speakers and then stayed for dinner following the session.

Attendance grew at each subsequent session. Topics such as how to organize a children's literature course, how to construct syllabi, favorite children's books used, the merits of various textbooks, assessment strategies, and other relevant topics drew increasingly larger numbers of attendees. A critical part of each program was the opportunity to talk with colleagues, sharing experiences, questions, and challenges related to the session topic for that year.

An interesting outgrowth of the Master Class after several years was the National Survey of Children's Literature Teaching Practices, sponsored by the Children's Literature Assembly. Amy McClure and Carl Tomlinson surveyed CLA members across the country who were teaching children's literature at the university level, asking them to identify their textbook, children's books used for common readings, teaching strategies, evaluation tools, and the like. Instructors were also asked to describe the attitudes of their students regarding the crushing workload of the typical children's literature course and how they handled the same workload themselves. "Teaching Children's Literature at the College Level: A National Survey of Practices" was first presented at a Master Class and then published in the Spring 2000 issue of the *Journal of Children's Literature*.

Since its inception, the Master Class has evolved to include authors and illustrators of children's books in addition to university children's literature instructors as presenters. Themes for each annual class have been generated from conversations among CLA members about challenging issues they face in teaching their college courses. As the Master Class has developed to match the interests and needs of its audience, its planners remain committed to providing a forum for professors of children's literature to share effective strategies for promoting a love of literature in ever-changing political climates and diverse academic contexts.

A Master Class in Children's Literature: Trends and Issues in an Evolving Field celebrates the Master Class in Teaching Children's Literature. We are so pleased and gratified that our idea has come to fruition. Readers will find chapters from selected master classes that provide helpful guidance for structuring and teaching their own children's literature courses. After you read this book, we invite you to come to the current classes at each NCTE Annual Convention for further conversation with colleagues. You will leave refreshed and encouraged to continue the important work of helping prospective and practicing teachers and librarians become passionate about books. They, in turn, will share that passion with children. What a wonderful legacy for the Master Class!

Introduction

Introducing the Master Class

APRIL WHATLEY BEDFORD, *University of New Orleans*

LETTIE K. ALBRIGHT, *Texas Woman's University*

In her preface to this book, Amy McClure described how the Master Class in Teaching Children's Literature originated and how it has evolved over the years. She mentioned that the Master Class is now an annual event sponsored by the Children's Literature Assembly (CLA) at each National Council of Teachers of English (NCTE) Annual Convention. As editors, we would like to build on Amy's introduction by discussing who we, the members of CLA, are; the intended audience for this book; why we believe children's literature is important; and what we hope to accomplish by teaching courses in children's literature at the university level. We also preview the structure of the book and each of its upcoming chapters.

Who We Are

Members of the Children's Literature Assembly have one thing in common: we feel passionately about children's literature. Our membership is made up primarily of university instructors of courses in children's literature; most of us work in teacher education programs, some in English departments, and some in schools of library science. We also count among our numbers classroom teachers and librarians, those who are already opening up children's worlds through books and those who hope to learn more about how to do so effectively within the present-day realities of kindergarten through eighth-grade classrooms and libraries.

Truthfully, though, this doesn't tell much about who we really are. We'd like to paint a portrait of ourselves as passionate readers and teachers of children's literature by sharing a little more about the work we do and the way we act when we're together. Each year, we look forward with fervent anticipation to the NCTE Annual Convention. Observers will find groups of us excitedly talking about the best book we just read, our friendships founded on our mutual love of children's books; touring the exhibits to discover new delights from each publisher; and standing in line to obtain a priceless autograph or snap a treasured photo of children's authors and illustrators who are like rock stars to us. We eagerly attend all of the CLA-sponsored events, beginning with the Saturday evening Master Class in Teaching Children's Literature, where we are fully absorbed in learning from our colleagues, the experts in our field, about how to include cutting-edge topics in our children's literature courses. We buy tickets to the Sunday morning breakfast and the all-day Monday workshop to bask in the presence of authors, illustrators, and editors who captivate us with behind-the-scenes peeks into their work and worlds. We enthusiastically join the crowd at the presentation of the Notable Children's Books in the Language Arts, furiously scribbling notes about which honored books we must read *immediately*. Many of us spend countless hours tirelessly planning and bringing these events to fruition, knowing that we ourselves will enjoy and learn from them immensely. We also look forward to receiving the twice-yearly *Journal of Children's Literature*, a wonderful benefit of membership in CLA, and read cover-to-cover its pages filled with previews or recaps of convention activities and dynamic articles about teaching with children's books. We are thoroughly addicted to children's literature!

Whom This Book Is For

This edited volume is for anyone who has a passion for children's books. The Master Class was created for university instructors of children's literature who prepare elementary and middle school teachers and librarians so that they might share ideas and learn from their colleagues. This book will allow this audience to do just that. It will also appeal to those students that we teach: preservice and practicing classroom teachers and librarians who work with children in kindergarten through eighth grade. Anyone who wants to learn more about critical current issues in the field of children's literature will find much to ponder within these pages. In addition to addressing critical issues, all of the chapters include teaching strategies. Most of these strategies have been developed in our college classes to deepen the knowledge of adults who introduce literature to children, and most were designed to be adapted and applied for use with elementary and middle school students.

Why We Teach Children's Literature

We teach children's literature, quite simply, because we love it. Most of us fell in love with reading at an early age and have cherished memories of books that made indelible impressions on us as children. Teaching children's literature allows us the opportunity to continue the magic of reading aloud, introducing books, and discussing texts with undergraduate and graduate students. All of us who teach children's literature at the college level have experienced the thrill of helping adults who didn't love reading or books as children to become passionate about children's books, and it is the books themselves that ignite this ardor. Our work as instructors of children's literature is challenging and exciting and deeply fulfilling.

Why We Love Children's Literature

We, the editors of this volume and speaking on behalf of the Children's Literature Assembly, know that we are not alone in recognizing the value of children's books. Anita Silvey, former publisher of children's books for Houghton Mifflin, editor-in-chief of *The Horn Book Magazine*, and president of the Children's Book Council, recently edited *Everything I Need to Know I Learned from a Children's Book* (2009). This collection of essays from celebrities, leaders, and "notable people from all walks of life" highlights the books that these eminent individuals read as children that have resonated with them throughout their lives, inspiring them, motivating them, helping them to understand the complexities of life, and teaching them lessons by which to live.

All of the essayists in Silvey's (2009) collection discuss the impact that specific books had on their lives; many of them also elaborate on the worth of children's books in general. Novelist Meg Wolitzer wrote, "Good children's books give you an early sense of the multiple textures of the world. They remind you that there is, in fact, no single world—but many of them" (p. 77). Caldecott winner for both *The Polar Express* (1985) and *Jumanji* (1981), Chris Van Allsburg learned from reading *Harold and the Purple Crayon* (Johnson, 1983) that he could create his own world by creating books. Beloved author Judy Blume stated, "Some books you never forget. Some characters become your friends for life" (p. 85). These are the books that many of us turn to again and again, just like visiting old friends. Revisiting the books of our youth also allows us to return to our childhoods. Eric Rohmann, Caldecott-winning author/illustrator, attested, "Today when I read *Charlotte's Web* [White, 1952], I am a boy again" (p. 185).

Jerry J. Mallett, curator of the Mazza Museum of International Art from Picture Books, didn't read his first "quality" children's book until after he became a teacher, while he was taking his first children's literature course. He commented:

> What a wonderful life I have had being surrounded by the most marvelous art and literature imaginable. It all started with *The Twenty-One Balloons*. From it I learned that it is never too late to have your life changed by a children's book. (Silvey, 2009, p. 211)

Renowned educator Jack Pikulski credits reading children's books to his daughter as the impetus for reorienting his career from focusing on children with reading problems to opening up the world of children's literature to all readers. He commented that even now, in his "mature years," he still reads children's books and always will (p. 145).

At the 1997 Master Class in Teaching Children's Literature, which focused on "Uses and Abuses of Children's Literature in the Classroom," presenter Dan Hade posed a theory "based on the need to reestablish a 'spirituality' in our approach to children's literature" (Pierce, 1998, p. 103). Hade's theory expresses the reverence that all of us who teach children's literature at the college level feel about the subject of our work. Hade proposed four paths by which adults can invite children to experience the literature created for them:

- The positive path of awe, wonder, mystery, and delight.
- The negative path of living through pain and suffering, daring the dark, and confronting our fears.
- The creative path of playfulness, imagination, and giving birth to new perspectives.
- The transformative path of justice and compassion, where pain is transformed into compassionate, just action. (Pierce, 1998, p. 103)

Undergraduate and graduate courses in children's literature provide opportunities for preservice and practicing teachers and librarians to encounter books from each of these paths. Recently named National Ambassador for Young People's Literature, Katherine Paterson (the second to hold this position, succeeding author Jon Scieszka) wrote of the wonder she felt when she read *The Secret Garden* (Burnett, 1911) as a child (Silvey, 2009). Many of us introduce such wonder-inducing books in the beginning of our children's literature courses because they produce the same sense of awe, mystery, and delight in adult readers as they do in children (Martino, 2008).

While children's literature has been criticized over the past few decades for producing books that are too "dark" or deal with subjects that are too "heavy" for their intended audience, all children have fears and bad days. Unfortunately, too many experience pain and suffering on a daily basis. The best children's books that confront the negative side of life do so in masterful, age-appropriate ways that allow readers to better understand themselves and the world around them, providing both mirror and window (Bishop, 1990). In our courses, we attempt to balance these books with those that inspire joy and creativity. *Salon* magazine founder Laura Miller, writing about her first reading of *The Lion, the Witch, and the Wardrobe* (Lewis, 1950), said that this was the book that turned her into a reader because she discovered that someone else had an imagination like hers. She continued, "It showed me how I could tumble through a hole in a world I knew into another, better one, a world fresher, more brightly colored, more exhilarating, more fully felt than my own" (Silvey, 2009, p. 65). Many adult readers make these new discoveries of imagination for the first time in their college children's literature courses.

Finally, we believe that children's literature can be transformative—for both children and adults—and we hope that the students who enter our classes will be moved to take action for social justice by the books we share with them and in turn will foster transformative reading in the children they teach. In her article "Taking Children's Literature Seriously: Reading for Pleasure and Social Change," our colleague Vivian Yenika-Agbaw (1997) argues that inviting children to read for pleasure is necessary but not enough, and she asserts that even young children can be taught to read critically and to identify racism, sexism, and other prejudices that reproduce an unjust society.

What We Hope to Accomplish

In 1997, Dan Hade challenged attendees at the Master Class in Teaching Children's Literature "to develop our own theories about the central importance of literature" in the classroom rather than relying on policymakers, school administrators, textbook publishers, or other constituencies to make these decisions for us (Pierce, 1998, p. 103). Members of the Children's Literature Assembly have been grappling with this challenge ever since, and developing—and sharing—our theories about the primacy of children's literature at the college level and in elementary and middle school classrooms has been at the heart of every Master Class and every other CLA-sponsored event. We, as editors, have also responded to Dan's call in creating a conceptual framework for the contents of this book. Based on our attendance at Master Classes over a number of years, our reading of the articles originally written about those classes, our work with chapter authors for this book, and hundreds of informal conversations with colleagues about our teaching habits and goals, we believe that college courses in children's literature should foster passion, connoisseurship, and generativity.

Passion

We have already discussed our passion for children's literature but want to reiterate here that we believe all elementary teachers and librarians should be passionate about children's literature to ignite that same passion in the children they do and will teach. The amazing body of children's literature that has been published and the creative and innovative publications that are currently being produced assure that teaching with children's literature should never get stale. It is in children's literature courses at the college level that preservice teachers discover—often for the first time—the wealth of books available to children and also where they learn how to make these books a vital part of classroom instruction and daily school life.

Those of us who teach college children's literature courses are shocked and disheartened when we encounter teacher candidates or practicing teachers who are not readers themselves, but unfortunately this happens far too often. Susan Gebhard (2006) writes movingly about when this happened to her the first time she taught children's literature at the college level and how she changed her teaching as a result of discovering that many of the students in her class had not had positive experiences with books or reading. By immersing her students in literature and allowing her own excitement for reading children's books to be evident to her students, a number of them became enthusiastic readers for the first time in their lives. Gebhard wrote about this experience: "It seemed imperative for me to instill in them a sense that reading can and should be fun—and that it was okay to display an over-the-top love for books!" (p. 459). Gebhard believed that her passion would be contagious to her students, and it was.

This "over-the-top love for books" is what we hope to demonstrate for our students and to instill in them, always with the ultimate goal that they will inspire the same passion in generations of elementary and middle school students. Children's literature researchers provide substantial evidence of the positive effects a teacher's reading behaviors can have on students' reading practices, and all of these researchers cite a teacher's knowledge, love, and sharing of children's books as the keys to producing these positive effects (Dreher, 2002–03;

Kolloff, 2002; Layne, 2009; Worthy, 2002). Applegate and Applegate (2004) surveyed 195 prospective teachers and found that 54.3 percent of the respondents were "unenthusiastic" or unengaged readers. We have seen similar proportions in our own teaching, but the good news, based in our experience and supported by all the previously cited studies, is that it is never too late to change an unenthusiastic, unengaged reader into an enthusiastic, engaged, passionate reader. This happens routinely in college children's literature courses, and forums such as the Master Class ensure that we will continue to strengthen our teaching so these transformations keep happening.

Connoisseurship

Nurturing teachers and librarians to be passionate about children's literature is not enough, however. The Master Class was designed for those instructors of college children's literature courses—already passionate about their chosen field—as a forum for connoisseurs of children's literature to share their expertise with one another. By definition, a connoisseur is "a person who is especially competent to pass critical judgments in an art, particularly one of the fine arts, or in matters of taste" as well as "a discerning judge of the best in any field." The chapters of this book address issues that will assist teachers, librarians, and children in becoming connoisseurs of children's literature.

The application of connoisseurship to the arena of education originated with Eliot Eisner (Smith, 2005), and we believe that his understandings of connoisseurship apply perfectly to the field of children's literature. We suggest that adults who are connoisseurs of children's literature read children's books first and foremost for their own aesthetic enjoyment. They appreciate what children's books have to offer them as adult readers. For Eisner (1998), connoisseurship and criticism work hand in hand, with the connoisseur appreciating a work of art (or an educational practice or a children's book) and the critic delving further to evaluate that same work of art and share that evaluation publicly.

We believe that even children as young as kindergarten age are capable of becoming children's literature connoisseurs. Former CLA board member Glenna Sloan wrote the seminal *Child as Critic* (2003), now in its fourth edition, and was one of the first to advocate for developing a kind of connoisseurship among child readers. Our goal as college instructors of children's literature is to prepare teachers and librarians who are such connoisseurs of children's literature themselves that they will ignite a passion in the children with whom they work so that, as adults, those children can look back and remember the children's books that changed their lives.

Generativity

At the 1996 Master Class in Teaching Children's Literature, Rudine Sims Bishop of The Ohio State University spoke about how the knowledge that preservice and inservice teachers gain in their college children's literature courses should enable them to become generative (Pavonetti, 1997), meaning "with productive capability." Specifically, she asserted that teachers need a knowledge base that allows them to become generative—capable of making productive decisions—in three areas: building a classroom library; creating themed instructional cycles based on children's literature and connected across genres; and selecting children's books to "enrich the total curriculum" (p. 67). Helping our students make informed decisions about building their classroom libraries is always a paramount goal for those of us who work with current and future teachers.

In our teaching, college instructors of children's literature in teacher preparation programs also thoroughly address the second and third areas introduced by Bishop, and many CLA members who contributed to this volume have also published widely on ways to incorporate children's literature throughout the elementary and middle school curriculum. Both Janelle Mathis and Kathy Short have focused much of their scholarship on text sets and thematic, literature-based curriculum (see, for example, Mathis, 2002; Short, Schroeder, Laird, Kauffman, Ferguson, & Crawford, 1996). *Children's Literature and Learning: Literary Study Across the Curriculum* by Barbara Lehman (2007); *Children's Literature in the Reading Program: An Invitation to Read,* edited by Deborah Wooten and Bernice Cullinan (2009); and *The Wonder of It All: When Literature and Literacy Intersect* by Nancy J. Johnson and Cyndi Giorgis (2007) all offer numerous theoretically based instructional strategies that foster both literary and literacy learning for diverse students. We would add to Bishop's recommendations that teachers and librarians both should possess the generativity to work together to incorporate children's literature throughout the elementary and middle school curriculum.

We would also add a fourth area in which both teachers and librarians should be generative: advocacy. We hope—and believe—that prospective and practicing teachers and librarians who are exposed to all that children's literature has to offer them as professionals and the students with whom they work will become advocates and activists for the inclusion of literature in the elementary and middle school literacy program; the importance of self-selected, independent reading for all students in kindergarten through grade 8; the building of classroom libraries; and even the existence of school libraries—all of which have been threatened, and in many places have disappeared, over the past decade. In 2000, Miriam Martinez (a contributor to this volume) and Lea McGee were asked by the editors of *Reading Research Quarterly* to examine the role of children's literature in past and present reading instruction and to make predictions about children's literature for the future decade. At that time, these authors were encouraged by the exponential growth in children's book publishing; the advances in quality of picture books, historical fiction, and nonfiction; and the increasing recommendations of reading researchers and textbook authors to include literature in literacy instruction, all of which had occurred during the previous decade. They predicted that an increasingly diverse student population would demand the publication and classroom inclusion of more books in which students could see themselves, and they also predicted that the development of online and digital literacies would influence both publication and instruction in ways that couldn't be imagined.

A decade has passed since Martinez and McGee conducted their review, and their two predictions have been realized. What they could not have predicted at the hopeful dawning of the new millennium was the way the political climate that dominated most of the next decade would result in a narrow, skills-based, standardized test–driven definition of reading founded on state and federally sanctioned and scripted instructional materials developed from "scientifically based reading research." Instead, the authors anticipated a broadened definition of literacy that "suggests that only literature provides the multiple layers of meaning necessary for acquiring the strategies, stances, and ways of deep thinking that we are coming to define as literacy" (Martinez & McGee, 2000, p. 167). While we believe that Martinez and McGee's assertion is true of the world in which we live, the schools in which teachers and librarians work and children learn have, for the most part, become more constricted in the past decade than ever before.

The national movement for teachers to use a skills-based, scripted curriculum to teach reading not only has resulted in a loss of time and space for literature in classrooms and schools but also has "trickled up" to influence the ways in which reading methods courses are taught at universities, with many universities being hounded by state departments of education and local school districts to design their courses based on these classroom realities. In some cases, university programs and professors have acquiesced; others have fought (Brenner, 2007). Coupled with changes in reading methods courses has been the elimination of children's literature courses in many teacher preparation programs (National Council of Teachers of English, 2001).

These movements led NCTE to reaffirm its commitment to literature-based teaching through two resolutions (National Council of Teachers of English, 2001, 2006). Hoewisch (2000) presents a thorough case for the importance of children's literature courses in teacher preparation programs. We believe that becoming advocates for children's literature will require teachers and librarians who are deeply knowledgeable about the theoretical, research, and policy supports for keeping children's literature vibrantly alive in schools, and we assert that this knowledge is most likely to be acquired through college courses in children's literature.

How This Book Is Organized

Rather than a chronological retrospective of the Master Classes in Teaching Children's Literature in the order in which they occurred, this book is divided into three sections: "Laying the Foundation," which includes three chapters; "Broadening Our Reading Worlds," which includes five chapters; and "Responding to Challenges, Celebrating Possibilities," which includes four chapters. Below is a brief introduction to each section and the chapters included. At the time each Master Class occurred, an article recounting its major points was published in the *Journal of Children's Literature*, and those references are included in the following overview.

Laying the Foundation

Chapters in this section focus on how educators might structure university-level children's literature courses; what some of the issues are that are currently at the forefront of the field; and how to encourage a variety of responses to literature. We begin this section the way the Master Class actually began, by looking at alternative ways of teaching children's literature at the college level. That Master Class was held in 1996, and speakers included Rudine Sims Bishop of The Ohio State University; Christine Francis of the University of Alberta; and Kathy Short of the University of Arizona (Pavonetti, 1997). In "What's Going On in Children's Literature Classes?" (Chapter 1), Miriam Martinez and CLA Past President Nancy Roser return to this topic more than a decade later by analyzing 55 children's literature syllabi and talking in depth with four noted professors about how they organize their courses.

In Chapter 2, "Uses and Abuses of Children's Literature," CLA Past President Evelyn B. Freeman looks closely at four current trends and issues in the field of children's literature—books as commodities; technology and books; genres of children's literature; and reading for pleasure—and evaluates the positives and negatives of each. The Master Class that originally considered uses and abuses of children's literature in the classroom was held in 1997, where speaker Dan Hade of Pennsylvania State University raised issues about how and by whom the importance of children's literature in the elementary classroom is established; Freeman of The Ohio State University discussed trends in nonfiction and informational texts for children; and Shirley Crenshaw of Westminster College urged participants to evaluate their own teaching and syllabi by reflecting on the values and theories they hoped to address in their courses (Pierce, 1998).

One of the foundations of all college-level children's literature courses is awareness of the myriad ways readers might respond to children's books. This was the theme of the 1999 Master Class, at which Rick Kerper of Millersville University shared a project he developed for responding to Caldecott Award–winning picture books; Janelle Mathis of the University of North Texas described her work with personal text sets; and Nancy Johnson of Western Washington University explained a strategy she developed in response to Lois Lowry's *The Giver* (1993), where students create a "story arc or story ray" (Giorgis, 2000, p. 75). In Chapter 3, CLA Past President Marjorie R. Hancock, known for her work in children's literature and response, revisits Louise Rosenblatt's (1938) reader response theory and considers how readers might respond to children's literature in the second decade of the 21st century and beyond.

Broadening Our Reading Worlds

This section focuses on the importance of children's literature professors knowing deeply the characteristics and elements of children's literature as well as ways to engage readers with literature. This knowledge is first communicated in college classrooms and then passed along to the children with whom students in these college courses will work. Chapters in this section move beyond the image of reader as engaged but passive to the role that reading plays in creating a more just and equitable—as well as interconnected—world. Each chapter in this section emphasizes a particular type of book or category of literature.

Chapter 4 highlights the art of the picture book, just as the 2000 Master Class did. At that class, Barbara Kiefer, then at Teacher's College, spoke about her experience as chair of the 2000 Caldecott Award committee; Michael Tunnell of Brigham Young University shared his experiences as a picture book author, and Barbara Elleman of Marquette University described her work on a biography about picture book author/illustrator Tomie dePaola (Giorgis & Johnson, 2001). In her chapter for this text, Cyndi Giorgis provides numerous strategies for studying and responding to picture books that teachers and librarians can use with children.

The focus of the 1988 Master Class was children's literature about mathematics, and CLA Past President Terrell Young and his colleagues Amy Roth McDuffie and Barbara Ward return to that topic in Chapter 5. At that class, Cyndi Giorgis of the University of Las Vegas shared the results of two action research studies she conducted about children's mathematical responses to literature, and Patricia Austin of the University of New Orleans discussed criteria that children's literature with mathematical dimensions should meet and analyzed specific examples of such books (Young, 1999). In their chapter, Young, Roth McDuffie, and Ward consider books with mathematical dimensions published in the past decade and provide a model for helping educators make thoughtful decisions about *which* books to share with children and *ways* to share those books that can be applied to other genres of literature as well.

Multicultural children's literature is a topic that was highly important when it was the focus of the Master Class in 2007 (Ernst & Mathis, 2008), and its importance has continued to grow since then. At the Master Class, author Sharon Flake and illustrator E. B. Lewis captivated the audience with stories about why they create books in which African American readers might see themselves. In Chapter 6 of this text, Janelle B. Mathis expands the topic to consider the increase in books published representing a range of cultures and ways to respond to multicultural literature within a contemporary context.

One specific culture beginning to be represented in children's books is the lesbian, gay, bisexual, transgender, and questioning/queer (LGBTQ) community. These books, though absolutely necessary, are still highly controversial. Why these books are important and ways in which college children's literature instructors handle the controversy that surrounds them were the subjects of the 2005 Master Class in Teaching Children's Literature. Speakers at that class included authors Nancy Garden and James Howe and professors Linda Lamme of the University of Florida and Patricia Austin of the University of New Orleans (Albright & Bedford, 2006). In Chapter 7, April Whatley Bedford reviews the body of children's literature with LGBTQ characters and ways to nurture gender diversity through children's books.

An area of interest to many children's literature instructors but a field of expertise to only a handful, international children's literature was the topic of the 2002 Master Class. Hazel Rochman, reviewer and editor for *Booklist*, opened that session with a moving speech about her experiences as an immigrant, followed by presentations from professors Junko Yokota of National Louis University, Barbara Lehman of The Ohio State University, and Elizabeth Poe, then of West Virginia University, about the ways in which they incorporate international children's literature into their teaching (Hancock, 2003). In Chapter 8, Kathy G. Short provides compelling reasons for including international literature in children's literature courses as well as guidance for how to do so effectively.

Responding to Challenges, Celebrating Possibilities

The final section in this volume focuses on recent trends in the field of children's literature that offer possibilities as well as dangers. All children deserve the right to read for pleasure, to read for their own purposes beyond those required in the classroom, and to have access to books that will make them more socially aware and active citizens. The last chapter in this section focuses on this notion as well as on the idea of "generativity"—teachers and librarians as capable, informed, and effective decision-makers about children's literature.

One challenge to the field of children's literature in the new millennium has been the phenomenon of children's books achieving the status of bestsellers. While this would seem to be a positive movement, it also has its drawbacks; thus, the impetus for selecting children's books as bestsellers was the subject of the 2003 Master Class. At the class, speakers included Patricia Austin of the University of New Orleans and Barbara Lehman of The Ohio State University, bestselling children's author Nancy Farmer, and children's book editor Judy O'Malley (Vardell, 2004). Each looked at the topic from a different perspective, and Barbara A. Lehman and April Bedford give an expanded view of each of those perspectives in Chapter 9.

Like the bestseller phenomenon, the ever-changing world of technology has influenced children's literature in countless ways. At the 2004 Master Class, Michael Joseph of Rutgers University and creator of the Child_Lit discussion list; Cynthia Leitich Smith, a children's author with an extensive and active website; Terry Borzumato, then representing Random House Publishing; and Sylvia Vardell, professor and CLA past president, each described how the Internet had changed their work in children's literature (Bedford, 2005). Sylvia M. Vardell revisits those topics, along with new technological advances, in Chapter 10.

Challenges to children's literature often come in the form of threats of censorship or demands to remove books from classroom or library shelves. Responding to censorship challenges was the subject of the 2001 Master Class, where author Lois Lowry spoke about her reactions to having some of her books challenged, and Ginny Moore Kruse, director of the Cooperative Children's Book Center, offered valuable advice to teachers and librarians dealing with threats of censorship (Pavonetti, 2002). Linda M. Pavonetti furthers those topics in Chapter 11.

The final challenge discussed in this section is how to foster children's love for literature in a high-stakes testing environment. This was the climate in which educators and children were ensconced at the time of the Master Class in 2006, and unfortunately, things have changed little since then. In 2006, four speakers shared their insights about keeping the love of literature alive in such an environment: authors Jim Murphy and Candace Fleming and professors Nancy Roser of the University of Texas and Kathy Short of the University of Arizona (Mathis & Albright, 2007). In Chapter 12 of this volume, Lettie K. Albright offers recommendations to help teachers and librarians advocate for the inclusion of children's literature in elementary and middle schools.

Conclusion

To conclude this text, we return to the conceptual framework we established in the beginning of this introduction and consider how to develop passion, connoisseurship, and generativity in response to each of the issues addressed in the preceding chapters. We also examine themes across Master Class topics and pose lingering questions related to each topic. Finally, we offer recommendations to help teachers interrogate their own teaching with the goal of making it increasingly literature-based.

Works Cited

Albright, L. K., & Bedford, A. W. (2006). Master class in teaching children's literature: From resistance to acceptance—introducing books with gay and lesbian characters. *Journal of Children's Literature, 32*(1), 9–15.

Applegate, A. J., & Applegate, M. D. (2004). The Peter effect: Reading habits and attitudes of preservice teachers. *The Reading Teacher, 57*, 554–563.

Bedford, A. W. (2005). Master class in the teaching of children's literature: From *Charlotte's Web* to the World Wide Web: The impact of the Internet on the field of children's literature. *Journal of Children's Literature, 31*(1), 11–17.

Bishop, R. S. (1990). Mirrors, windows, and sliding glass doors. *Perspectives: Choosing and Using Books for the Classroom, 6*(3), ix–xi.

Brenner, D. (2007). Strategies for becoming involved in policy: What was learned when faculty opposed a stand-alone course in phonics. *Journal of Literacy Research, 39*, 163–171.

Dreher, M. J. (2002–2003). Motivating teachers to read. *The Reading Teacher, 56*, 338–340.

Eisner, E. W. (1998). *The enlightened eye: Qualitative inquiry and the enhancement of educational practice.* Upper Saddle River, NJ: Merrill.

Ernst, S. B., & Mathis, J. B. (2008). Multicultural literature: Reading, writing, and responding within a "new" literacy context. *Journal of Children's Literature, 34*(1), 10–12.

Gebhard, S. (2006). The lost boys (and girls): Readers in Neverland. *Journal of Teacher Education, 57*, 454–463.

Giorgis, C. (2000). Supporting student responses to literature: A master class in the teaching of children's literature. *Journal of Children's Literature, 26*(1), 74–77.

Giorgis, C., & Johnson, N. J. (2001). Gaining insight into picture book illustration and design: A master class in the teaching of children's literature. *Journal of Children's Literature, 27*(1), 62–63.

Hancock, M. R. (2003). Incorporating international children's literature into college level children's literature courses: A master class in the teaching of children's literature. *Journal of Children's Literature, 29*(1), 14–19.

Hoewisch, A. K. (2000, February). Children's literature in teacher-preparation programs. *Reading Online*. Retrieved from http://www.readingonline.org/critical/hoewisch/childrenlit.html

Johnson, N. J., & Giorgis, C. (2007). *The wonder of it all: When literature and literacy intersect.* Portsmouth, NH: Heinemann.

Kolloff, P. B. (2002). Why teachers need to be readers. *Gifted Child Today, 25*(2), 50–54, 64.

Layne, S. L. (2009). *Igniting a passion for reading: Successful strategies for building lifetime readers*. Portland, ME: Stenhouse.

Lehman, B. A. (2007). *Children's literature and learning: Literary study across the curriculum.* New York: Teachers College Press.

Martinez, M. G., & McGee, L. M. (2000). Children's literature and reading instruction: Past, present, and future. *Reading Research Quarterly, 35*, 154–169.

Martino, A. (2008). Wonder rediscovered in children's books. *Chronicle of Higher Education, 55*(17), B-28.

Mathis, J. B. (2002). Picture book text sets: A novel approach to understanding theme. *Clearing House, 75*(3), 127–131.

Mathis, J. B., & Albright, L. K. (2007). Keeping the love of literature alive in this high-stakes testing environment. *Journal of Children's Literature, 33*(1), 14–19.

National Council of Teachers of English. (2001). *Resolution on preparing and certifying teachers with knowledge of children's and adolescent literature*. Retrieved from http://www.ncte.org/positions/statements/childrensadollit

National Council of Teachers of English. (2006). *Resolution on the essential roles and value of literature in the curriculum*. Retrieved from http://www.ncte.org/positions/statements/valueofliterature

Pavonetti, L. (1997). Conversations among colleagues: A master class in teaching children's literature. *Journal of Children's Literature, 23*(1), 66–69.

Pavonetti, L. M. (2002). It seems important that we should have the right to read . . . . *Journal of Children's Literature, 28*(1), 9–15.

Pierce, K. M. (1998). Uses and abuses of children's literature in the classroom: Master class for teaching college level children's literature courses. *Journal of Children's Literature, 24*(1), 103–105.

Rosenblatt, L. M. (1938). *Literature as exploration*. New York: Appleton-Century.

Short, K. G., Schroeder, J., Laird, J., Kauffman, G., Ferguson, M. J., & Crawford, K. M. (1996). *Learning together through inquiry: From Columbus to integrated curriculum*. Portland, ME: Stenhouse.

Silvey, A. (Ed.). (2009). *Everything I need to know I learned from a children's book: Life lessons from notable people from all walks of life*. New York: Roaring Brook Press.

Sloan, G. (2003). *The child as critic: Developing literacy through literature, K–8* (4th ed.). New York: Teachers College Press.

Smith, M. K. (2005). Elliot W. Eisner, connoisseurship, criticism and the art of education. *The Encyclopedia of Informal Education*. Retrieved from www.infed.org/thinkers/eisner.htm

Vardell, S. M. (2004). Children's books as best sellers: Their impact on the field of children's literature. *Journal of Children's Literature, 30*(1), 13–18.

Wooten, D. A., & Cullinan, B. E. (Eds.). (2009). *Children's literature in the reading program: An invitation to read*. Newark, DE: International Reading Association.

Worthy, J. (2002). What makes intermediate-grade students want to read? *The Reading Teacher, 55*, 568–569.

Yenika-Agbaw, V. (1997). Taking children's literature seriously: Reading for pleasure and social change. *Language Arts, 74*, 446–453.

Young, T. (1999). Master class: Children's literature and mathematics—an unhealthy alliance? *Journal of Children's Literature, 25*(1), 70–71.

Children's Books Cited

Burnett, F. H. (1911). *The secret garden*. New York: F.A. Stokes.

Johnson, C. (1983). *Harold and the purple crayon*. New York: HarperCollins.

Lewis, C. S. (1950). *The lion, the witch, and the wardrobe*. New York: MacMillan.

Lowry, L. (1993). *The giver*. Boston: Houghton Mifflin.

Van Allsburg, C. (1981). *Jumanji*. New York: Houghton Mifflin.

Van Allsburg, C. (1985). *The Polar Express*. New York: Houghton Mifflin.

White, E. B. (1952). *Charlotte's web* (G. Williams, Illus.). New York: Harper.

1

Laying the Foundation

What's Going On in Children's Literature Classes?

MIRIAM MARTINEZ, *University of Texas at San Antonio*

NANCY L. ROSER, *University of Texas at Austin*

In its "Resolution on Preparing and Certifying Teachers with Knowledge of Children's and Adolescent Literature," the National Council of Teachers of English (2001) called for the preparation of teachers "with strong content and pedagogical knowledge of children's and/or adolescent literature." In particular, this resolution advocated that teacher preparation programs provide candidates with broad knowledge of children's literature, as well as strategies for installing that literature in classrooms. Although we (and others) have described the waxing and waning roles of children's literature in elementary classrooms (Martinez & McGee, 2000; Roser & Martinez, 2000; Walmsley, 1992), it seems somewhat more difficult to document just how today's teachers are being equipped with this "strong content and pedagogical knowledge" of children's literature. We chose to examine a portion of the "infrastructure" of teacher knowledge by surveying the syllabi of college and university classes that introduce children's literature to the children's teachers. We also interviewed a small sample of college and university level professors of children's literature—in an attempt to learn how they work to make teachers both knowing and deeply appreciative of books for children.

For this chapter we asked: What do current children's literature courses designed to prepare and certify teachers contain and require? How are teachers being made competent for teaching with and through literature? How are courses attempting to supply the understandings that will make literature study serious, purposeful, satisfying, and essential for children's learning? But first, we attempted to pin down what might be some central, agreed-on, and clear goals of teaching children's literature to teachers.

What Should Teachers Know about Children's Literature?

When Sam Sebesta (2001), a dynamic, knowledgeable, and veteran professor of children's literature, addressed "what teachers need to know about children's literature" in *The New Advocate,* he reminded readers of the need to use selection aids and to read, read, read. Sebesta also emphasized the importance of teachers developing a set of defensible criteria for book selection; of learning to deeply enjoy children's books; of keeping abreast of the "underground" movement in children's literature; and of providing space and time for young readers' responses in classrooms. Based on experts like Sebesta and the creators of dozens of syllabi we examined, we offer three central goals for children's literature courses. Courses designed to develop knowing and strategic teachers whose classrooms thrive on children's literature should do the following:

- Help teachers develop familiarity with quality children's books broadly representative of our world.
- Support teachers' deeper understandings of literary texts (e.g., texts' power to engage, their qualities and craft, their invitations to respond).
- Guide teachers toward acquiring instructional strategies that help children to read deeply, interpretively, and joyfully.

We next elaborate each of these goals as a way of contextualizing how contemporary college and university courses seem to regard the tasks of preparing teachers who both lean on literature to teach and who teach children about literature. In the final section, we describe our procedures for procuring and examining course syllabi for children's literature—and some promising practices.

Goal 1: Children's literature courses should help teachers develop familiarity with quality children's books broadly representative of our world.

If teacher candidates are to be prepared to connect children with books that appeal, to select books for the curriculum, and to share books in ways that stretch the experience of being human, there are implications for their coursework. Surely, courses in literature and literacy must surround teacher candidates with well-chosen exemplars, give them plenty of opportunities to read and reflect, and offer ways to read and talk with children about books.

There was a time in our nation's history when there was little (if any) need to take deliberate steps to prepare teachers in a specific course titled Children's

Literature due to the paucity of published literature for children. Although literacy was expanding markedly in the nineteenth century in the United States, schoolchildren read predominantly moralistic and didactic texts (soon gathered into graded series) designed to ensure a uniformity of values, ideas, and experiences for a new nation.

In the lifetimes of our own parents and grandparents, however, US publishers produced substantially more books for children and, increasingly, those books have begun to reflect the diversity of classrooms. In 1930, fewer than a thousand books for children were published in the United States, but by 2006 that number exceeded 13,000 (American Library Association, 2007). Given the volume of children's books in print, keeping fully apprised of books for children is next to impossible—even for those who work full-time in the field of children's literature. Anita Silvey, editor emerita of *The Horn Book*, professes to reading 2,000 children's books a year. At that rate, it would take Silvey 125 years to read the quarter million children's books currently in print (Bowker, 2008). Even if a teacher intended to do a lot of skimming, or to read only books that appeared on award lists, the challenge would still be huge. As Sebesta (2001) wryly noted, if there were just an agreed-on canon of children's books that all teachers should know, knowledge demands would be much simplified. Yet, given the range of readers, curricula, and interests in today's classrooms, there is (thankfully) no one list. Rather, teacher candidates (through their coursework) not only need introduction to a wealth of compelling books to read deeply, but also acquaintance with book selection tools that help them to select quality books for their classrooms. In today's diverse classrooms, ripe with potential for new literacies, even selection aids are not a simple set. Instead, teachers need familiarity with a variety of print and electronic resources that steer them toward books for *all* the children and across the day.

Goal 2: Children's literature courses should support teachers' deeper understandings of literary texts (e.g., their power to engage, the qualities of their crafting, their invitations to respond).

Not so long ago, secondary teachers claimed the larger stake in the teaching of literature, often defining their task as helping students analyze texts based on literary elements and merits. Meanwhile, inside elementary schools, teachers saw their role as monitoring (largely through questions) their children's comprehension of adopted texts. One explanation for the differences in teachers' stances across levels of schooling lay with the texts themselves. Those available to elementary teachers were often purposefully constructed with planful vocabulary repetitions, adapted to match readability formulae, and gathered into grade-level volumes intended to serve literacy. Another explanation for differences in the treatment of texts may have been that elementary teacher preparation focused on teaching reading rather than on guiding thoughtful encounters with literature.

In our own historical analysis of reading methods textbooks and courses of study used to educate elementary teachers across 100 years (Martinez & Roser, 1982), we found that the teachers' textbooks made little mention of trade books in the classroom. With the single exception of teacher education textbooks of the late 1800s, authors of reading methods textbooks appeared to view children's literature as playing only a peripheral or enrichment role in instruction.

From the late 1980s to the mid-1990s, in concert with the whole language movement and scattered state initiatives, came a dramatic change in the role of authentic literature in US classrooms. In this golden period for children's literature—perhaps more than any time before or since—children's trade books received unprecedented attention by educators (Martinez & McGee, 2000). Trade books were promoted as key instructional tools both in the literacy program and across the curriculum. Researchers, intent on children's meaning making through talk, writing, and other means, initiated classroom studies that gave support for a curriculum with literature as its center. State standards began to prescribe that children and young adults be introduced to a wide range of literary genres and discourse types. Teachers themselves began to look at story time and literature study not as peripherals or enrichment, but as critical spaces for classroom inquiry.

It seemed an agreed-on goal that courses in literature and literacy should expose teacher candidates to the complexities (and concomitant satisfactions) of genuine literary experiences so that children, too, could explore literature because they simply couldn't help themselves. Contemporary children's literature courses, set amid today's more narrowed curricula and concerns for measurable outcomes, tend to hold fast to the goals of providing time, resources, and rationale for teacher candidates to explore their own ideas about the demands of particular texts, their own ways of observing language and images closely, and their own useful patterns for participating in communities of meaning makers.

Current models of literary meaning-making, based on the work of theorists such as Louise Rosenblatt (1995), give the reader equal footing with the text. Readers become critical contributors to what Rosenblatt terms the evoked poem. Nevertheless, if teacher candidates themselves have been taught that texts have an obtuse central theme and that their job as readers (or teachers) is to ferret that theme, they have learned to privilege the text over the reader. Courses in children's literature, then, must reteach teachers to trust children (and themselves) to make supportable meanings that will astound.

We have learned about astonishing meaning making through observation and classroom studies of literary transactions. Perhaps young readers' richest understandings are made possible through social interactions—what Fish (1980) has called interpretive communities. Instructors of children's literature must also aim toward helping teacher candidates understand the nature of the reader/text transaction and its implications for classroom instruction.

Goal 3: Guide teachers toward acquiring instructional strategies that help children to read deeply, interpretively, and joyfully.

As mentioned above, there has been only limited research focused on teacher preparation in children's literature. In 1968, National Council of Teachers of English (NCTE) published a report on *Teaching Children's Literature in Colleges and Universities* (Landau, 1968), reporting responses of 573 instructors of children's literature courses. Nearly two decades later, the Children's Literature Assembly of NCTE conducted a national survey of teachers of Children's Literature in English, Education, and Library Science departments in US colleges and universities (CLA, 1968, as cited by McClure & Tomlinson, 2000). In 2000, McClure and Tomlinson surveyed members of the Children's Literature Assembly who were teaching graduate and undergraduate courses in children's literature.

Inferring from the results of these surveys, it is possible to conclude that teachers of children's literature choose meaty, award-winning books, and plan for both individual response and group discussions of those books. To ensure those same sorts of interpretive communities in elementary classrooms, it seems logical that teacher candidates must become familiar with different approaches for organizing for literature study (e.g., Many & Wiseman, 1992; Wiseman, Many, & Altieri, 1992); with ways of guiding literature discussion (e.g., Eeds & Peterson, 1991; Raphael & McMahon, 1994; Smith, 1990); and with ways of interpreting, analyzing, and extending children's thoughtful, responsive talk and actions (Short, 1993; Sipe, 2008). In particular, children's literature courses must help teachers develop facility in using particular instructional invitations—such as journals, visual representations, and dramatic enactments—that support children's transactions with literature.

Taking a Closer Look at Children's Literature Courses

The central tenet of all three goals is that teacher candidates be prepared to select quality literature, organize for literature study, and support and guide children's transactions with literature. Inherent in these goals is that teachers themselves become joyful readers of children's literature. To learn more about how these goals are represented in the preparation of future elementary teachers, we requested, gathered, and analyzed syllabi used in children's literature courses across the United States. We recognize the limitations of the sample in terms of its volunteer status. We recognize, too, the limitations of any syllabus to transmit the life force of a course or a classroom. Surely no syllabus, however detailed in its presentation of course goals, required readings, and course assignments, can reflect the enthusiasm of a group becoming bookworms and bibliophiles together. Even so, after sorting out the goals and required readings, we found descriptions of course assignments that pointed toward rich learning experiences that seemed to stretch beyond traditional assignments. To elaborate the information we gleaned from the syllabi, we contacted and interviewed selected instructors of children's literature whose syllabi revealed particularly fresh, original (and sound) approaches to preparing teachers.

Data Collection and Analysis

As a window on current practices in teaching children's literature, we searched the Internet for postings of current syllabi used in children's literature courses and used discussion lists of organizations, such as the Children's Literature Assembly, to request course syllabi from instructors. Both requests and follow-up attempts netted a total of 55 syllabi, representing 37 different institutions in 22 states. Of these syllabi, 39 were used in undergraduate courses and 16 in graduate courses. We then contacted and interviewed instructors both by email and telephone so as to learn more about some of the most intriguing course requirements.

We inspected the 55 course syllabi to learn about the nature of teaching children's literature in today's university courses, including such course features as the titles, genres, and authors students are required to read, as well as the nature and purposes of typical course requirements. In this chapter, we report common practices in the field and elaborate on some particularly fresh, original, and sound instructional ideas/approaches drawn from these syllabi.

Findings

Required Reading

Reading children's books was a requirement in every syllabus we scrutinized. Some instructors required students to select books within parameters (e.g., five works of historical fiction, five works of modern fantasy), often providing a set of titles representative of varying genres. The average number of self-selected titles required by instructors was 11, with a range from 1 to 107. Other instructors required all their students to read a set of core books. Still others required a combination of self-selected and core titles. The average number of core books (required for all students) was five.

There was little overlap in the required titles for courses in children literature. A total of 440 different books were listed as required reading in the syllabi we inspected. Of that total list, 57 percent (n = 252) were included on only *one* syllabus, while 22 percent (n = 97) were required by only *two* instructors. Of the remaining titles (21 percent of the set), eight were required by five or more instructors (see Table 1.1). Two of those titles, *Alice's Adventures in Wonderland* (Carroll, 1866) and *Charlotte's Web* (White, 1952), are regarded as classics in children's literature. Two others, *The Watsons Go to Birmingham—1963* (Curtis, 1995) and *Esperanza Rising* (Ryan, 2000), are labeled works of multicultural literature. One title, *A Kick in the Head: An Everyday Guide to Poetic Forms* (Janeczko, 2005), is a poetry compilation. Of the remaining three titles, two are contemporary realistic fiction and one is science fiction.

In addition to identifying titles from course syllabi, we also tried to discern whether works by particular authors were frequently required. We found a total of 70 authors whose works were required reading by three or more instructors. The works of 10 children's authors were required by eight or more instructors. A list of those 10 authors and the frequency with which their books were required appears in Table 1.2.

Finally, we identified the genre of the core readings (see Table 1.3). The genres most frequently required were contemporary realistic fiction and modern fantasy. Poetry and informational titles were required infrequently as common readings. In addition, approximately 16 percent of the instructors required their students to read particular picture books.

Table 1.1: Frequently Required Core Readings

Title	No. of Instructors * Requiring
Girl, 15, Charming but Insane	16
Charlotte's Web	11
The Watsons Go to Birmingham—1963	10
Alice's Adventures in Wonderland	10
A Kick in the Head	6
Esperanza Rising	6
Joey Pigza Swallowed the Key	5
The Giver	5

*Instructors = 42

Table 1.2: Most Frequently Required Authors*

Authors	Number of Instructors Requiring Author's Work(s)
Leo Lionni	17
Frances Temple	13
Katherine Paterson	12
E. B. White	10
Maurice Sendak	10
Lewis Carroll	11
Christopher Paul Curtis	18
Kate DiCamillo	8
Robert Munsch	8
J. K. Rowling	8

Total number of authors assigned in all syllabi = 305

Table 1.3: Percentage of Required Core Readings by Genre

Genre	Percentage
Contemporary realistic fiction	24.6
Modern fantasy	18.2
Picture books	16.8
Historical fiction	12.2
Traditional literature	6.2
Informational	5.4
Period novel	5.4
Autobiography/biography/memoir	4.6
Poetry	4.3
Science fiction	1.6
Mystery	.7

Course Assignments in Children's Literature Classes

Because course requirements and tasks hint at the richness of learning experiences, we also read the syllabi to collect and code the kinds of tasks that instructors required *in addition to* reading children's books. Because assignments are sometimes briefly sketched within syllabi, our analysis may have misconstrued the purposes and nature of some of those assignments. Table 1.4 provides a list of the most frequently required tasks as we interpreted them.

Nearly half the instructors included an assignment that required the students to document their trade book reading through either individual or group

Table 1.4: Assignments Required by Instructors (n = 42)

Assignment	Number of Instructors
Written papers	23
Documentation of reading	20
Author study	15
Talking with others about books	13
Literary response journal	6
Field work	6
Creation of book for children	6
Reflection on self as reader	4
Exams	4

annotated bibliographies or resource files. A like number of instructors required papers of one kind or another. These were described variously as essays, analytical papers, review papers, research papers, book reviews, and critiques of picture books.

One frequently mentioned written assignment was the literary response journal. In one class, students were asked to bring their journal entries to class to share with peers in literature circles as a means of launching conversations. Another instructor extended a response journal assignment by inviting the students to closely inspect their own responses to a novel by viewing their responses through the lens of Judith Langer's (1996) envisionment-building theory. Still other instructors engaged students in self-reflection through literacy memoirs.

In addition to asking students to read widely and to document their reading, many instructors appeared to honor the social construction of meanings by requiring students to interact with others around books. These assignments took different forms. For example, a number of instructors asked their students to engage in face-to-face discussion in book clubs or literature circles. One instructor asked her students to gather in small groups at a coffee shop or some other informal venue to talk about a book. Then, with an apparent eye toward better understanding the nature of literary discussion, this instructor required her students to analyze and compare their coffee-shop book conversation with classroom conversations. Other instructors connected their students with pen pals with whom they communicated about books they were reading. Still others asked their students to participate in electronic communities via discussion boards.

Author and illustrator studies were another frequently mentioned require-ment in the syllabi we examined. Approximately 25 percent of instructors included this particular assignment. A number of instructors required students to share their author studies with peers, a requirement that served to broaden students' familiarity with the authors and illustrators of children's books. Still other instructors asked their students to create a book for children. Perhaps sur-prisingly, only four instructors included assignments that involved fieldwork.

Talking Over Teaching with Some Untraditional Profs

Acknowledging that syllabi may offer a fairly limited portrait of what actually transpires in a course, we closely read the descriptions of course requirements to identify examples of what seemed to be especially thick learning experi-ences. We asked four willing professors of children's literature courses whose syllabi contained intriguing approaches—Junko Yokota, Charles Temple, Linda Pavonetti, and Kathy Short—to "tell us more."

Junko Yokota: Infusing Technology at National Louis University

Use of basic technology (e.g., PowerPoint presentations, word-processed assign-ments) was an expectation of nearly all the course syllabi we examined. How-ever, at National Louis University, Junko Yokota has taken her class beyond minimal expectations for incorporating technology. Although many teachers of children's literature require students to keep logs of their readings in some sort of database, Junko introduces her students to software downloads that enhance those databases in scope and flexibility. For example, a number of years ago she introduced Macintosh users to Delicious Library, a cataloging application that helps users enter, sort, and manage their own collections. Delicious Library per-mits users to enter ISBN and other bibliographic information manually, but also to use Isight webcams to scan an item's barcode for instant cataloging of books, movies, music, and games. (MediaMan is the PC user's equivalent of Delicious Library.)

More recently Junko has begun having her students use LibraryThing.com, a site available to users of both Macintosh and PC platforms. The site enables users to automatically add bibliographic data to their own catalog of reading, drawing from Amazon.com or hundreds of libraries, including the Library of Congress. Not only can users of LibraryThing.com painlessly obtain ISBN and other bibliographic information by entering a few words from a book's title, they can also instantly add book covers into their developing "bookshelf" with a click. The free Web application also allows users to catalog, sort, and rate the books they read—and to share their reviews with classmates. Students leave the course with the beginnings of a virtual classroom library shelf. Important to teachers of children's literature is that the template pages are designed so that students can enter their own reviews and summaries, as well as access others' reviews. Important for teachers is the option to assign teacher-devised "tags" for each book, so that teachers can mark "books to read aloud," or a book's location ("in my home library"), books for particular units, or even student favorites. The database is readily searchable by the tags.

Rather than having university students respond to the books they read in journals, Junko offers opportunities to explore digital venues for responding to literature. For example, she requires her students to join an electronic book discussion group on a social networking site (where she, too, is able to "listen in" and add to discussions). Students are expected to post their responses to books and also respond to others' posts. One of her favorite sites for this assignment is Goodreads.com because, unlike Blackboard, students have access to Goodreads after they graduate. She also asks her students to visit children's literature blogs to learn how other professionals are responding to children's books. In addition, Junko gives students the option of setting up their own blogs or for creating a blog for a classroom.

Recognizing the increasingly wide range of books in digital format, she requires students to inspect and critically analyze digital books. The assignment requires students to locate and compare a book that is available in both print and digital formats so as to evaluate the potential influences of formats on readers' comprehension and response. Students typically choose from books they locate using Tumble Books, One More Story, or ICDLbooks. To make issues of access more concrete, Junko's students must also find a resource online they cannot easily obtain in print. For this assignment, many go to ICDLbook, where they have access to international books in their original language.

Charles Temple: Storytelling at Hobart and William Smith Colleges

Typical preservice teachers may shy away from storytelling, but not so the students taking children's literature with Charles Temple at Hobart and William Smith Colleges. Traditional literature and storytelling are the launching points for Charley's course. Together professor and students do an in-depth exploration of folktales from around the world and the ways communities have historically shared those stories. Charley then invites his own students to become storytellers. Using a variety of storytelling and dramatic exercises to help his college students develop their confidence and skill as storytellers, Charley engages the students in a unit on storytelling that culminates with classmates telling their own stories in class.

Class work is followed by the field component of the project. In collaboration with a local elementary school librarian, Charley sends small teams of teachers into a school to coach third, fourth, and fifth graders in storytelling. For five weeks, teams of preservice teachers work twice a week with their assigned class in the school library. First, they tell the students stories themselves—ones they have learned for the children's literature class. Next, they help the children read through many selected stories to find a story that each really enjoys—one that will hold their interest (and that of their parents) over weeks of practice. Finally, the teachers help the children learn their stories—coaching the children to focus on the story's overall structure, memorizing only the beginning, the ending, and a few key phrases.

University students report that the most enjoyable part may be conducting storytelling exercises, i.e., helping children stand before an audience and tell an engaging story. The teachers coach for the basics of speaking confidently before an audience, overcoming shyness, and projecting voices. They demonstrate techniques for making stories come to life through voice and gestures. They help children make performance decisions based on the mood of stories and the personalities of characters. They guide children to be mindful of an audience attempting to visualize the action through the storyteller's craft. They teach about pacing to create suspense and surprise. Through all these activities and instruction, the preservice teachers draw on experiences from Charley's children's literature class, and from the resource text, *Children Tell Stories: A Teaching Guide* (Hamilton & Weiss, 2005). Storytelling workshops culminate in presentations at gatherings to which parents and other students are invited. Some performers also participate in a Storytelling Gathering sponsored by the local teachers' center. The intensive storytelling opportunities that Charley Temple provides in his children's literature class seem to ensure that his students not only develop skill as storytellers but also learn to help children become knowledgeable about the frames and functions and meanings of stories.

Linda Pavonetti: Required Reading at Oakland University

Although our analysis revealed that the average number of core books was five, a few instructors included a significantly longer list of core books. We asked Linda Pavonetti to talk about the reasons she asks her students to read 25 core books each semester. Linda explained that she organizes most of her class sessions around core books she describes as "mentor texts." For example, in one session, Linda's preservice teachers come to class having read the same three

Cinderella variants. Organized into small groups, the students worked to identify common threads across the books. These commonalities then became the basis for a graphic organizer that preservice teachers could use to guide children in exploring Cinderella variants.

For another session, Linda required students to read five contemporary realistic fiction books: *Walk Two Moons* (Creech, 1994), *Because of Winn Dixie* (DiCamillo, 2000), *If You Come Softly* (Woodson, 1998), *Joey Pigza Swallowed the Key* (Gantos, 1998), and *Maniac Magee* (Spinelli, 1990). Soon the students were posing commonalities across these titles as well: abandonment, resistance, and relationships. Again, the preservice teachers collaborated to design a graphic organizer to represent their insights. This activity stimulated conversation about the nature of realistic fiction. Finally, Linda asked her students to generate their own criteria for evaluating the genre based on the discoveries they had made through their shared focus. Only at this point did she offer her students evaluation criteria proposed by experts.

When asked how class sessions might be different if she aimed for the same understandings without using a shared corpus of mentor texts, Linda was quick to reply that she had tried it both ways. That is, she had also tried having students read different titles and come to class prepared to discuss their individual reading. She explained she found sharing different books less effective. Too often conversation remained at a surface level, with students spending most of their time summarizing the plots of stories for their peers rather than digging beneath the surface of plots to arrive inductively at a deeper understanding of a particular genre (motif, structure, etc.). Linda also observed that this inductive approach to exploring children's literature around core books, coupled with the construction of a variety of graphic organizers and other conversation starters, offers other advantages as well: Preservice teachers are more likely to remember the books they have read because of the way in which class activities continue to reference and revisit the shared books, allowing for collective delving and deeper meaning making. Further, by sharing their graphic organizers, students seemed to gain insights into the nature of literary reading, discovering that readers sometimes interpret the same book in dissimilar but defensible ways. Finally, Linda's preservice teachers are introduced to tools they will be able to use in their own classrooms to engage children in taking up layers of meaning.

Most teachers cannot afford to buy their own copies of the 25 core readings for Linda's course, so they rely on the public or university library to obtain copies. However, Linda also provides support by putting the core books on reserve in the university library, ensuring that students can come to class fully prepared to participate in the engaging and challenging activities that she designs around core children's books.

Kathy Short: Giving Students the Reins on the Course Syllabus at the University of Arizona

Most survey courses in children's literature are organized by genre, and on one level, observes Kathy Short of the University of Arizona, this structure makes sense. After all, this approach can serve to broaden the reading of students who might otherwise tend to stay with their favorite genre, and it also allows time to build an understanding of evaluation criteria which vary by genre. And virtually all children's literature textbooks are organized around genre. Yet Kathy argues that only occasionally in working with children would she engage them in genre study. Instead, she believes that organizing books around themes is much more significant for children. For that reason she questions the value of teaching a children's literature course for teachers (and future teachers) organized only around genre.

Instead, Kathy has explored an alternative to the traditional genre structure. She begins her children's literature course with an activity that engages students in reflection on their early experiences with children's literature: creating a time line of how they have changed as readers, mapping their literacy journeys, writing short stories about literacy memories, writing a journal entry from memory about a favorite childhood book and then rereading the book and writing a new response, etc.

Kathy and her students then move on to talk about children's literature as a vast field that requires ways of organizing the books to look for connections and patterns across books. This leads to several class sessions spent looking at the major ways in which children's literature is often organized—by genre, by literary elements, by authors/illustrators, by awards, and by theme. A class session focuses on each organizational structure to give the students an overview of these different ways of organizing books. Kathy always focuses on thematic organization last, and it is this structure that defines the remainder of the course.

In exploring a thematic approach with her students, Kathy chooses a broad umbrella concept as a frame—broad concepts such as journeys, sense of place, change, etc. She then chooses two class novels to help develop the broad concept, one of which was written by the author who will be presenting that year at the annual University of Arizona children's literature conference (which is organized around the same broad concept). For example, "Crossing Borders" was the organizing concept when Pam Muñoz Ryan was the featured author, and when Jacqueline Woodson was featured, "Change" was the undergirding concept. Once Kathy and her students begin to explore the broad concept, she immerses the students in literature and literary response activities through which they explore the concept, first with personal connections and then more broadly. Through these experiences, which extend across several class sessions, the class develops a web of themes related to the broad concept. Together Kathy and her students group these themes and ideas and negotiate ones they want to explore more deeply. The negotiated themes are then explored in the remaining class sessions—with one theme becoming the defining focus in each class session. Once the class has chosen focus themes, Kathy pairs each theme with a genre that seems to have a good fit.

To facilitate this innovative organizational structure, Kathy has built a large collection of multiple copy books so that for each theme she can choose five to six novels related to the theme for the next class session, which students then sign out to read. In this final phase of the semester, the first part of each class session is organized around the featured theme: Kathy does a thematically related read-aloud and students then meet in small-group literature circles to discuss the books they have read. Then the class moves into browsing the books Kathy has brought in; some of the books are related to the theme; others are exemplars of the featured genre, while still other books have been selected to highlight particular authors and illustrators who work in the genre. So while thematic connections provide the central structure for these final class sessions, each class session actually uses all three ways of organizing literature—theme, author, and genre.

Kathy acknowledges that this organizational structure is challenging. It requires access to a wide range of resources and instructor familiarity with those resources. Further, even though Kathy gives students a tentative course schedule once themes have been negotiated for the latter portion of the course, the schedule must still be constantly adjusted based on what students write in their literature logs and on what has transpired in the previous class session. All of this requires time and reflection. However, the payoff in student learning is such that Kathy is committed to this innovative way of organizing her children's literature course.

Conclusions

When Sean Walmsley (1992) interviewed teachers, school librarians, and administrators to uncover their views on literature in the elementary school, he found that the most frequently cited purposes for the teaching of literature included "for fun" and "to teach reading skills." Walmsley concluded that a "bigger picture" seemed to be missing as the educators talked about children's literature in the classroom. Not surprisingly, Walmsley found that most of the teachers he interviewed "had little formal training in literature" (p. 510). We believe children's literature courses must be the vehicle through which teachers and teachers-to-be acquire this bigger picture.

We began this chapter by posing some global aims for children's literature courses that might help a new generation of teachers be more informed, strategic, and articulate about why and how they include literature in daily classroom routines. The first goal we stated—the intent that teachers develop familiarity with a wide range of quality children's books—appears pervasive in the children's literature syllabi we examined. There was extensive evidence that teachers and teacher candidates are reading widely, as well as reading the works of acclaimed authors and illustrators. However, the appearance of only two multicultural titles on a compilation of the most commonly required core books suggests required readings may not fully reflect the diversity of our classrooms or our global society. Further, teacher candidates may not be reading across all genres of children's literature. Titles representing contemporary realistic fiction and modern fantasy continue to be the most frequently required in today's children's literature courses. It is also less clear whether many teachers are being taught self-sufficiency with resources (human, print, and digital) for identifying and keeping apprised of the wealth of books for children. Technology seems at the ready to help with these tasks.

A second goal of teaching Children's Literature is to help teachers understand the nature of literary texts so that classroom literary experiences can be made even more engaging and satisfying. Written course assignments identified in syllabi (e.g., essays, analytical papers, book reviews) suggest that close analysis of children's books is expected in many courses. Those written assignments may be outgrowths of fulsome book discussions and thoughtful analyses of professional readings—leading toward better understanding of the artistry and crafting of quality texts. It may be more challenging to provide course experiences and assignments in which teachers learn to reflect on their own thoughtful processes as readers of literary texts, or learn to observe and interpret children's engagement and response.

The third goal we identified for Children's Literature courses was that of helping teachers acquire instructional strategies that guide children's deepened explorations of literature. Certainly the course syllabi we examined provided evidence that teachers are being engaged in experiences they can adapt to their own classrooms—experiences such as writing responsively in journals or participating in literature circles. There was less evidence in the syllabi that students were being given fieldwork opportunities focused on becoming more adept with literature inquiry in classrooms.

Evidence suggests that Children's Literature courses have historically been focused most directly on ensuring that future teachers know quality literature for children; our own examination of current syllabi suggests that this goal may still dominate. Those who design and teach the courses may need to continue to consider and plan strategies for achieving thoughtful, collaborative discourse about shared texts; for deliberation about the role of children's literature in high-stakes classrooms; for consideration of current interpretations of genre studies in classrooms; for dialogue about what it means to engage in literary readings; and for the provision of tools and insights for the close observation of children's literary responses.

Works Cited

American Library Association. (2007). *Number of children's books published.* Retrieved from http://wikis.ala.org/professionaltips/index.php/Number_of_Children's_Books_ Published

Bowker. (2008). *Subject guide to children's books in print 2009: A subject index to books for children and young adults.* New Providence, NJ: Author.

Eeds, M., & Peterson, R. (1991). Teacher as curator: Learning to talk about literature. *The Reading Teacher, 45,* 118–126.

Fish, S. (1980). *Is there a text in this class? The authority of interpretive communities.* Cambridge, MA: Harvard University Press.

Hamilton, M., & Weiss, M. (2005). *Children tell stories: Teaching and using storytelling in the classroom.* Katonah, NY: Richard C. Owen.

Landau, E. D. (1968). *Teaching children's literature in colleges and universities.* Champaign, IL: National Council of Teachers of English.

Langer, J. A. (1996). *Envisioning literature: Literary understanding and literature instruction.* New York: Teachers College Press.

Many, J. E., & Wiseman, D. L. (1992). The effects of teaching approach on third-grade students' response to literature. *Journal of Reading Behavior, 24,* 265–287.

Martinez, M. G., & McGee, L. M. (2000). Children's literature and reading instruction: Past, present, and future. *Reading Research Quarterly, 35,* 154–169.

Martinez, M. G., & Roser, N. L. (1982). Literature in the reading program: Tracing roots. *The Reading Professor, 8,* 23–30.

McClure, A. A., & Tomlinson, C. M. (2000). Polling the profs: A national survey of teachers of children's literature in universities and colleges. *Journal of Children's Literature, 26*(2), 40–49.

National Council of Teachers of English. (2001). *Resolution on preparing and certifying teachers with knowledge of children's and adolescent literature.* Retrieved from http://www.ncte.org/positions/statements/childrensadollit

Raphael, T. E., & McMahon, S. I. (1994). Book club: An alternative framework for reading instruction. *The Reading Teacher, 48,* 102–116.

Rosenblatt, L. M. (1995). *Literature as exploration* (5th ed.). New York: Modern Language Association.

Roser, N. L., & Martinez, M. G. (2000). What Alice saw through the keyhole: Visions of children's literature in elementary classrooms. *Journal of Children's Literature, 26*(2), 18–27.

Sebesta, S. (2001). What do teachers need to know about children's literature? *The New Advocate, 14,* 241–249.

Short, K. G. (1993). Making connections across literature and life. In K. E. Holland, R. A. Hungerford, & S. B. Ernst (Eds.), *Journeying: Children responding to literature* (pp. 284–301). Portsmouth, NH: Heinemann.

Sipe, L. R. (2008). *Storytime: Young children's literary understanding in the classroom.* New York: Teachers College Press.

Smith, K. (1990). Entertaining a text: A reciprocal process. In K. G. Short & K. M. Pierce (Eds.), *Talking about books: Creating literate communities* (pp. 17–31). Portsmouth, NH: Heinemann.

Walmsley, S. A. (1992). Reflections on the state of elementary literature instruction. *Language Arts, 69,* 508–514.

Wiseman, D. L., Many, J. E., & Altieri, J. (1992). Enabling complex aesthetic responses: An examination of three literary discussion approaches. In C. K. Kinzer & D. J. Leu (Eds.), *Literacy research, theory, and practice: Views from many perspectives. Forty-first yearbook of the National Reading Conference* (pp. 283–290). Chicago: National Reading Conference.

Children's Books Cited

Carroll, L. (1866). *Alice's adventures in wonderland.* New York: D. Appleton.

Creech, S. (1994). *Walk two moons.* New York: HarperCollins.

Curtis, C. P. (1995). *The Watsons go to Birmingham—1963.* New York: Delacorte Press.

DiCamillo, K. (2000). *Because of Winn-Dixie.* Cambridge, MA: Candlewick Press.

Gantos, J. (1998). *Joey Pigza swallowed the key.* New York: Farrar, Straus and Giroux.

Janeczko, P. B. (2005). *A kick in the head: An everyday guide to poetic forms* (C. Raschka, Illus.). Cambridge, MA: Candlewick Press.

Lowry, L. (1993). *The giver.* Boston: Houghton Mifflin.

Paterson, K. (1977). *Bridge to Terabithia*. New York: Crowell.

Ryan, P. M. (2000). *Esperanza rising*. New York: Scholastic.

Spinelli, J. (1990). *Maniac Magee*. Boston: Little, Brown.

White, E. B. (1952). *Charlotte's web* (G. Williams, Illus.). New York: Harper.

Woodson, J. (1998). *If you come softly*. New York: G. P. Putnam's Sons.

2

Uses and Abuses of Children's Literature

Evelyn B. Freeman, *The Ohio State University–Mansfield*

"I open up the book I'm holding, a new one brought this very day. Just chicken scratch, I used to figure, but now I see what's truly there, and I read a little out." So speaks Cal, who lives in a remote area of the Appalachian mountains, as he thanks *That Book Woman* (Henson, 2008) for bringing him books and opening up the world of reading to him. This picture book is a tribute to the Pack Horse Librarians who were called "Book Women" and who traveled to homes in the Appalachian mountains of Kentucky, bringing books to families during the 1930s. These inspiring women believed in the ability of children's books to bring the world to children. For children in the 1930s, books were objects to be cherished, and the Book Women braved snow, rain, and cold to share books with isolated children.

The 1997 Master Class focused on the "uses and abuses of children's literature in the classroom." This chapter builds on the content of that class and reflects, more than a decade later, current trends and issues in children's literature. Since it would be impossible to fully analyze every trend in the field of children's literature over the last decade, I have chosen to focus on the following four topics: books as commodities, new technologies, expanding genres of children's literature, and changes in reading for pleasure. While all of these topics overlap, to varying degrees, with the focus of other chapters, each trend has significantly changed the writing, publishing, marketing, or reading of children's books since the Master Class was begun. The limits of space prevent these discussions from being all-encompassing, but for each topic, the current uses (positive things that are happening), as well as abuses (challenges and concerns), are discussed.

Books as Commodities

Children's books have become commodities with movie spin-offs, toys, games, and other merchandise. In addition, characters who are popularized on television and in the movies have spawned their own children's books. This trend can certainly be considered positive as it encourages parents to purchase books and children to read them. Yet, this trend also raises some troubling questions.

Children's books have been adapted for the screen for more than 70 years. In 1937, Shirley Temple starred in the film version of *Heidi*, and in 1939, Judy Garland portrayed Dorothy in the beloved *The Wizard of Oz*, a movie that still appears on television. In recent years, however, there has been a proliferation of movies based on award-winning and popular children's books. *The Spiderwick Chronicles*, released in 2008, is based on the five-book fantasy series by Holly Black and Tony DiTerlizzi. Philip Pullman's Carnegie Award–winning *The Golden Compass* (originally titled *Northern Lights* in England) was released as a film and video game in 2007. *Inkheart*, based on the book by Cornelia Funke (2003), hit the big screen in 2009. And all seven Harry Potter books have film adaptations, with the final book split into two movies.

In addition, favorite book characters are featured in several popular children's television shows. Clifford the Big Red Dog, the character created by Norman Bridwell in 1963, and Arthur, the aardvark, developed by Marc Brown, are stars in their own PBS television shows and have their own webpages on the PBS Kids website. Favorite characters from books have been used for many kinds of commercial products. *Olivia* by Ian Falconer (2000) has become a popular pig who is now a plush doll as well as a children's lamp. Curious George, the beloved monkey, first appeared in *Curious George* by H. A. Rey in 1941. Still popular with young children today, Curious George boasts his own line of products that include party supplies, pajamas, and paper dolls.

While this trend of books and the media can be viewed positively—books are being promoted and children are encouraged to read the books upon which movies and TV shows are based—concerns have also been raised regarding children's literature as a commodity. For instance, many people have no idea that the wildly popular Shrek is actually based on the picture book *Shrek* by award-winning author/illustrator William Steig (1990). The contribution of the book itself has been minimized as the commercialization has proliferated.

Hade (2002) cautions against this trend and notes: "The mass marketplace selects which books will survive, and thus the children's book becomes less a cultural and intellectual object and more an entertainment looking for mass appeal" (p. 511). He further expresses concern that children are being viewed as consumers rather than readers. Children's books and their characters have become "brands" to be marketed and popularized in a variety of ways. Big corporations seek to make money from these offshoots of children's books. Hade concludes his article by posing the question: "What parts of our children are not for sale?" (p. 517).

Still another trend in children's books as commodities occurs when a movie or TV show comes first, and then books are written based on the series or characters. Some common examples include all the Sesame Street books, Mickey Mouse books, Golden Books about Bob the Builder, those based on Walt Disney movies, Handy Manny books, and Dora the Explorer books. Again, one can ask, "Why is this a problem?" We are getting kids to read. Yet, many librarians and educators have questioned the literary quality of these books, concerned that richness of language, engaging plot, and compelling themes may not be well developed in these books. Further, one may wonder, if these kinds of books are being published and mass-marketed, what other books may not be? Will there be room for new authors? Will publishers take a chance on books that are more of a risk in terms of mass appeal yet may represent outstanding literature for children?

Award-winning children's author Jane Yolen reflects on this trend of children's books as commodities. In the article "Ten Things I No Longer Enjoy about Publishing but Am Willing to Endure," Yolen (2007) discusses branding as the fourth issue: "All of us—writers, illustrators, editors, publishers, teachers, librarians—are trying to create a literature of childhood" (p. 63). Yolen asserts that "publishing children's books is a big business" (p. 63) and that many children's books and their characters are now identified as their own brand with sheets, book-bags, clothes, and other merchandise featuring their images. She laments that the merchandise "becomes even more important than the book, the concept more important than the story, the brand more important than characterization" (p. 64).

Technology and Books

The impact of technology on our lives continues to expand daily. The relationship of technology to children's literature is no exception. Vardell's chapter about how technology has changed the field of children's literature (Chapter 10) discusses a broad range of issues, while this chapter focuses more narrowly on the impact of technology in three areas: how the use of online information and materials has affected reading of the printed book; how audiobooks have increased in popularity; and how software programs such as Accelerated Reader and Scholastic Counts have affected reading instruction.

Online Reading

In 2008, Scholastic and Yankelovich conducted a study, *2008 Kids and Family Reading Report,* of 1,002 people, 501 children ages 5–17 and one parent or guardian for each child. Results revealed that "after age eight, more children go online daily than read for fun daily" (p. 4). The fact that students go online daily can lead them to find websites and resources that relate directly to children's books. Children's book publishers host websites, and many children's authors have developed their own websites. Some publishers have even begun releasing video book trailers—just as producers do for movies—and "webisodes" to accompany the publication of new titles (Davila & Patrick, 2010). Other websites feature activities involving children's books that provide children interactive experiences with literature. Children can email authors, ask questions about books, and start their own blogs to discuss books with each other and interact with authors on their blogs. The ways to find book information and communicate with others about books have expanded rapidly in recent years and will continue to do so. The challenge becomes how to capitalize on this reality as a positive factor to encourage children to read books.

Another aspect of the *2008 Kids and Family Reading Report* (2008) focused on children's preferences for reading books electronically or in print. Findings revealed that 75 percent of the children surveyed agreed with the statement, "No matter what I can do online, I'll always want to read books printed on paper." In addition, 62 percent of the children indicated that they "prefer to read books printed on paper rather than on a handheld device or computer" (p. 4). Nonetheless, publishers are producing books for children in e-formats, and the creation of devices such as the Kindle and the iPad may have an impact on children's reading preferences. They are also marketing books such as Patrick Carman's *Skeleton Creek* and its sequel, *Ghost in the Machine*, both published in 2009. These books engage readers in reading both traditional, printed text and viewing video clips by logging onto the Internet and using a password provided in the books.

How publishers continue to capitalize on online reading opportunities for children remains to be seen. This is also a trend ripe for scholarly exploration. Some scholars have already begun studying the possibilities that online reading and multimodal texts afford college courses in children's literature (Larson, 2008; Thompson, 2008) as well as the ways in which these reading practices create readers' identities (Stone & Veth, 2008). Davila and Patrick (2010) state, "As current research regarding digital book media is limited, it will be interesting to see what scholars observe about children's book preferences and digital book media in upcoming years" (p. 207). They also predict that "it is inevitable that children's reading preferences will continue to shift with the evolution of new media and technologies" (p. 207).

Audiobooks

According to a recent survey, "Young listeners are the fastest growing market segment" for audiobooks (Audio Publishers Association, 2008). The increased production of audiobooks has provided children the opportunity to listen to books in a variety of settings such as at home, at school, and in the car, and through formats such as CDs and mp3 files. The Kindle will even read a book to you. Some may question whether listening to recorded books is the equivalent of "real" reading. Yet others conjecture that books on tape simply provide another format for children to listen to books being read aloud. Jim Trelease (2006) notes that "[t]he recorded book is a perfect example of how technology can be used to make this a more literate nation" (p. 171). Pam Spencer Holley (2010) provides research-based educational benefits of listening to recorded books, including a positive correlation between "listening to audiobooks and reading improvement." She describes audiobook listening as "an important step in becoming a life-long reader" (para. 1). The popularity of this media as a way to share books with children is evidenced by the number of professional journals, such as *Horn Book Magazine*, the *Journal of Children's Literature*, and *Publishers Weekly*, that routinely provide reviews of children's audiobooks and include regular columns about audiobooks. Additionally, the American Library Association has been recognizing the best audiobooks for children and young adults produced annually since 1999.

Computerized Reading Incentive Programs

Over the past decade the adoption of computerized management systems for reading instruction, such as Scholastic Reading Counts and Accelerated Reader, has gained in popularity in school districts. The most widely used of these systems, Accelerated Reader, has been the subject of much debate and discussion. Developed by Renaissance Learning, Accelerated Reader is a computerized method to assess reading skills. Over 115,000 books can be found in Accelerated Reader's database. Basically the process includes three steps:

1. Students select a book to read either at school or at home.
2. Students take a computerized quiz (or quizzes) after reading that book.
3. The teacher determines how the data from quizzes will inform instruction.

When students pass the computerized quizzes, they receive points that later entitle them to various kinds of rewards, determined by individual districts/schools.

The Fall 2003 issue of the *Journal of Children's Literature* focused on these reading incentive programs and provided diverse points of view about their benefits. In this issue, Stephen D. Krashen and Lynn Rogers present opposing viewpoints about the benefits of Accelerated Reader and the research studies about the program's outcomes. Comments from students, parents, librarians, teachers, and authors highlight both positive and negative aspects of reading incentive programs.

So while some studies have indicated positive outcomes and enhanced reading comprehension with Accelerated Reader (Ross, Nunnery, & Goldfeder, 2004; Nunnery, Ross, & McDonald, 2006), there have also been strong criticisms of these programs. One philosophical issue revolves around the tension between intrinsic versus extrinsic rewards for successfully reading a book. Trelease (2006) raises concerns about how these programs may impede class discussion of books and limit children's book choices to those included in the database. Renita Schmidt (2008), a fourth-grade teacher who used Accelerated Reader for seven years, conducted an analysis of the program and discussed four related areas that included developing a lifelong love of reading, social reading, reading management, and motivation for reading. She concluded, "When schools use reading to quiet children and create quiet classrooms, when schools teach children long books are worth more points than short books, and when schools teach children to consume books and regurgitate answers, we are doing parents and students a grave disservice" (p. 210). The What Works Clearinghouse, hosted by US Department of Education Institute of Educational Sciences, reported in 2008 that "Accelerated Reader was found to have no discernible effects on reading fluency, mixed effects on comprehension, and potentially positive effects on general reading achievement" (para. 4).

Genres of Children's Literature

Changes in the genres of children's literature have also produced trends observed during the past decade. Changes noted involve the following genres: nonfiction, picture books, fantasy, and poetry. Additionally, hybrid genres, multiple genre formats, and "new" genres have emerged in children's literature during recent years.

Nonfiction

The 1997 Master Class highlighted nonfiction and the increased attention given to that genre. Recent studies have countered previous research and indicate that young children of both genders are choosing nonfiction over fiction (Mohr, 2006). The importance of nonfiction as a genre in reading and writing instruction has continued to increase. A review of journal articles related to children's literature in the classroom revealed 15 articles from 2000–05 that focused specifically on nonfiction. These articles indicated the value of nonfiction in primary classrooms and questioned the perception that children prefer fiction (Scharer, Freeman, & Lehman, 2008). However, fiction continues to dominate classroom collections, summer reading lists from libraries, and children's book awards. Colman (2007) describes the myths and misconceptions surrounding nonfiction as a genre. She laments "defining fiction as reading for pleasure and nonfiction as reading for information—that miseducates students about what to expect from fiction and nonfiction" (p. 259). Now, as in 1997, there is the concern that nonfiction as a genre will be viewed as the utility player—books that are used for research or to teach specific skills, rather than ones that can satisfy a child's curiosity and interest in a topic. Further, nonfiction children's books can be savored and enjoyed for pleasure, just like fiction.

Picture Books

Picture books are the staple of children's literature, and the past decade has witnessed many changes in this popular genre. First, picture books are no longer limited to fictional stories for young children. The picture book format can now be found in all genres, including informational books and biography, and for a range of readers other than the youngest. Recent Caldecott Award–winning books include *The Man Who Walked between the Towers* by Mordicai Gerstein (2003) that recounts the daring tightrope walk of Philippe Petit between the World Trade Center twin towers in 1974. A biography about Harriet Tubman, *Moses: When Harriet Tubman Led Her People to Freedom*, by Carole Boston Weatherford (2006) with illustrations by Kadir Nelson, was named a Caldecott Honor Book in 2007. In addition, the interest, content, and reading levels of many picture books are clearly for older students in the upper-elementary and middle school, such as *The Wall: Growing Up Behind the Iron Curtain* by Peter Sís (2007), an illustrated memoir of his early years in Czechoslovakia. Magnificent paintings by Bagram Ibatouline support the text in the fascinating informational book *Secrets of the Sphinx* by James Cross Giblin (2004).

The emergence of the postmodern picture book has changed the way children approach picture books, as authors and illustrators no longer limit themselves to a linear presentation of text and illustrations (Goldstone, 1999, 2002, 2004; Sipe & Pantaleo, 2008; Wolfenbarger & Sipe, 2007). In the postmodern picture book, multiple storylines occur concurrently or contain multiple perspectives. Other characteristics of these books include irony and contradiction and uncovering the artistic process of book making (Goldstone, 2004). The Caldecott Medal winner *Black and White* by David Macaulay (1990) is one of the first examples of this kind of picture book. Other prominent examples include John Scieszka's (1992) *The Stinky Cheese Man and Other Fairly Stupid Tales* and David Wiesner's (2001) *The Three Pigs*, also a recipient of the Caldecott Medal. Wolfenbarger and Sipe (2007) give the example of the Caldecott Honor Book *Knuffle Bunny: A Cautionary Tale* by Mo Willems (2004) that combines computer-manipulated photographs with hand-drawn sketches. They describe that "the effect of juxtaposing real and invented space and characterization presents a departure from the norm of maintaining a singular, coherent time and place" (p. 276).

Fantasy

The genre of fantasy has witnessed a huge renaissance caused by the Harry Potter phenomenon. Harry Potter has led to another trend—that of longer books being written for children. Fantasy dominates the list of chapter books, series books, and paperbacks for children on the *New York Times* bestseller list. For example, the list of March 22, 2009, includes the fantasy series The Twilight Saga by Stephenie Meyer (84 weeks on the list), House of Night by P. C. and Kristin Cast (2009; 29 weeks on the list), the Inkheart Trilogy by Cornelia Funke (24 weeks on the list), and the Harry Potter books by J. K. Rowling (215 weeks on the list). Examples of longer books (more than 300 pages) on the list for children include *The Mysterious Benedict Society* by Trenton Lee Stewart (2007), 512 pages; and *Seekers: Great Bear Lake* by Erin Hunter (2009), 320 pages, both of which are fantasy.

Poetry

Poetry as a genre has emerged as a crossover with other genres. One example of this crossover is the verse-novel, which has gained in popularity over the past decade. Alexander (2005) discusses the verse-novel in which "the entire story is told in the form of non-rhyming free verse" (p. 270). In these books, the story is often told in the first person and organized around short sections that usually have a heading or title. They lend themselves to being read aloud.

Several award-winning children's authors have penned verse-novels. Karen Hesse's verse-novel *Out of the Dust* (1997) received the 1998 Newbery. Told in the first person by narrator Billie Jo, a girl living in Oklahoma during the Dust Bowl, the novel powerfully conveys Billie Jo's thoughts and emotions from winter 1934 to autumn 1935. The family experiences an unspeakable tragedy, and Billie Jo must find a way to forgive her father and herself. Zarnowski (2010) calls these historical fiction novels in verse a "fusion genre."

In addition to historical fiction verse novels, a number of noted authors have written verse novels of contemporary realistic fiction. In the National Book Award Finalist *Locomotion*, author Jacqueline Woodson (2003) reveals the story of Lonnie C. Motion through poems he has written. Lonnie is seven when his parents die in a fire leaving his sister and himself orphans. Although his sister is adopted, Lonnie lives with a foster mother. His fifth-grade teacher introduces him to poetry and through his poems, readers witness his pain and grief and also his resiliency. In *Love That Dog*, Newbery Award–winning author Sharon Creech (2001) combines the diary form with the verse novel as Jack learns about poetry and writes about his dog Sky. This book would be a wonderful mentor text for children as they learn to write their own poems.

Another link between poetry and other genres is nonfiction that is written in verse. Marilyn Nelson, former poet laureate of the state of Connecticut, has written several award-winning poetry books on nonfiction topics. *Carver: A Life in Poems* (Nelson, 2001) chronicles the life of George Washington Carver through poems, many written in the voice of individuals who knew him. Most poems are accompanied by archival photographs. A timeline of significant dates in Carver's life appears throughout the book. Nelson (2009) has teamed with illustrator Jerry Pinkney in *Sweethearts of Rhythm*. Subtitled *The Story of the Greatest All-Girl Swing Band in the World*, this book introduces readers to the integrated all-women's band formed in the 1940s through a series of poems written from the perspective of their musical instruments. Pinkney's illustrations are rendered in watercolor and collage. The book includes a timeline of events, author's and illustrator's notes, and an extensive bibliography of resources.

Another crossover book between poetry and nonfiction is Carole Boston Weatherford's (2007) *Birmingham, 1963*. The author's note indicates that while the narrator of the poem is fictional, the events described in the book—the September 15, 1963, bombing of the Sixteenth Street Baptist Church in Birmingham—actually occurred. This free-verse poem is illustrated with archival photographs. Individual poems about the four girls who died in the bombing are accompanied by a photograph of each girl.

A related trend in poetry is to craft with poetic language, or organize a collection of poems around a nonfiction topic in science or social studies. For instance,

Thomas Locker's (2000) poetic text, illustrated with oil paintings, describes clouds in *Cloud Dance*. Back matter text by Candace Christiansen provides additional factual information about various types of clouds and how clouds are formed. *Tour America: A Journey through Poems and Art* by Diane Siebert (2006) guides readers across the United States. Each double-page spread includes a poem about the place, an illustration by Stephen Johnson, and a boxed inset that discusses the poem's topic in more detail. Some examples of places include the Gateway Arch in St. Louis, Missouri, and the Badlands of South Dakota.

Hybrid Genres

Another trend related to genre involves the categorization of children's books into the traditional genre categories. Many books published in the last few years defy such easy classification. For example, the most recent Newbery winner, *When You Reach Me* (Stead, 2009), includes elements of historical fiction, realistic fiction, and fantasy. The editors of the *Journal of Children's Literature* developed the theme for its Spring 2010 issue based on this trend. In addition to the "fusion genre" of historical verse novels already identified by Myra Zarnowski—indeed, any of the "crossover" poetry genres discussed previously could also be considered fusion genres—other hybrid genres explored in this journal issue include a genre identified by Frank Serafini (2010) as "expository fiction" and books termed by Sharon Kane (2010) as "fictionalized nonfiction." In the former, picture book authors apply the characteristics of nonfiction to such fictional topics as dragons or wizards. In the latter, authors insert their imaginations into biographies or informational texts in ways that prevent such books from being classified strictly as nonfiction. Kane acknowledges the complexity of these hybrid genres as well as the debate their creation has sparked among children's literature enthusiasts.

Multigenre Formats

An interesting recent trend involves novelists incorporating multiple formats and media to convey the story. Jeff Kinney (2007) in his best-selling *Diary of a Wimpy Kid* and its sequels combines a basic diary format with cartoons. Sisters Kate and M. Sarah Klise have collaborated on "Regarding the" series. In *Regarding the Trees: A Splintered Saga Rooted in Secrets* (Klise, 2005), the novel is presented in letters, newspaper articles, drawings, advertisements, and notes. While both of these series are humorous, a serious book, *Ways to Live Forever* by Sally Nicholls (2008), also incorporates journal entries, lists, and questions as the main character, 11-year-old Sam, is facing death from leukemia.

"New" Genres

A new genre of literature for children has developed over the past decade since the 1997 Master Class and is gaining in popularity: the graphic novel. Basically a graphic novel is a story told through sequential art with a combination of text, panels, and images. Yang (2008) believes that the value of graphic novels is that they are visual and "bridge the gap between media we watch and media we read" (p. 187). Graphic novels for readers ages 8 to 14 can now be found in virtually every genre including fantasy, realistic fiction, and memoir. *Bone: Out from Boneville* by Jeff Smith (2005), an example of a popular upper elementary graphic novel, is book one in a nine-book series. It is a fantasy adventure about three cousins filled with humor and action. The wordless graphic novel *The Arrival*, by Shaun Tan (2007), chronicles the immigration of a fictional character to a new country. *To Dance: A Ballerina's Graphic Novel* is the memoir of Siena Cherson Siegel (2006). The artwork by her husband Mark Siegel was done with watercolor paints and ink.

In addition to these graphic novels for upper elementary and middle school readers, the youngest readers can also enjoy graphic novels created just for them. The Baby Mouse series by sister and brother team Jennifer Holm and Matthew Holm is wildly popular with primary grade children; as of 2010, 12 books in the series had been produced with more to follow. The winner of the 2010 Theodore Seuss Geisel Award, given annually since 2006 to the most distinguished American book for beginning readers, was the graphic novel *Benny and Penny in the Big No-No!* by Geoffrey Hayes (2009).

Although many question whether the comic book format should be considered literature, the fact that graphic novels have been awarded such honors as the Geisel, as well as the 2007 Michael L. Printz Award to Gene Luen Yang's (2006) graphic novel, *American Born Chinese* (also a 2006 finalist for the National Book Award), seems to confirm their literary merit. In 2006, the Children's Book Council published a list of Graphic Novels for Young People that included seven pages of annotated titles of graphic novels for elementary and middle school readers published in 2005 and spring of 2006. To further the rising popularity of graphic novels among young readers, several publishers have created graphic novel imprints, such as Graphix of Scholastic and First Second of Roaring Brook.

Reading for Pleasure

At the Master Class in 1997, Dan Hade posed the question of how and by whom the importance of children's literature in the classroom is determined (Pierce,

1998). A decade later, Anita Silvey raised a similar kind of issue with her highly debated article, "Has the Newbery Lost Its Way?" (Silvey, 2008). In this article, Silvey questions the choice of certain books that have received the Newbery Medal since 2004, noting their lack of popularity with both children and children's librarians. She interviewed more than 100 media specialists, children's librarians, teachers, and booksellers in 15 states and concluded that many individuals believe the recent Newbery Medal books do not appeal to children. Further, the children with whom these professionals interact do not have any interest in reading the award books. The article caused quite a stir and generated discussion and debate on many blogs and discussion lists. The fundamental issue of what makes a book for children distinguished has focused attention on children's interests and how important that criterion should be in award selection.

The same concern raised in the 1997 Master Class remains today—How do we encourage children to read for pleasure and become lifelong readers? The *2008 Kids and Family Reading Report* (2008) found that "[a] majority of kids say they like to read books for fun and that reading books for fun is important" (p. 4). A study by Rideout, Roberts, and Foehr (2005) found that 73 percent of 2,032 respondents ages 8–18 read for pleasure daily. But *what* are they reading for pleasure? If the texts that bring children pleasure are not the same as those designated as distinguished by adult children's literature experts, is there a way to bridge the gap? In their 2010 review of research on children's reading preferences, Davila and Patrick concluded that children, both boys and girls, prefer adventure, humor, and scary stories. How many award-winning children's books fall into one of these categories? A closer analysis is needed.

We also need to ask, "*Where* are children reading for pleasure?" When the National Reading Panel questioned the scientific evidence for sustained silent reading in classrooms in 2000, many decried that reading for pleasure and providing students opportunity to self-select books and read for enjoyment in schools was threatened. Krashen (2004) counters the claim of the panel and presents a compelling case for the value of free voluntary reading in literacy development. Jim Trelease (2006) suggests that teachers respond to naysayers about sustained silent reading and children: "My classroom may be the *only* place where some of them ever see other people reading silently to themselves, and it might be the only place they ever see an adult reading for pleasure and not just for work. My classroom is a laboratory for positive role modeling" (p. 82).

Specific concern has risen during the last decade about the reading habits of boys and the perception that boys do not enjoy reading, do not read as much as girls, and are overrepresented in special education programs. Many educators and librarians have suggested ways to encourage boys to read. This is an interesting backlash to studies from the previous decade that concluded there were not enough strong female characters in children's books to serve as positive role models for girls and girls were therefore being shortchanged (see, for example, Sadker & Sadker, 1994). That body of scholarship led to the establishment of the Amelia Bloomer Project, an annual bibliography of feminist books appealing to young readers from birth to 18, which has been selected and published since 2002 by the Feminist Task Force of the Social Responsibilities Round Table of the American Library Association.

In 2001, author Jon Scieszka, named the National Ambassador for Young People's Literature by the Center for the Book at the Library of Congress, initiated the Guys Read program. The mission of this initiative, as described on the website, "is to motivate boys to read by connecting them with materials they will want to read, in ways they like to read" (www.guysread.com). Zbaracki (2008) points out that boys do read for pleasure, but they are often reading texts other than books such as magazines, manuals, and online materials. He has identified five factors to consider in selecting books for boys: "interest, choice, social factors, involvement, and text types" (p. 2). He further notes that humorous books appeal to boys, as does the emerging genre of graphic novels.

Davila and Patrick (2010, p. 201) cite a study of children's reading preferences conducted by Boracks, Hoffman, and Bauer (1997), that concludes "while boys prefer books with male protagonists, girls will read stories with either heroes or heroines." This kind of evidence, coupled with the perspective that reading has traditionally been viewed as more "feminine" than "masculine," has led many teachers and librarians to search for books they think will appeal to boys since girls will "read anything," but this is not always the best practice for either gender. In their review of research on children's reading preferences, Davila and Patrick offer much advice about encouraging reading for pleasure that is both gender-specific and gender-neutral. Based on their analysis, girls prefer romance, realistic fiction, and series fiction, and boys "show a preference for comics, joke books, news, informational texts, and other stereotypically masculine reading materials" (p. 206). Boys also prefer fantasy and science fiction, crime/detective stories, fiction about war and spies, and "gross and gory" topics (p. 206). However, boys and girls equally enjoy adventure, comedy, and ghost or horror stories; moreover, "among avid readers, there may be fewer differences between genders" (p. 204).

Certainly, finding out children's reading preferences, helping children select books that correspond with their interests, and providing time for children to actually read their self-selected texts are the tasks of teachers and librarians. One way that children's literature specialists can help young readers develop their personal tastes and preferences, as well as broaden their reading horizons, is by introducing them to authors and illustrators who might become favorites. A recent trend in the field of children's literature has been the emergence of creating children's books as a "family business." For example, illustrator Jerry Pinkney, along with wife Gloria Jean Pinkney, son Brian Pinkney and his wife Andrea Davis Pinkney, and son Myles Pinkney and his wife Sandra Pinkney, have created a children's literature "dynasty," with over 100 picture books featuring the Pinkney family name (Minzesheimer, 2010). Children's literature critic and historian Leonard Marcus's 2006 publication, *Pass It Down: Five Picture Book Families Make Their Mark*, highlights the work of Jerry and Brian Pinkney as well as four other families who have collaborated on picture books. Families who create children's books was the focus of the 2008 CLA Workshop at the NCTE Annual Convention; a list of authors and illustrators that was created for the workshop, though probably no longer exhaustive, is included as Figure 2.1. It seems likely that if a child enjoys the work of a particular author, that same child might also enjoy being introduced to the work of the author's spouse or sibling or child. Being knowledgeable of families in the "children's literature business" can assist teachers and librarians in placing in children's hands those books that will open their reading worlds.

Conclusion

And so we return to where we began. In summary, this chapter has highlighted some current trends and issues in children's literature. As those who prepare teachers and librarians to share books with children, we must remain continually aware of how the field of children's literature is evolving. Although we no longer have book women traveling the hills of Appalachia, we still have dedicated adults who believe in the power of books, who cherish the written word, and who strive to bring children and books together.

Marc Aronson, Marina Budhos
Herm Auch, Mary Jane Auch
Arnold Adoff, Virginia Hamilton, Jaime Adoff
Molly Bang, Monika Bang-Campbell
Ludwig Bemelmans, John Bemelmans Marciano
Phil Bildner, Kevin Lewis
Donald Crews, Ann Jonas, Nina Crews
Jean de Brunhoff, Laurent de Brunhoff
Penda Diakite, Baba Wague Diakite
Leo and Diane Dillon
Ed Emberley, Rebecca Emberley, Michael Emberley, Marie-Louise Fitzpatrick
Sid Fleischman, Paul Fleischman
Shannon Hale, Dean Hale
Craig Hatkoff, Isabella Hatkoff, Juliana Hatkoff
Kevin Henkes, Laura Droznek
Tad Hills, Lee Wade
Jennifer Holm, Matthew Holm
Clement Hurd, Edith Thacher Hurd, Thacher Hurd
Justine Larbalestier, Scott Westerfeld
Kathryn Lasky, Christopher Knight
Betsy and Ted Lewin
Anita Lobel, Arnold Lobel
Tracy Mack, Michael Citrin
Kam Mak, Mari Takabayashi
Frederick McKissack, Patricia McKissack, Frederick McKissack Jr.
Walter Dean Myers, Christopher Myers
Mark Newgarden, Megan Montague Cash
Frances Park, Ginger Park
Jerry Pinkney, Gloria Jean Pinkney, Brian Pinkney, Andrea Davis Pinkney, Myles Pinkney,
    Sandra Pinkney
Sean Qualls, Selina Alko
Gloria and Ted Rand
James Ransome, Lesa Cline-Ransome
Harlow Rockwell, Anne Rockwell, Lizzy Rockwell
Robert Sabuda, Matthew Reinhart
Mark Siegel, Siena Cherson Siegel
Cynthia Leitich Smith, Greg Leitich Smith
Lane Smith, Molly Leach
Jerry Spinelli, Eileen Spinelli
Janet Stevens, Susan Stevens Crummel
Sarah Stewart, David Small
Jeanette Winter, Jonah Winter
Don Wood, Audrey Wood, Bruce Wood
Lawrence Yep, Joanne Ryder
Jane Yolen, Adam Stemple, Jason Stemple, Heidi Stemple

Figure 2.1: A sampling of literary families.

Works Cited

Alexander, J. (2005). The verse-novel: A new genre. *Children's Literature in Education, 36*,
    269–283.

Audio Publishers Association. (2008). *More Americans are all ears to audiobooks.* Retrieved from http://www.audiopub.org/pdfs/2008%20sales%20consumer%20final.pdf

Boraks, N., Hoffman, A., & Bauer, D. (1997). Children's book preferences: Patterns, particulars, and possible implications. *Reading Psychology, 18*, 309–341.

Children's Book Council. (2006). *Graphic novels for young people 2005–2006.* Retrieved from www.cbcbooks.org

Colman, P. (2007). A new way to look at literature: A visual model for analyzing fiction and nonfiction texts. *Language Arts, 84*, 257–268.

Davila, D., & Patrick, L. (2010). Asking the experts: What children have to say about their reading preferences. *Language Arts, 87*, 199–210.

Goldstone, B. P. (1999). Brave new worlds: The changing image of the picture book. *The New Advocate, 12*, 331–343.

Goldstone, B. P. (2002). Whaz up with our books? Changing picture book codes and teaching implications. *The Reading Teacher, 55*, 362–370.

Goldstone, B. P. (2004). The postmodern picture book: A new subgenre. *Language Arts, 81*, 196–204.

Hade, D. (2002, September/October). Storyselling: Are publishers changing the way children read? *The Horn Book Magazine, 78*, 509–517.

Holley, P. S. (2010). *Top ten educational benefits of audiobook listening.* Retrieved from http://school.booksontape.com/s_promo_pam_spencer.cfm

Kane, S. (2010). A dozen great books: Is fictionalized nonfiction an oxymoron? *Journal of Children's Literature, 36*(1), 23–26.

Krashen, S. (2003). The (lack of) experimental evidence supporting the use of Accelerated Reader. *Journal of Children's Literature, 29*(2), 9, 16–30.

Krashen, S. D. (2004). *The power of reading: Insights from the research* (2nd ed.). Portsmouth, NH: Heinemann.

Larson, L. C. (2008). Electronic reading workshop: Beyond books with new literacies and instructional technologies. *Journal of Adolescent and Adult Literacy, 52*, 121–131.

Minzesheimer, B. (2010, February 4). For Pinkney's bunch, books bind a literary dynasty. *USA Today.* Retrieved from http://www.usatoday.com/life/books/news/2010-02-04-pinkney04_CV_N.htm?POE=click-refer

Mohr, K. A. J. (2006). Children's choices for recreational reading: A three-part investigation of selection preferences, rationales, and processes. *Journal of Literacy Research, 38*, 81–104.

Nunnery, J. A., Ross, S. M., & McDonald, A. (2006). A randomized experimental evaluation of the impact of Accelerated Reader/Reading Renaissance implementation on reaching achievement in grades 3 to 6. *Journal of Education for Students Placed at Risk, 11*(1), 1–18.

Pierce, K. M. (1998). Uses and abuses of children's literature in the classroom: Master class for teaching college level children's literature courses. *Journal of Children's Literature, 24*(1), 103–105.

Rideout, V., Roberts, D. F., & Foehr, U. G. (2005). *Generation M: Media in the lives of 8–18 year-olds. Executive summary.* Menlo Park, CA: The Henry J. Kaiser Family Foundation.

Rogers, L. (2003). Computerized reading management software: An effective component of a successful reading program. *Journal of Children's Literature, 29*(2), 9–15.

Ross, S. M., Nunnery, J., & Goldfeder, E. (2004). *A randomized experiment on the effects of Accelerated Reader/Reading Renaissance in an urban school district: Preliminary evaluation report.* Memphis, TN: The University of Memphis, Center for Research in Educational Policy.

Sadker, M., & Sadker, D. (1994). *Failing at fairness: How America's schools cheat girls.* New York: Scribner.

Scharer, P. L., Freeman, E. B., & Lehman, B. A. (2008). Children's literature in the classroom: Essential or marginal? In S. S. Lehr (Ed.), *Shattering the looking glass: Challenge, risk, and controversy in children's literature* (pp. 15–26). Norwood, MA: Christopher-Gordon.

Schmidt, R. (2008). Really reading: What does Accelerated Reader teach adults and children? *Language Arts, 85,* 202–211.

Serafini, F. (2010). Expository fiction: Blurring the boundaries between fiction and nonfiction in *Dragonology* and *The Discovery of Dragons. Journal of Children's Literature, 36*(1), 44–50.

Silvey, A. (2008). Has the Newbery lost its way? *School Library Journal, 54* (10), 38–41.

Sipe, L. R., & Pantaleo, S. (Eds.). (2008). *Postmodern picturebooks: Play, parody and self-referentiality.* New York: Routledge.

Stone, J. C., & Veth, E. S. (2008). Rethinking the new literatures of childhood: Cultural models of gender in popular websites. *Journal of Language and Literacy Education* [Online], *4*(2), 21–39. Retrieved from http://www.coe.uga.edu/jolle/2008/rethinking.pdf

Thompson, M. (2008). Multimodal teaching and learning: Creating spaces for content teachers. *Journal of Adolescent and Adult Literacy, 52,* 144–153.

Trelease, J. (2006). *The read-aloud handbook* (6th ed.). New York: Penguin Books.

2008 kids and family reading report: Reading in the 21st century: Turning the page with technology. (2008). New York: Scholastic.

What Works Clearinghouse. (2008). *Intervention: Accelerated Reader.* Retrieved from http://ies.ed.gov/ncee/wwc/reports/beginning_reading/arrr/index.asp

Wolfenbarger, C. D., & Sipe, L. R. (2007). A unique visual and literary art form: Recent research on picturebooks. *Language Arts, 84,* 273–280.

Yang, G. (2008). Graphic novels in the classroom. *Language Arts, 85,* 185–192.

Yolen, J. (2007). Ten things I no longer enjoy about publishing but am willing to endure. *Journal of Children's Literature, 33*(1), 62–67.

Zarnowski, M. (2010). Historical novels in verse: A fusion genre. *Journal of Children's Literature, 36*(1), 37–43.

Zbaracki, M. D. (2008). *Best books for boys: A resource for educators.* Westport, CT: Libraries Unlimited.

Children's Books Cited

Carman, P. (2009a). *Ghost in the machine (Skeleton Creek).* New York: Scholastic.

Carman, P. (2009b). *Skeleton Creek.* New York: Scholastic.

Creech, S. (2001). *Love that dog.* New York: HarperCollins.

Falconer, I. (2000). *Olivia.* New York: Atheneum.

Funke, C. (2003). *Inkheart* (A. Bell, Trans.). New York: Scholastic.

Gerstein, M. (2003). *The man who walked between the towers.* Brookfield, CT: Roaring Brook Press.

Giblin, J. C. (2004). *Secrets of the Sphinx* (B. Ibatoulline, Illus.). New York: Scholastic.

Hayes, G. (2009). *Benny and Penny in the big no-no!* New York: Toon Books.

Henson, H. (2008). *That book woman* (D. Small, Illus.). New York: Atheneum.

Hesse, K. (1997). *Out of the dust.* New York: Scholastic.

Hunter, E. (2009). *Seekers: Great Bear Lake.* New York: HarperCollins.

Kinney, J. (2007). *Diary of a wimpy kid.* New York: Amulet Books.

Klise, K. (2005). *Regarding the trees: A splintered saga rooted in secrets* (M. S. Klise, Illus.). Orlando, FL: Harcourt.

Locker, T. (2000). *Cloud dance.* Orlando, FL: Harcourt.

Macaulay, D. (1990). *Black and white.* Boston: Houghton Mifflin.

Marcus, L. S. (2006). *Pass it down: Five picture-book families make their mark.* New York: Walker Books for Young Readers.

Nelson, M. (2001). *Carver: A life in poems.* Asheville, NC: Front Street.

Nelson, M. (2009). *Sweethearts of rhythm: The story of the greatest all-girl band in the world* (J. Pinkney, Illus.). New York: Dial.

Nicholls, S. (2008). *Ways to live forever.* New York: Scholastic.

Pullman, P. (1998). *The golden compass.* New York: Knopf.

Rey, H. A. (1941). *Curious George.* Boston: Houghton Mifflin.

Scieszka, J. (1992). *The stinky cheese man and other fairly stupid tales* (L. Smith, Illus.). New York: Viking.

Siebert, D. (2006). *Tour America: A journey through poems and art* (S. T. Johnson, Illus.). San Francisco: Chronicle Books.

Siegel, S. C. (2006). *To dance: A ballerina's graphic novel* (M. Siegel, Illus.). New York: Atheneum/Richard Jackson Books.

Sís, P. (2007). *The wall: Growing up behind the Iron Curtain*. New York: Farrar, Straus and Giroux.

Smith, J. (2005). *Bone: Out from Boneville*. New York: Scholastic.

Stead, R. (2009). *When you reach me*. New York: Random House.

Steig, W. (1990). *Shrek*. New York: Farrar, Straus and Giroux.

Stewart, T. L. (2007). *The Mysterious Benedict Society*. New York: Little, Brown.

Tan, S. (2007). *The arrival*. New York: Arthur A. Levine/Scholastic.

Weatherford, C. B. (2006). *Moses: When Harriet Tubman led her people to freedom* (K. Nelson, Illus.). New York: Hyperion.

Weatherford, C. B. (2007). *Birmingham, 1963*. Honesdale, PA: Wordsong.

Wiesner, D. (2001). *The three pigs*. New York: Clarion Books.

Willems, M. (2004). *Knuffle bunny: A cautionary tale*. New York: Hyperion.

Woodson, J. (2003). *Locomotion*. New York: G. P. Putnam's Sons.

Yang, G. L. (2006). *American born Chinese*. New York: First Second.

3

Re-imagining the Possibilities of Reader Response to Literature

MARJORIE R. HANCOCK, *Kansas State University*

The focus of the 1999 Master Class in Teaching Children's Literature was response to children's books. Five years later, at the 2004 National Council of Teachers of English Annual Convention, participants crowded into a small session room to celebrate the vision, wisdom, and democratic principles of Louise M. Rosenblatt, the creator of the transactional theory of reader response and the language arts icon of generations of readers. This theoretical genius was approaching her 100th birthday, and rigorous applause ceased as the voice of this respected scholar who had the greatest impact on literature in the classroom spoke. Rosenblatt spent her entire life teaching educators that our personal transactions with literature can change both lives and society. Her theoretical works and engaging ideas changed teachers' philosophies about the role of literature in literacy instruction.

Rosenblatt's presence reminded the audience of her beliefs, her legacy of followers, and her goal to retain literature as key to the reading process in schools and homes. Her accompanying panel of doctoral students, now noted professors at major universities, celebrated 70 years of generational commitment to literature as the foundation of democratic education. Rooting her theory in authentic classroom practice, teachers experienced how the transactions between literature and unique readers created lifelong commitment to both literacy and critical thinking.

In classrooms across the country today, even under the boundaries of No Child Left Behind, children talk, draw, write, or use technology to create their response to literature choices. Through this continuing perspective, the theoretical platform of Rosenblatt continues to thrive as each reader personalizes his or her own response to literature, sharing thoughts within a learning community and striving toward becoming a democratic citizen in a global society. Rosenblatt's fingerprints remain forever on classroom reading across all instructional levels. Her legacy lies in those professionals who connect her theory to practice, assuming differentiated practices as the new literacies shift reader response to a new era. New literacy genres, varied formats of literary presentation, and fresh modes of response built on new technology provide opportunities for current and future teachers to engage in the innovative, unfolding modes of reader response.

Legacy of Rosenblatt's Theory

Since its publication in 1938, Louise Rosenblatt's *Literature as Exploration* has provided the theoretical basis for research in the teaching and study of literature and the way it is shared in school settings (Dressman & Webster, 2001). Although supported by university and secondary teachers for years, it was only in the past three decades that children's literature advocates have discovered, processed, and implemented her theory, which granted natural permission to include literature as a part of the elementary/middle level curriculum (Cai, 2001). Rosenblatt's work eternally supports teachers' desires to surround readers with quality children's literature experiences so ongoing personal emotions, connections, and responses result in creating lifelong readers.

The transactional theory of reader response focuses on the reciprocal relationship between the reader and the literature, resulting in individual responses to the text throughout the reading process. As the reader brings a wealth of life and literature experiences to reading, the personal response evokes the literary work of art as a truly personal experience for the reader. In *The Reader, the Text, the Poem* (1978), Rosenblatt artfully described the evolving balance between the roles of reader and text by likening reading to a role performed on the stage. Imagine a darkened stage with the author stage left, the reader stage right, and the book at center stage. Years ago, the spotlight focused on the author; then it shifted to the text with the reader totally obscured. After many years, however, the spotlight began to shine on the reader, gaining earned importance as an active member of the reading event. Today, the spotlight focuses on all three characters—the reader, the author, the text—as they blend together to create meaning. Rosenblatt's passionate words painted a vivid transaction between the reader and the text in the minds of elementary/middle level practitioners.

Aesthetic and Efferent Response

An awareness between *efferent* and *aesthetic* reading is necessary to fully understand transactional theory. In efferent reading, the reader's attention is primarily focused on acquiring information. For example, perhaps a student is reading *M. L. K.: Journey of a King* by Tonya Bolden (2007) to find out pure facts about

Dr. Martin Luther King—his birthdate, birthplace, connections to the Civil Rights Movement, and details of his assassination. Aesthetic reading, however, is primarily concerned with the lived through experiences that occur during interaction with the text. Aesthetic reading focuses on feelings and thoughts that flow through the reader's mind and heart during the reading process. In this case, a student may be reading Christopher Paul Curtis's (2007) *Elijah of Buxton*, based on the history of the Elgin Settlement in Canada that served as a home for escaped slaves and freed people during the mid-1800s. A reader might lean emotionally toward Elijah's sense of humor, the questionable status of a lying preacher, or the challenging attempt to bring an Underground Railroad family to freedom. The sensitivity of the reader abounds in the reading of quality literature in which personal interaction, rather than isolated comprehension, reigns.

Both the terms *aesthetic* and *efferent* apply to a selective stance the reader adopts toward a literary text. The efferent stance showcases the cognitive, factual, public, and quantitative aspects of meaning. The aesthetic stance, on the other hand, focuses on the reader, the ongoing reading process, emotions, enjoyment, personal connections, and the qualitative aspects of meaning. While the reading of a particular book can become fixed somewhere on a continuum between both of these stances, readers typically slide back and forth between these two stances, depending on the text itself. In *M. L. K.: Journey of a King*, for example, the reader may relate to being discriminated against in one's own life, not necessarily by ethnicity/race but by gender, socioeconomic status, or language. In *Elijah of Buxton*, the reader may actually link to websites from the author's notes on Buxton, Canada, to locate more information about Frederick Douglass or to access a map to sense the distance of the Elgin settlement from Detroit. The constant fluctuation between the aesthetic and the efferent are characteristic of highly qualified readers.

Application of Response Theory to New Literacies

The new literacies (Leu, Kinzer, Coiro, & Cammack, 2004) have moved response to literature beyond the traditional paper-and-pencil responses of the previous reader response era. The new literacies are defined as the skills, strategies, and dispositions necessary to adapt to continuously changing, emerging technologies. Forms of response now extend to the visual, informational/Internet, or media literacies. Literature-based literacy and reader response now often lean toward clustering around the Internet and other information and communication technologies in an online, networked classroom. For educators who value the impact and uniqueness of reader response, the preparation of students to address the new literacies is central to keeping reader response dominant, yet simultaneously assuring student preparedness for a technology-based future as both readers and citizens.

The transactional theory of reader response still has the theoretical potential to blend with the philosophical belief of the new literacies. Readers continue to read but now often respond to a text by participating in an online discussion, locating related informational websites or actually creating response-based presentations through new media including PowerPoint, iMovies, or podcasts. Some of the traditional phases of reader response continue to capture the responses of readers in valued ways. Blending the new versus the traditional response modes, reader response to literature still reigns empowered to dominate a classroom utilizing quality literature and expecting the voices and thoughts of reader responders to fill the classroom context.

Paving the Way to the Future of Reader Response

Besides the infusion of new technologies into reader response, the extension of genres of literature into reader response also has led to the expansion of reader response to wordless books, hybrid narrative/expository text and nonfiction literature, poetic formats, and graphic novels. While early elementary/middle level reader response in the 1980s and 1990s leaned toward picture storybooks and realistic and historical fiction chapter books, the trend in the new century is to inspire response to *all* genres.

The purpose of this chapter is to briefly revisit the traditional and honored view of reader response across several decades. The nostalgic view of oral and written response actually lays the foundation for the inclusion of the new literacies as a mode of response. Establishing an in-depth understanding of the foundation of reader response is essential prior to paving the road to future venues of response. Following the foundational view of reader response transactions, this chapter celebrates the re-imagined modes of reader response that have begun to emerge as our world shifts to a global perspective and a technology base. If Rosenblatt were still with us, she likely would thrive on an expanding, fluctuating, and accelerated reader response perspective. While she might place high value on the traditional reader and text, she would unquestionably support the power of the new literacies to provide expanded genres to which to respond and extended technology as venues with which to express unique reader response.

Established Response Modes

An appreciation for response to literature begins with theory but continues with an awareness of the wide range of responses that children exhibit as they interact with books. Janet Hickman (1981) originally observed and described patterns in elementary children's responses to literature as they occurred in a fifth-grade classroom setting.

Listening behavior, the first childhood mode of response, evidences itself during a parent/teacher read-aloud as a child stretches to view illustrations, produces spontaneous laughter, or chants a repetitive phrase. *Contact with books*, whether browsing in the library, reading in a comfortable pillow chair, or attending to books at their desks, reflects reader interest, intent, and immersion in literature. Pulling books off the shelf, hugging titles, reading a familiar author while keeping books "within reach" showcases the importance of literature in a child's life and warrants selective preferences as response. The *impulse to share*, an instinctive need to share the textual event with others in a community of readers, reflects response through retellings, sharing textual discoveries, and relating personal connections to another title (text-to-text), an event in life (text-to-life), or a global perspective (text-to-world). Some readers respond through *action and drama* as puppet shows, improvisation, movement, and plays based on literature foster active comprehension and a deeper personal, literary connection. *Art, musical, and constructive response* take the form of drawings, multimedia presentations, musical accompaniment, or constructed models, reflecting a hands-on approach to response. Drawing or visual replication of a story, baking a recipe related to a title, selecting or playing background music for a read-aloud, or folding a model of an animal all reflect this active, engaged mode of response.

As children listen or read literature, *oral response* encourages their fleeting responses in which the voice of the reader is valued and respected for its individuality, spontaneity, or structured response to a teacher-generated prompt. The *written response* mode captures and records a permanent record of the reader's personal transaction with literature. Personal expression of thoughts, feelings, and opinions are typically recorded in a journal format, exchanged with a partner, or shared with a teacher, thus providing an impetus for interaction with literature that reconstructs higher-level reading images and advanced personal thoughts.

These established modes of response tend to weave, overlap, and build on each other. While these introductory modes provide a framework for exploring the possibilities of response, any mode can be generated through a distinctive piece of quality literature. Yet the oral and written modes require further discussion to clarify, elaborate, and celebrate these research-documented response extensions over the past two decades.

Talking about Books

The most natural response to literature, either read aloud or read independently, is to talk about it. A developmental perspective begins with childhood in which literature encounters result in spontaneous reactions, personal connections, and likes/dislikes about the story. Intermediate/middle level readers look forward to verbal and social interactions with peers, gaining new perspectives from fellow readers. These natural responses capture individualized response through the oral medium, encouraging risk-taking, developing oral communication skills, while showcasing the individuality of the reader.

Early childhood read-alouds encourage active engagement in reading, thus moving readers toward positive reading experiences and instilling the desire to learn to read. Listening to the *language of literature* involves alliterative titles, rhyming texts, playful language, and text demanding repetition. These responses beg children to experiment with language, providing inspiration for emergent readers.

Oral response prompts provide the first structured yet open-ended approach to encourage thought and expand response offerings, inviting readers to focus, feel, connect, and relate to literature. The power to challenge readers to stretch their thinking is based on three original open-ended response prompts (Bleich, 1978):

- What did you notice in the story?
- How did the story make you feel?
- What does the story remind you of from your own life?

As readers move forward in their thinking, prompts can be expanded toward even further independent thought:

- What special meaning or message did the story have for you?
- What did you like/dislike about the story?
- What would it feel like to have been (character's name)?
- What do you think will happen to (character's name) in the future?

A steady diet of the same prompts, however, can become inhibiting, so choosing prompts wisely, tailoring them according to individual titles, and providing a consistent environment in which book talk is valued throughout the entire school day is essential for quality oral response. Oral response is not built though a daily routine, but through a natural environment of acceptance, unique thoughts, and valuing response to literature.

Literature conversations within small groups are based on the belief that reading is a social transactional process as students bring, construct, and take meaning from the text. Collaborative listening, thinking, and responding lead to new perspectives on a book. A sense of a community of readers and an acceptance of risk taking lead to the success of literature conversations. Each session is viewed as dialogue among readers in which personal impressions are valued, honored, and used as a springboard to ongoing conversations. The emphasis on student-generated talk driven by minimal teacher facilitation provides a setting for authentic and unique expression. Socially empowered response finds an appropriate audience within literature conversations.

Literature circles (Daniels, 2002) may assign roles that serve as directed response to literature because each student focuses on a specific aspect of a literature experience: discussion director, literary luminary, connector, illustrator, vocabulary enricher, and summarizer. Another means of guiding students toward higher-level response is to provide written guidelines for response following the sharing of personal response (Hancock, 2008a). These provide a roadmap for conversations for novice conversationalists. Extended research in this area led to an advanced organizational framework for book clubs (Raphael, Florio-Ruane, George, Hasty, & Highfield, 2001). Regardless of the term applied to informal literary talks, the opportunity for oral response encourages and preserves the authenticity of response leaning toward growing mature conversations as lifelong readers.

Written Response

Written response provides recorded documentation of thoughts elicited throughout the reading of a literary text. Innermost responses to literature occur mostly in a journal format, but responses can also make their way into creative writing by following literature as a model for writing. Both of these written reflections serve a meaningful purpose as personal interpretation and voice align with student written response to quality literature.

A *literature response journal* is a repository of wanderings, wonderings, speculations, questions, and explorative thoughts recorded throughout the reading process (Hancock, 1993). Journals reflect the reader making discoveries, letting the mind ramble, and creating room for the evolving text. The literature response journal can assume different formats, but all are geared toward capturing the unique response of each reader. A dialogue journal, for example, can foster continuous dialogue between the reader and another reader, creating a continuous written conversation throughout the entire book. A character journal implies a first-person interaction with the book as the reader assumes the guise of the book's main character. The "I" stance creates strong involvement with the character and events of the book. A reading log, on the other hand, implies brief entries, usually at the end of a book, providing less authentic response, but documenting an ongoing reading list throughout the school year.

The freedom and commitment to write in a literature response journal results in a full range of reader responses to quality, emotionally focused literature. Teacher modeling of written response inspires and raises expectations to thinking beyond the texts to one's own life. With teacher encouragement and feedback, children develop their own response styles and internalize the written response process. The interplay between reading and writing becomes a natural part of the reading process (Hancock, 2008a).

Literature can easily serve as a model for writing when following a format or genre structure of a book. Many researchers have pinpointed the relevant connections between reading and writing (Graves, 1983/2003; Hansen, 1987/2001). Whether modeling a fairy tale variant, a journal diary, or letter writing, for example, aligned titles provide gracious models that actually improve the quality of children's writing in that particular genre. Literature as a model for writing serves to internalize genre, literary elements, and the craft of writing as an essential part of a child's writing process.

Re-imagined Modes of Literature Response

With the ongoing expansion of both literary genres and technological connections to literature, new modes of reader response are emerging with strong potentials and innovative possibilities. This section focuses on the most recent research supporting new responses to literary genres and through new technologies. Both these genres and the technological modes of response provide the groundwork for expanding the literature *to which* to respond and the media *through which* to respond. The transactional theory of reader response (Rosenblatt, 1938, 1978) celebrates a sound, timeless theoretical foundation as it readily aligns with the newest genres of literature and extended response modes.

Global/Multicultural Reader Response

The role of multicultural/global literature in eliciting reader response as well as the use of this genre to achieve response from second language learners opens a fresh perspective on reader response (Hancock, 2008b). For years, many teachers avoided the use of multicultural literature in classrooms lacking diversity. However, the population changes in America have opened the door to the use of multicultural texts and global literature for English language learners, children of military families, and international learners residing in the United States. The new trend in multicultural response to literature has grown from multiethnic literature such as literature about African Americans, to a population focus such as literature about Hispanic/Latino individuals, and even a more global perspective for response such as those awarded the Mildred Batchelder Book Award for outstanding children's books written in a foreign language and translated into English.

Research supports the link between reader response and the multicultural/global genre. Dressel (2005) implemented a multicultural, middle-level unit that explored the link between reader response and social responsibility across cultures. Surveys, dialogue journals, and a book club provided response data from seven multicultural novels including Suzanne Fisher Staples's (1989) *Shabanu: Daughter of the Wind* and Sherry Garland's (1993) *Shadow of the Dragon.* The study indicated the need for teachers of dominant culture students to include more multicultural literature in their curriculum so students can gain experience with different views within our global society. Students need to read beyond who they are and move toward changing cultural attitudes and behaviors from what they read.

Belinda Louie (2005) conducted an observational case study on response to Jicai Feng's (1995) Chinese novella, *Let One Hundred Flowers Bloom.* Embedded in a historical, cultural, and political context, the findings identified emotional and cross-cultural empathy reflected in response. Response journal entries and an emotional timeline of the character provided data that concluded that multicultural literature and response options helped readers develop empathy for characters who lived in a different world. Ruth Elizabeth Quiroa (2005) investigated the oral, written, and artistic response of young Mexican-origin children to Mexican-related story books. The culturally specific literature intersected with the cultural background of the participants, thus eliciting high levels of aesthetic response, critical thinking, and familiar cultural aspects related to readers' lives.

Overall, these studies serve as a first step toward utilizing the multicultural genre to implement a broader curriculum addressing a global perspective and encouraging a deeper understanding and empathy of international and cultural differences. Reading and responding to a cultural and/or global setting, character, problem, and solution may contribute to creating a global citizenry and a lifetime of reading books beyond our borders.

Nonfiction Reader Response

The growth of the quantity and the quality of the nonfiction genre in the past decade has brought expository text to the forefront of literature in the classroom. While nonfiction traditionally sat on the shelf until the assignment of an annual research project, today's readers choose nonfiction for independent reading, revel in the varying structure of expository text, and challenge reader response to nonfiction by viewing these texts through a fresh perspective. While the advent of the Orbis Pictus Award for Nonfiction from the National Council of Teachers of English has advocated the increased use of nonfiction for expository text reading, its quality titles have resulted in increased response research in this genre.

Porter (2006) celebrated the blending of interdisciplinary curriculum (science/social studies/literacy) through Orbis Pictus nonfiction. Oral and written responses to related nonfiction indicated a conceptual understanding beyond textbook information. Pappas (2006) targeted the information book genre and its use in blending science and literacy. Identifying seven hybrid types of information text provides a tool for investigating the responses of young children to the increased popularity of blending narrative/expository texts.

Nonfiction stands at the threshold of response-based reading across the curriculum. Hancock (2008a) provides several classroom-based possibilities for reader response to nonfiction including responding to authentic quotes, book excerpts, and lesser-known historical facts and figures. Response to biography includes connecting oneself to the subject, authoring a bio-poem blending facts and personality traits, and responses to first-person accounts of discoveries and expeditions. Responses to nonfiction through photographic essays blend visual literacy and its impact on descriptive writing and leading thoughts outside the photo frame to include imagined or verified details (Van Horn, 2008). Finally, response to nonfiction through a multigenre research project (Putz, 2006) nurtures the use of nonfiction text and related websites to creatively share facts through writing genres including recipes, birth certificates, licenses, résumés, greeting cards, or lists. The empowered choices of genres and the personal responses to factual information through creative writing successfully bypass the traditional informational report while thriving on the power of reader response.

Interdisciplinary/Content Area Reader Response

With the definition of literacy and literature extending into cross-disciplinary realms, reader response holds the potential to compare/contrast itself to both realistic/historical fiction and nonfiction titles. Responding aesthetically and efferently to contrasting genres could elicit a variety of personal responses, unrestricted to a single genre as in the past. Even poetry related to a content area topic might generate the possibility of unique response in a cross-genre/cross-disciplinary response perspective.

The advent of content area literacy (Vacca & Vacca, 2007) justifies the use of literature across disciplines. As No Child Left Behind has leaned toward prioritization of literacy over content area subjects, knowledgeable educators have chosen to expand literacy into social studies, science, and mathematics. Instead of separating literacy and the content areas, the new trend leans toward embedded literacy in topical areas of varied disciplines, thus allowing students to gain subject area knowledge as well as improving literacy skills, and even responding to multigenre literature within a contextual scenario.

An example from social studies includes the study of the Middle Ages as a global period in history. Reading Laura Amy Schlitz's (2007) *Good Masters! Sweet Ladies! Voices from a Medieval Village,* a recent Newbery Medal winner, provides a mix of both expository and narrative texts blending background knowledge of the period with the voices of the serfs, the lords, and the merchants who inhabited this time period in history. Reading Karen Cushman's (1994) *Catherine, Called Birdy*, an earlier Newbery Medal winner, extends the informational background of the previous text to provide a deeper level of comprehension of an individual residing in the Middle Ages and the daily life and personal challenges of a young woman during this period. While a textbook may be available for research, these titles provide an optimal, information-based adventure in a social studies curricular context, thus providing motivation, inspiration, and interest, often not present in a traditional classroom setting. Response journals to both of these titles may provide insight into both the efferent and aesthetic response reflecting knowledge and personal connections to a valued period of world history.

Poetic Response to Reading Poetry

With the advent of creative and lesser-known poetic forms, poetry books for children and young adults have warranted an option of actually creating self-written poetry as a form of response. Leaning on the framework and format of the examples shared in the literary title, young writers can respond to a poet's format, function, and style through one's own poetic writing. For example, Linda Sue Park's (2007) *Tap Dancing on the Roof: Sijo (Poems)* provides a traditional six-line form of Korean poetry that is related to Japanese haiku. Each of its four lines contains 14 to 16 syllables. The first two lines introduce the topic, the third and fourth lines elaborate on it, while the fourth and fifth lines contain a concluding humorous or ironic perspective. The newness of the format to the reader builds on prior knowledge of haiku and tends to inspire outstanding, creative writing in the form of personal response to a fresh poetic format.

While this form of written response may stretch the foundational definition of reader response, it does allow the individual reader/writer to focus on a self-selected topic, use the literature title as a model, and then expand and explain through a self-created poem in the newly designed format. As in reader response, no two products will be the same, thus sharing the ideals of reader response by forging both a literary model and personal writing choices into the response mode. While research in poetic response is limited, literature-based classroom teachers apply this option with almost every new poetry book that introduces a fresh poetic format to their language arts curriculum.

Visual Literacy as Reader Response

The advent of the new technologies in the creation of digital artwork as both illustration and story have paved the way for a new generation of subgenres of literature. Today's digital native generation of readers have a background of visual learning as a result of their exposure to a digital/video world. The creation of postmodern picture books (Kevin O'Malley's 2005 *Once Upon a Cool Motorcycle Dude*), the visual impression of wordless books (David Wiesner's 2006 *Flotsam)*, the enhancement of the use of illustrations in chapter books (Brian Selznick's 2007 *The Invention of Hugo Cabret*), and the popularity of graphic novels (*The Arrival* by Shaun Tan, 2007) provide an entirely new venue for reader response. The shift toward emphasizing illustrations themselves as *meaning making* sources and response related, nonlinear and non-sequential organization, interactive formats, and multiple levels of both visual and textual perspectives serve to broaden the scope of reader response. While an entire chapter in this volume is devoted to visual literacy (Chapter 4), it is addressed here in relation to reader response theory.

Postmodern picture books (Goldstone, 2002; Panteleo, 2004) provide literature with multiple story lines, narrators, and perspectives. Unexpected formats present challenges in text structure, multiple meaning, and opportunities for critical analysis. This subgenre was recently documented through a case study of a fourth-grade book club response to a plethora of postmodern titles including Kevin O'Malley's (2001) *Humpty Dumpty Egg-Splodes* and Anthony Browne's (2004) *Into the Forest* (Lohfink, 2006). The responses to these visual picture books lean toward promoting higher-level thinking and unique responses not related to other literary genres.

Another aspect of visual literacy is the option of responding to literature through artistic response. Opat (2008) recently worked with struggling readers through Caldecott Medal and Honor illustrated picture books to masterfully encourage artistic response as a means of determining listening comprehension. For some young readers, the artistic learning style and art response option appealed to them more than sharing written response through words. Whitin (1996, 2005) previously and continuously utilized visual representation as a means of response in response journals with middle school readers and showed the reflection of response through artistic representation as appropriate for sharing detailed information derived from literature. Many literature titles reflect art and artists, therefore providing a venue for artistic response for older readers as well.

Technology as an Extended Mode of Reader Response

Online reading, literature discussion, and reader response through multimedia enter the realm of the new literacies, providing a new venue for eliciting and analyzing reader response. Print texts are now transitioning to e-books; literature response journals are now being created electronically and posted on blogs; literature circles are now extended to chat rooms and orchestrated through threaded discussion groups. Literature-based projects have extended to technology-based projects incorporating multimedia, Internet, and online publishing. Yet these new technology-based options accurately align with the theoretical foundation of reader response.

The Electronic Reading Workshop approach (Larson, 2007, 2008) was based on the four common components of a reading workshop: literature selection, literature response journals, literature conversations, and project response options (Hancock, 2007). The new phase of the Electronic Reading Workshop views these components as electronic books or online reading materials, electronic journals or blogs, online threaded discussion groups or chat rooms, and technology-based projects (Larson, 2008).

Electronic books or e-books provide online accessible/downloadable books, which can be viewed on computers, cellular phones, or electronic readers such as the Kindle. E-books include tools allowing visual highlighting of text and additional comments through electronic sticky notes. *A House of Tailors* by Patricia Reilly Giff (2004) formed the foundation of Lotta Larson's (2008) preservice teacher study. Opportunities for individual response journals can be incorporated through email correspondence or blogs. Teacher feedback can occur through an email reply or "track changes" in regard to reader online responses. Online literature conversations can be conducted through email exchanges, message board threaded discussion groups, or real-time online chats. Moving beyond the book to a technology-based project can involve options including a virtual guide to the literature (PowerPoint with Internet links to background information), a digital oral history (multimedia presentation of sound, interviews, and information), or a podcast that replicates the sights and sounds of the setting of the historical text. The Electronic Reading Workshop provides a framework for teachers who strive to merge literacy and technology through literature.

The use of technology forms the cutting edge of reader response research. Any studies or experiences in the blending of reader response and technology will pave the way for new venues assuring that digital natives continue to be literature readers throughout their lifetimes.

Future Dimensions of Reader Response Research and Practice

To keep Rosenblatt's theory of reader response aligned and expanding in the coming decade requires new genres, new venues for response, and new media for sharing response to literature. Rosenblatt's legacy and theory will remain alive and thriving because continuing response-based research and classroom-based response activities will forge ahead to create independent, critical thinkers for tomorrow's world. Research blending the trends of a consistently changing society with the power of reader response research will create a vision for the future that Rosenblatt spent a lifetime establishing, articulating, and sharing with the educational community. While she may not have foreseen the new literacies, the expanding global initiative, and the vast array of fresh visual literacy genres, a sound theory is destined to align with changing times.

The theoretical voice of Rosenblatt continues to be heard by literature-based teachers. Rosenblatt's impact on both research and practice continues to inspire countless dissertation studies and teacher action research projects in school settings. The impact of these studies evidences itself in university level teacher preparation programs and teacher professional development seminars. Its impact is felt in the hearts, minds, talk, and writing of children and young adults as they build a lasting relationship with literature. Literature-based classrooms continue to serve as a tribute to the theoretical voice of Rosenblatt when the individuality of the reader and the uniqueness of response flourish, both through response to new literary genres and through new response modes influenced by technology.

Both researchers and teachers must continue to explore the potential and the variety of modes of response. Response supports active engagement, verbal acuity, the power of the written word, artistic creations, technology prowess, and the human need to share. Response addresses the varied learning styles of students and allows all readers to experience the freedom of sharing their unique thoughts during and following a literature experience. When researchers and teachers provide continuing opportunities for response, models of response, and receptiveness toward response, readers and literacy will both flourish (Hancock, 2008a).

Ultimately, the link between Louise Rosenblatt's transactional theory of reader response of the past and its coherent connections to the literature, reading, and response trends leaning toward the future provides a pathway for the voice of Rosenblatt to continue to echo in the educational realm. With ongoing research documentation and teacher implementation, reader response will continue to reign as a prioritized academic and democratic theory. The transactional theory of reader response will thrive by supporting reading in a new educational era by embracing the freedom of individual readers to express themselves with unique enthusiasm, thoughts, and voices in a changing global and technological society.

Works Cited

Bleich, D. (1978). *Subjective criticism*. Baltimore, MD: Johns Hopkins University Press.

Cai, M. (2001). Reflections on transactional theory as a theoretical guide for literacy and literature education. *The New Advocate, 14,* 19–32.

Daniels, H. (2002). *Literature circles: Voice and choice in book clubs and reading groups* (2nd ed.). Portland, ME: Stenhouse.

Dressel, J. H. (2005). Personal response and social responsibility: Responses of middle school students to multicultural literature. *The Reading Teacher, 58,* 750–764.

Dressman, M., & Webster, J. P. (2001). Retracing Rosenblatt: A textual archeology. *Research in the Teaching of English, 36,* 110–145.

Goldstone, B. P. (2002). Whaz up with our books? Changing picture book codes and teaching implications. *The Reading Teacher, 55,* 362–370.

Graves, D. H. (1983/2003). *Writing: Teachers and children at work*. Portsmouth, NH: Heinemann.

Hancock, M. R. (1993). Exploring the meaning-making process through the content of literature response journals: A case study investigation. *Research in the Teaching of English, 27*, 335–368.

Hancock, M. R. (2007). *Language arts: Extending the possibilities.* Upper Saddle River, NJ: Merrill/Prentice Hall.

Hancock, M. R. (2008a). *A celebration of literature and response: Children, books, and teachers in K–8 classrooms* (3rd ed.). Upper Saddle River, NJ: Prentice Hall/Merrill.

Hancock, M. R. (2008b). The status of reader response research: Sustaining the reader's voice in challenging times. In S. S. Lehr (Ed.), *Shattering the looking glass: Challenge, risk and controversy in children's literature* (pp. 91–108). Norwood, MA: Christopher-Gordon.

Hansen, J. (1987/2001). *When writers read.* Portsmouth, NH: Heinemann.

Hickman, J. (1981). A new perspective on response to literature: Research in an elementary school setting. *Research in the Teaching of English, 15*, 343–354.

Larson, E. L. C. (2007). *A case study exploring the "new literacies" during a fifth-grade electronic reading workshop* (Doctoral dissertation). Retrieved from http://krex.k-state.edu/dspace/handle/2097/352

Larson. L. C. (2008). Electronic reading workshop: Beyond books with literacies and instructional technologies. *Journal of Adolescent and Adult Literacy, 52*, 121–131.

Leu, D. J., Jr., Kinzer, C. K., Coiro, J. L., & Cammack, D. W. (2004). Toward a theory of new literacies emerging from the Internet and other information and communication technologies. In R. B. Ruddell & N. J. Unrau (Eds.), *Theoretical models and processes of reading* (5th ed., pp. 1570–1613). Newark, DE: International Reading Association.

Lohfink, G. S. (2006). *Responses to postmodern picture books: A case study of a fourth grade book club* (Doctoral dissertation). Kansas State University, Manhattan.

Louie, B. (2005). Development of empathetic responses with multicultural literature. *Journal of Adolescent and Adult Literacy, 48*, 566–578.

Opat, A. M. (2008). *Alternative pathways: Struggling readers utilize art elements for listening/viewing comprehension and artistic response* (Doctoral dissertation). Kansas State University, Manhattan.

Pantaleo, S. (2004). Young children and Radical Change characteristics in picture books. *The Reading Teacher, 58*, 178–187.

Pappas, C. C. (2006). The information book genre: Its role in integrated science literacy research and practice. *Reading Research Quarterly, 41*, 226–250.

Porter, D. L. (2006). *The impact of interactive read alouds of Orbis Pictus nonfiction on sixth graders' oral and written responses during integrated curricular units* (Doctoral dissertation). Kansas State University, Manhattan.

Putz, M. (2006). *A teacher's guide to the multigenre research project: Everything you need to get started.* Portsmouth, NH: Heinemann.

Quiroa, R. E. (2005). *Literature as mirror: Analyzing the oral, written, and artistic responses of young Mexican-origin children to Mexican American-themed picture storybooks* (Doctoral dissertation). University of Illinois, Urbana-Champaign.

Raphael, T. E., Florio-Ruane, S., George, M., Hasty, N. L., & Highfield, K. (2004). *Book club plus! A literacy framework for the primary grades*. Lawrence, MA: Small Planet Communications.

Rosenblatt, L. M. (1938). *Literature as exploration*. New York: Appleton-Century.

Rosenblatt, L. M. (1978). *The reader, the text, the poem: The transactional theory of the literary work*. Carbondale: Southern Illinois University Press.

Vacca, R. T., & Vacca, J. L. (2007). *Content area reading: Literacy and learning across the curriculum*. Boston: Allyn and Bacon.

Van Horn, L. (2008). *Reading photographs to write with meaning and purpose, grades 4–12*. Newark, DE: International Reading Association.

Whitin, P. (1996). Exploring visual response to literature. *Research in the Teaching of English, 30*, 114–140.

Whitin, P. (2005). The interplay of text, talk, and visual representation in expanding literary interpretation. *Research in the Teaching of English, 39*, 365–397.

Children's Books Cited

Bolden, T. (2007). *M. L. K: Journey of a king*. New York: Abrams Books.

Browne, A. (2004). *Into the forest*. Cambridge, MA: Candlewick Press.

Curtis, C. P. (2007). *Elijah of Buxton*. New York: Scholastic.

Cushman, K. (1994). *Catherine, called Birdy*. New York: Clarion Books.

Feng, J. (1995). *Let one hundred flowers bloom*. New York: Viking.

Garland, S. (1993). *Shadow of the dragon*. San Diego: Harcourt.

Giff, P. R. (2004). *A house of tailors*. New York: Wendy Lamb Books.

O'Malley, K. (2001). *Humpty dumpty egg-splodes*. New York: Walker.

O'Malley, K. (2005). *Once upon a cool motorcycle dude*. New York: Walker.

Park, L. S. (2007). *Tap dancing on the roof: Sijo (poems)* (I. Banyai, Illus.). New York: Clarion Books.

Schlitz, L. A. (2007). *Good masters! Sweet ladies! Voices from a medieval village* (R. Byrd, Illus.). Cambridge, MA: Candlewick Press.

Selznick, B. (2007). *The invention of Hugo Cabret*. New York: Scholastic.

Staples, S. F. (1989). *Shabanu: Daughter of the wind*. New York: Knopf.

Tan, S. (2007). *The arrival*. New York: Arthur A. Levine/Scholastic.

Wiesner, D. (2006). *Flotsam*. New York: Clarion Books.

2

Broadening Our Reading Worlds

4

Speaking from the Art

Children's Book Illustration and Design

CYNDI GIORGIS, *University of Nevada, Las Vegas*

The Caldecott Medal was first presented in 1938, having been established the year before by a man named Frederic G. Melcher, who in 1921 had also created the Newbery Medal. For the Caldecott, his intention was to honor the work done in picture books by American illustrators. But right from the start, there was a question of what exactly defined a picture book. In her *History of the Newbery and Caldecott Medals*, Irene Smith states that Melcher believed that the "dominant feature must be the work of the artist." When I began work on *The Invention of Hugo Cabret,* I had no idea that the "dominant feature would be the work of the artist"; that the story would be told so prominently through images. So tonight, members of the Caldecott committee, esteemed colleagues, fellow honorees, friends, and family, I'd like to talk a little bit about how I came to make a 550-page picture book.

—BRIAN SELZNICK, 2008 CALDECOTT MEDAL AWARD ACCEPTANCE SPEECH

A decade ago, the Master Class in the Teaching of Children's Literature focused on the topic of picture book illustration and design. At that time, few would argue that a picture book is defined as that in which text and illustration work in concert to create meaning in the span of 32 to 48 pages. When Selznick's 550-page *The Invention of Hugo Cabret* received the Caldecott Medal in 2008, it pushed educators, librarians, parents, and even kids to rethink the definition of a picture book and the role of illustration in reading. The boundaries of illustration in children's books have been further extended by recent titles such as Sherman Alexie's *The Absolutely True Diary of a Part-Time Indian* (2007) and Jeff Kinney's *Diary of a Wimpy Kid* (2007) series, which includes drawings interspersed with text throughout these popular chapter books. Illustrations, or drawings in the case of Alexie's and Kinney's books, provide much more than an artistic reprieve but rather enhance and extend readers' interpretations of the text as they read the art they encounter in picture and chapter books.

Visual Literacy and Picture Walking

In today's society, images play a dominant role in our lives and the ability to interpret these images has become increasingly important. *Visual literacy* is a term that has gained widespread use and refers to the ability to discriminate and interpret images. In 1989, Betty Goldstone stated:

> Children come to school with the ability to interpret on a literal level and perceive the image as a whole. However, the higher order thinking skills of analyzing, synthesizing, and interpreting the visual image does not come naturally. To be able to interpret visual images from pictorial or media sources, the viewer must use abstract thinking skills. This is ultimately what the educational system is trying to promote. (p. 592)

More than two decades later, Goldstone's (1989) perspective of promoting visual literacy is still relevant and something that is often overlooked in schools. Children need to have the ability to critically analyze visual text and also to understand the way art elements are used to create them. Sipe (1998) states that, "We should not underestimate what children are capable of when they talk about picture books; even young children can be very sophisticated as literary critic" (p. 6).

A popular strategy that is used in many elementary classrooms is that of the picture walk. Typical questions asked of students include, What's going on here? Why does the character look excited? How do you think the story is going to end? These types of questions ask children to use illustrations as clues to the text as they attempt to guess the storyline. Students are not truly engaging in a picture walk because analysis of the illustrations is not the focus. Questions for a picture walk examining illustrations might include the following:

- What do you see?
- What catches your eye first?
- How do the colors make you feel?
- What point of view does the illustrator give you?
- What do you see in the foreground? middle ground? background?

- What do you think the illustrator used to create the art?
- What questions are bubbling up for you about the illustrations?

Richards and Anderson (2003) have narrowed this list by suggesting the STW strategy of asking, *What do I See? What do I Think? and What do I Wonder?* These questions encourage students to extend their initial observation of the illustrations and to hone in on the positioning and facial expressions of the characters, the mood or tone conveyed by color, or the media used by the illustrator to create a sense of time or place. Developing an understanding of the elements used by artists enables readers to express their analysis of the art and to make meaning from their interpretation.

Elements of Art

Often teachers do not discuss illustrations in picture and chapter books because they don't feel comfortable in their own knowledge about art. Illustrations may be referred to as "cute" rather than using more descriptive terms such as *luminous, expressive, comical, cheery,* or *clever*. Rosemary Wells, illustrator of numerous picture books including the Max and Ruby series, believes that referring to her art as "cute" is nothing short of demeaning (Giorgis, 2000). So, it is important for adults and children to not only read the text but to be competent readers of illustrations as well.

Understanding Elements of Art Is One Place to Begin

The elements of art are the visual tools that illustrators use. Some of these elements include line, color, shape, texture, and perspective (Serafini & Giorgis, 2003). These elements coming together creates the composition of the illustration and page. In turn, the elements assist readers in generating meaning from the story.

> *Line*—Thick, thin, straight, jagged, short, repeated, blunt, choppy, long, curled, dark, light, soft, sharp, squiggly, tapered, fine, even, and exaggerated are some of the types of lines used by artists to create illustrations and portray ideas (Erbach, 2007). Horizontal lines suggest peace or relaxation while vertical lines indicate stability. Other lines such as diagonal, jagged, or squiggly convey motion or sometimes chaos. Lines also assist the reader's eye in navigating the page from side to side or top to bottom.

Color—Color brings focus to the elements in a story, is critical in creating mood or tone, emphasizes a character and his or her actions, and contributes to the aesthetics of a visual experience. Complementary (colors opposite each other on the color wheel), analogous (colors next to each other on the color wheel), or tertiary (colors produced by mixing two secondary colors) are schemes used as a way of organizing color. Red is an attention-getting color while blue is more restful. Yellow is viewed as a happy color, green is associated with nature, and purple suggests power and importance. The intensity or dullness also contributes to the color's effect on the reader.

Shape—Circles, ovals, triangles, diamonds, rectangles, and squares are found everywhere in nature and in the world around us. Three-dimensional forms such as spheres, cylinders, pyramids, or cubes can be translated two-dimensionally into shapes on the page. Shape can be thought of as created by an artist's use of line, color, and value.

Texture—Artists use texture as a way to communicate a tactile sensation. The page may appear rough or smooth, hard or soft depending on the way paint is applied or materials are placed, such as with collage. Readers are often tempted to touch the page in an attempt to feel the texture that has been produced.

Perspective—One of the most interesting elements that artists use is perspective to present a point of view or to focus the reader's eye on a specific action in the illustration. A bird's-eye view occurs when the reader has a sense of looking down on a scene while a worm's-eye view provides a view looking up. Artists also use the foreground or bottom third of an illustration, the middle ground or middle third of the picture, and background presented in the top third of the page to place emphasis on a specific character or scene. Perspective creates an illusion of depth on a two-dimensional surface.

Artists use the placement of color, line, shape, and texture to "compose" the picture. This composition is the working of the elements of art together to create an interesting and memorable illustration. Molly Bang's *Picture This: How Pictures Work* (2000) presents a superb explanation of how art elements function to convey meaning by using the story of Little Red Riding Hood. Another book that is excellent for exploring art elements is Maurice Sendak's *Where the Wild Things Are* (1963). Students in both my undergraduate and graduate children's literature courses are amazed at the way Sendak employs cross-hatching, which is the use of parallel lines drawn closely together to create the illusion of shade or texture in a drawing. This technique created with pen-and-ink over colored paint creates a balance of silliness and subtlety. Sendak's use of space is also effective as the world of Max grows from a small square to full-page to finally the double-page spread featuring the wild rumpus. Awareness of these art elements becomes intriguing as we linger over illustrations to capture a sense of how these elements are applied.

Media Used in Creating Illustrations

Children often ask, "How did they make those pictures?" They are fascinated by the art they are viewing and want to know more. Fortunately, there are several children's book publishers who are including this information for readers, generally on the back of the title page. Other times, it is up to the adult to try to determine the media used to create the illustration. This becomes more complicated when illustrations are computer-generated or digitally altered or enhanced. David Wiesner has used programs such as Photoshop to manipulate illustrations in his books, particularly the 2002 Caldecott Medal winner *The Three Pigs* (2001) where watercolor paintings were crunched up and lettering was sent flying.

Artists use a variety of media to create illustrations. A few of them include the following:

Painterly Techniques

Watercolor is finely ground-up pigments of color with a natural or chemical base that is mixed with water. It is transparent in that you can see the surface beneath, and it is able to be layered to change colors or to allow other colors to show through. Illustrators that primarily work in watercolor are Gail Gibbons, Jerry Pinkney, Emily Arnold McCully, Chris Soentpiet, and David Wiesner.

Oil paints have varying degrees of thickness, which allows different textures to be created. It is possible to obtain both opaque and transparent effects and matte and gloss finishes. Eric Rohmann's 1995 Caldecott Honor book *Time Flies* (1994) is a wordless journey back in time as a bird flies into a museum filled with dinosaur skeletons. The double-paged spreads using warm burnished browns and red as well as cooler colors of blue and green create unusual perspectives and striking compositions. Don Wood's misty blue artwork that bleeds off the pages of *The Napping House* (Wood, 1984) and Joe Cepeda's comical perspectives of both human and rodent in *Mice and Beans* (Ryan, 2001) are excellent examples of books illustrated using oil paints.

Acrylics produce vibrant, almost glowing colors that appear even and somewhat flat in comparison to oil paints. Acrylics have a synthetic base with colored pigments added for an opaque finish. Floating figures, fantastical creatures and celestial bodies with human features cavort across the pages in *Frida* (Winter, 2002) illustrated in acrylics by Ana Juan. Lynn Curlee's stunning acrylic paintings in *Skyscraper* (2007) provide a chronological history of the world's tallest buildings.

Gouache (pronounced *gwash*) describes a type of watercolor paint. The pigments are bound by liquid glue and can be applied thinly or thickly. Gouache dries to a matte finish and generally does not allow the whiteness of the paper to show through. *Old MacDonald Had a Woodshop* (Shulman, 2002) was illustrated by Ashley Wolff with gouache and brown pencil outlines.

Drawing

Pastels are soft, chalky sticks with an oil or chalk base that enables them to be blended and layered. Ed Young's *Foolish Rabbit's Big Mistake* (Martin, 1985) depicts both drama and fear in this retelling of Chicken Little. In the 2001 Caldecott Medal book *So You Want to Be President?* (St. George, 2000), David Small uses watercolor and ink along with pastels to create comical, caricatured artwork that emphasizes some of the presidents' best-known qualities.

Charcoal is made from wood that is slowly burned and carbonized in an airtight container to prevent it from turning to ash. Ian Falconer's *Olivia* (2000) contains endearing charcoal portraits of his porcine heroine along with illustrations highlighted by fire-engine red. Many of Claire Turlay Newberry's books have been re-issued including *April's Kittens* (1940) portraying an aptly named cat, Charcoal.

Pen-and-ink is often combined with watercolors to provide details in the illustrations such as in Uri Shulevitz's autobiographical *How I Learned Geography* (2008) with its folk-style illustrations rendered in collage, watercolor, and pen-and-ink. *Diary of a Wimpy Kid: Dog Days* (Kinney, 2009) continues in its trademark style of text and cartoon drawings lamenting the life of middle schooler Greg Heffley. *Pencil* drawings are interspersed with text in books such as Eileen Spinelli's (2007) free verse novella *Where I Live,* which includes warm and expressive illustrations by Matt Phelan.

Collage and Mixed-Media

Collage is three-dimensional design created by gluing elements such as newspaper, wallpaper, fabric, string, photographs, feathers, etc. onto an illustration. Lois Ehlert is well-known for her collage illustrations in *Boo to You!* (2009), *Oodles of Animals* (2008), and *Snowballs* (1995). Simms Taback and David Diaz both received Caldecott Medals for their collage illustrations—*Joseph Had a Little Overcoat* (1999) and *Smoky Night* (Bunting, 1994), respectively. Denise Fleming makes her own paper for her picture book illustrations, which is detailed on her website at http://www.denise fleming.com.

Mixed-media illustrations use two or more media combined in a single composition. Patricia Polacco incorporates pencil, watercolor, markers, and photographs into her illustrations. In *Knuffle Bunny,* Mo Willems (2004) combines muted sepia-toned photographs with bright cartoon drawings. Impressionistic, mixed-media illustrations portraying a loving mixed-race family earned Chris Raschka a 2006 Caldecott Medal for *The Hello, Goodbye Window* (Juster, 2005).

A number of websites and blogs provide information about children's book illustration and design including *Picturing Books* and *Picture Books for Visual Art.* The National Center for Children's Illustrated Literature has numerous illustrators listed for browsing as well as examples of their art. *The Eric Carle Museum of Picture Book Art* website provides information on current exhibitions of children's book illustrators as well as resources about picture books.

Responses to Literature through Art

As students become aware of the elements and media used in creating illustrations and drawings in picture and chapter books, they are able to apply this knowledge to their own responses to particular books. During the 1999 Master Class, Richard Kerper of Millersville University and Nancy J. Johnson from Western Washington University shared strategies for artistic response to literature. These strategies can be revised and adapted for all grade levels, including undergraduate and graduate students at the college level.

The Art of Caldecott Award Winners

Over three weeks, Kerper introduces students to various art styles used in children's picture books along with examples of fine art. His purpose for doing so is to lead students into creating a poster featuring a Caldecott Award or Honor Book recipient. Kerper provides this time for students to linger over illustrations and to learn more about art elements and techniques of illustrators. This process results in the creation of a poster in this way:

1. Read the Caldecott Award winners and Honor Books. As you read the books, you must also view them. Pay as much attention to the illustration as you do the text. Since we are so text oriented, it is often best to look at the illustration on a page and consider what is communicated before reading the print. After you have read the text, look at the illustrations again. Consider what the illustrations are telling you and what the text is providing. What aspects of one is the other extending? What gaps in one is the other filling? What narrative elements do the illustrations introduce that the text does not reveal?

2. Compare each of the books read to the following definitions of the picture book format. Picture books "are predominantly pictures. . . . The pictures in a picture book should do more than simply reinforce the words of the story; they should also add to the story, give it new dimensions, even tell an additional story. Sometimes there are few words or no words at all and the pictures 'tell' the entire story" (Marantz, 1992, p. 2). Picture books have a "dual narrative, in which both pictures and text work interdependently to tell the story. It is a tale told in two media, the integration of visual and verbal art" (Bishop & Hickman, 1992, p. 2).

3. Select one book that you feel best achieves the ideal of what a picture book should be. Use the above definitions to guide your decision making.

4. Create an 18" □ 24" poster that includes the title, author, and illustrator. The poster should reflect a theme and the content of the book and should be original in design. It should not be a replication of the illustrator's work; no images may be copied from the book. Use the pictorial style or media of the book's illustrations as you design and create your poster.

5. Images and print must be sized appropriately and bold enough for distant viewing.

6. On the back of the poster attach the following:

   a. A rationale explaining why this book best exemplifies the definition of a picture book, and

b. An explanation of how the poster reflects the content, theme, and pictorial style or media of the book.

If time does not permit for a lengthy exploration and project, another strategy is for students to be engaged in a workshop-type approach that allows them to learn about art elements and media along with the parts of a book such as the cover, endpapers, title page, etc. Provide text sets of books for each element and medium. Then have students select a Caldecott Medal winner and conduct an analysis focused on the cover art, endpapers, use of art elements, media and layout and design of the book. Slowing down to examine each component enables students to gain a better understanding of the art as well as an appreciation for it.

Story Arc/Story Ray Response

Nancy J. Johnson assigns her students a story arc project using *The Giver* (Lowry, 1993), though this strategy could be used for any chapter book or novel. Each student is responsible for creating one visual ray representing a selected chapter from the book. The story ray is to provide a strong sense of the chapter with a focus on ideas, themes, characters, setting, mood, even tone. Before beginning their story rays, Nancy strongly encourages students to revisit their selected chapter and to pay attention to images, symbols, colors, as well as words or phrases that seem especially significant. Then students plan their story ray cognizant of the following questions:

- How can I offer a visual essence of the chapter?
- What color(s) do I use for the background and for the images I choose to represent? Why are these colors important/significant to the chapter?
- What images (symbols, artifacts, and items) should I represent on this strip of paper? What is the significance of each? Should I repeat any images? What layout should I use to capture a strong sense of my chapter?
- Should I include words? A quote? A short phrase? If so, where do words belong on my chapter's story ray? Do I repeat them? If so, why?

Nancy also advises students to leave little to no white space unless it is essential to what they are creating. She requests that they use media that are bold and colorful. They can also consider using more than one medium such as collage, torn paper, pen-and-ink, or paints.

Once the story ray is completed, Nancy asks that students reflect on their finished product and to explain their use of words and colors as well as layout and design. She then displays the story rays on the wall to resemble an arc of the rays of the sun and anchored by a photocopy of the book jacket.

This response strategy is not done in isolation but is informed by the examination of picture books and the discussion of art elements and media. It enables students to experience the reading of picture books and novels and to discover literary and artistic components of both.

Theme Images

This strategy was not presented during a Master Class but has been one I have used effectively as a visual response to both picture and chapter books. It was adapted from middle school teacher Janine A. King and located on the website *Literature Circles Resource Center*. A theme image can be generated from one book or from several based on the same theme or topic. From the book(s), students select one word representing a central concept. Then, they illustrate the concept, weaving the word into the image in some manner. For example, after reading *The Other Side* by Jacqueline Woodson (2001), a story about two girls racially divided by a physical barrier, Tracie, a graduate student, chose the word *friendship* as her theme. She thought carefully about the pastel colors E. B. Lewis used for the watercolor illustrations, but also about the somber time of the civil rights era. Tracie also considered the barrier of the fence and the line that was drawn physically and figuratively to keep the girls apart. In generating her response, Tracie relied on watercolors, collage, and markers and spoke about her use of the art elements of space, line, color, and perspective with others in the class.

Visual responses to literature are enhanced when there is an awareness and understanding of children's book illustration and design. Visual representation can reflect comprehension, emotions, attention to story detail, and personal interpretation of text (Hancock, 2004).

Last but Not Least, the New "Kid" in Children's Literature

A chapter on book illustration and design would not be complete without discussing the explosion and popularity of graphic novels. Children are enamored with them, and adults are perplexed as to whether they constitute "real" literature. Added to this, teachers are confused as to what to do with them in classrooms. When we talk about visual literacy, graphic novels present some of the best in design and artistic renderings. While the illustrations in graphic novels possess many of the art elements presented in this chapter, they also create opportunities for thinking about visual literacy in other ways.

James Bickers points out in an article appearing in *Publishers Weekly* (2007) that today's children are the first generation to grow up more accustomed to digital screens than the printed page. Kids increasingly understand and appreciate data that are transmitted to them in visual form. In this same article, Marlaine Maddux, editor-in-chief of Penny-Farthing Press, states, "We live in a visual society and providing illustration to support storytelling is extremely appealing to young readers" (para. 7). This storytelling that appears in graphic novels is designed in a different manner, which sets them apart somewhat from picture or chapter books.

At the website *ReadWriteThink* that is generated by the International Reading Association and the National Council of Teachers of English, a "Comic Book Primer" (Carter) is provided that emphasizes the uniqueness of graphic novel production by discussing the following roles:

- *Writer* writes the script from which the story will emerge.
- *Artist* draws the script, usually using pencils.
- *Inker* goes over the artist's pencil lines with ink to make them stand out.
- *Colorist* colors the inker's and artists' work, sometimes by hand and sometimes using software.
- *Letterer* puts the words in the right places and makes them clearly legible. The letterer might also put in the sound effects.
- *Editor* looks over the stories for errors as well as helps the creative team find direction for telling the stories.

The parts of the comic book or graphic novel that generate layout and design include the following:

- *Script* contains the written directions for how the comic book or graphic novel will be put together along with the dialogue.
- *Pages* are parts in the script where the writer tells what should be on each page.
- *Panels* are rectangles or squares where the action of the script will go.
- *Word balloons* show where people speak.
- *Thought balloons* show when people are thinking.

- *Narratory blocks* are little rectangles or squares where a narrator, maybe a character from the story, shares special information with the reader.
- *Open panels* are panels where one or more, or even all, of the sides are open to help show dramatic effect.
- *Splash page* is usually a panel that takes up the whole page, used to help introduce stories or give special attention to battles or particular events.

Graphic novels published for adolescents include such titles as *American Born Chinese* by Gene Luan Yang (2007), *Coraline: The Graphic Novel* (2008) written by Neil Gaiman and illustrated by P. Craig Russell, and *Rapunzel's Revenge* (2008) written by Shannon Hale and Dean Hale and illustrated by Nathan Hale. Jennifer Holm and Matthew Holm's Babymouse series provides an excellent starting point for younger children interested in graphic novels. Recommended lists of graphic novels can be located at the websites of the American Library Association and the Cooperative Children's Book Center.

Responding to Graphic Novels

Just as picture books provide artistic images and chapter books and novels generate visual images and symbols, graphic novels present another form of design. Therefore, it makes sense to have students respond to this genre in a way that is unique. Readers consider the color, size, and style of the font, the layout and design of the page using panels and boxes, and the use of speech balloons and bubbles to convey text. Here are a few strategies for responding to graphic novels at any age.

Graffiti Wall

The following lesson is adapted from "Comics and Graphic Novels" (Carter) on the *ReadWriteThink* website. As the graphic novel is read, students should keep a graffiti journal that contains the following:

- Graffiti: drawings, shapes, symbols, colors that help you remember each element of fiction in your novel
- Words and phrases that come to your mind while you read
- Direct quotations from the novel that reveal your thoughts on the setting, characters, plot structure, point of view, themes, and symbols developed in the novel

To create the graphic either in small groups or individually:

- In groups or with one other person, discuss the section of the novel that you are choosing to respond to, how it fits in with what goes before in the novel, and what comes after.
- Discuss how the elements of plot, setting, character, point of view, theme, and symbol are developed in this part of the novel.
- Choose a title for your section of the novel.
- Choose words, quotations, and graphics (doodles, drawings, shapes, colors, symbols) from your journals to include on your graffiti graphic.
- Using butcher paper or newsprint and crayons or markers to create your group or individual graffiti graphic.

Storyboards

A storyboard is often used by book illustrators to visually sketch out the action of a story. Storyboards are linear because they tell a story that goes from beginning to end. To create a storyboard in response to a graphic novel, students can do the following:

- Read and record the main points of action within the story.
- Determine how many panels to create. Generally 12 or fewer keep the focus on key points of the books.
- Select the character(s), setting, conflict, and resolution that will be depicted in the storyboard. A planning sheet to think through ideas can be used such as:

Scene or action	Characters	Landscape	Props	Caption

- Fold a piece of 11" □ 18" paper to make 12 sections. Draw the storyboard in response to the graphic novel focusing on personal response and connections.

These responses consider the graphic and visual nature of the books that students are responding to in addition to considering how the story is visually told.

Conclusion

As I view my collection of seven decades of Caldecott Medal winners, it becomes apparent that children's book illustration and design have changed tremendously from the three-color separation process that was prevalent years ago to the die-cut marvel of *Joseph Had a Little Overcoat* (Taback, 1999). And then there is Selznick's 550-page picture book. Technology has also changed the face of children's literature, something that David Wiesner acknowledges in his ability to create text and alter illustrations in *The Three Pigs* (2001). The advent of graphic novels along with illustrated chapter books—such as the Diary of a Wimpy Kid series, as well as Lois Lowry's *The Birthday Ball* (2010) containing drawings from Julies Feiffer—helps us realize the visual nature that children's books are displaying today.

Gaining an understanding and appreciation of the visual components that make up picture books, illustrated chapter books, and graphic novels assists in students' ability to comprehend and interpret visual images. In conclusion, it seems appropriate to return to Caldecott Medal winning illustrator Brian Selznick (2008) and his acknowledgment of Remy Charlip's impact on his artistic journey by quoting from the Charlip essay, "A Page Is a Door":

> A book is a series of pages held together at one edge, and these pages can be moved on their hinges like a swinging door. They could also be half-doors, doors with windows, double doors, like fold-outs, doors with attachments, pop-ups, textures or moving parts, and shaped doors. Of course, if a door has something completely different behind it, it is much more exciting. The element of delight and surprise is helped by the physical power we feel in our own hands when we move that page or door to reveal a change in everything that has gone before, in time, place or character. A thrilling picture book not only makes beautiful single images or sequential images, but also allows us to become aware of a book's unique physical structure, by bringing our attention, once again, to that momentous moment: the turning of the page.

Works Cited

Bang, M. (2000). *Picture this: How pictures work.* New York: SeaStar Books.

Bickers, J. (2007, February 19). The young and the graphic novel. *Publishers Weekly, 254*(8). Retrieved from http://www.publishersweekly.com/pw/print/20070219/4884-the-young-and-the-graphic-novel-.html

Bishop, R. S., & Hickman, J. (1992). Four or fourteen or forty: Picture books are for everyone. In S. Benedict & L. Carlisle (Eds.), *Beyond words: Picture books for older readers and writers* (pp. 1–10). Portsmouth, NH: Heinemann.

Carter, J. B. *Comics and graphic novels.* Retrieved from http://www.readwritethink.org/parent-afterschool-resources/activities-projects/comics-graphic-novels-30296.html?main-tab=2#tabs

Charlip, R. (n.d.). *A page is a door.* Retrieved from http://www.theinventionofhugo cabret.com/remy_essay.htm

Erbach, M. M. (2007). Illustration as art—line. *Book Links, 16*(5), 29–32.

Giorgis, C. (2000). "A book is forever:" A conversation with Rosemary Wells. *The New Advocate, 13*(2), 107–115.

Goldstone, B. P. (1989). Visual interpretation of children's books. *The Reading Teacher, 42,* 592–595.

Hancock, M. R. (2004). *A celebration of literature and response: Children, books, and teachers in K–8 classrooms.* Upper Saddle River, NJ: Pearson.

Marantz, S. S. (1992). *Picture books for looking and learning: Awakening visual perceptions through the art of children's books.* Phoenix, AZ: Oryx Press.

Richards, J. C., & Anderson, N. A. (2003). What do I see? What do I think? What do I wonder? (STW): A visual literacy strategy to help emergent readers focus on storybook illustrations. *The Reading Teacher, 56,* 442–444.

Selznick, B. (2008). *Caldecott Medal acceptance* [Speech transcript]. Retrieved from http://www.theinventionofhugocabret.com/brian_speech.htm

Serafini, F., & Giorgis, C. (2003). *Reading aloud and beyond: Fostering the intellectual life with older readers.* Portsmouth, NH: Heinemann.

Sipe, L. R. (1998). How picture books work: A semiotically framed theory of text-picture relationships. *Children's Literature in Education, 29*(2), 97–108.

Children's Books Cited

Alexie, S. (2007). *The absolutely true diary of a part-time Indian* (E. Forney, Illus.). Boston: Little, Brown.

Bunting, E. (1994). *Smoky night* (D. Diaz, Illus.). San Diego: Harcourt.

Curlee, L. (2007). *Skyscraper*. New York: Atheneum.

Ehlert, L. (1995). *Snowballs*. San Diego: Harcourt.

Ehlert, L. (2008). *Oodles of animals*. Orlando, FL: Harcourt.

Ehlert, L. (2009). *Boo to you!* New York: Beach Lane Books/Atheneum.

Falconer, I. (2000). *Olivia*. New York: Atheneum.

Gaiman, N. (2008). *Coraline: The graphic novel* (P. C. Russell, Illus.). New York: Harper Collins.

Hale, S., & Hale, D. (2008). *Rapunzel's revenge* (N. Hale, Illus.). New York: Bloomsbury.

Juster, N. (2005). *The hello, goodbye window* (C. Raschka, Illus.). New York: Hyperion.

Kinney, J. (2007). *Diary of a wimpy kid*. New York: Amulet Books.

Kinney, J. (2009). *Diary of a wimpy kid: Dog days*. New York: Amulet Books.

Lowry, L. (1993). *The giver*. Boston: Houghton Mifflin.

Lowry, L. (2010). *The birthday ball* (J. Feiffer, Illus.). New York: Houghton Mifflin.

Martin, R. (1985). *Foolish rabbit's big mistake* (E. Young, Illus.). New York: Putnam.

Newberry, C. T. (1940). *April's kittens*. New York: HarperCollins.

Rohmann, E. (1994). *Time flies*. New York: Crown Books.

Ryan, P. M. (2001). *Mice and beans* (J. Cepeda, Illus.). New York: Scholastic.

Selznick, B. (2007). *The invention of Hugo Cabret*. New York: Scholastic.

Sendak, M. (1963). *Where the wild things are*. New York: Harper and Row.

Shulevitz, U. (2008). *How I learned geography*. New York: Farrar, Straus and Giroux.

Shulman, L. (2002). *Old MacDonald had a woodshop* (A. Wolff, Illus.). New York: G. P. Putnam's Sons.

Spinelli, E. (2007). *Where I live* (M. Phelan, Illus.). New York: Dial.

St. George, J. (2000). *So you want to be president?* (D. Small, Illus.). New York: Philomel Books.

Taback, S. (1999). *Joseph had a little overcoat*. New York: Viking.

Wiesner, D. (2001). *The three pigs*. New York: Clarion Books.

Willems, M. (2004). *Knuffle bunny: A cautionary tale*. New York: Hyperion.

Winter, J. (2002). *Frida* (A. Juan, Illus.). New York: Scholastic.

Wood, A. (1984). *The napping house* (D. Wood, Illus.). San Diego: Harcourt.

Woodson, J. (2001). *The other side* (E. B. Lewis, Illus.). New York: G. P. Putnam's Sons.

Yang, G. L. (2007). *American born Chinese*. New York: First Second.

5

Deepening Mathematical Thinking

Building Bridges between Children's Literature and Mathematics

TERRELL A. YOUNG, AMY ROTH MCDUFFIE, AND BARBARA A. WARD
Washington State University

In November 1998 a group of educators left the labyrinth of Nashville's vast Opryland Hotel to attend the CLA Master Class in Teaching Children's Literature. Entitled "Children's Literature and Mathematics—An Unhealthy Alliance?," the special session responded to the renewed interest in integrating children's literature and mathematics. Two presenters, Patricia Austin of the University of New Orleans and Cyndi Giorgis of the University of Nevada, Las Vegas, critically analyzed the roles of context and book quality in students' response and learning.

The relationship between children's literature and math is still pertinent today. Indeed, we noted the following in looking at recently published articles related to children's literature and mathematics: (1) more articles on integrating children's literature and mathematics are published in mathematics journals than in language arts journals in general, and children's literature journals in particular; (2) published articles about how teachers can utilize literature in mathematics instruction far outweigh those about how students can respond mathematically to the literature they read; (3) issues of book quality are still relevant; and (4) guidelines for selecting literature for math integration are frequently provided.

This chapter will begin with a rationale for the integration of literature and mathematics. We will then present a table illustrating the potential of literature to evoke mathematical responses and learning. We will finish the chapter with discussions on selecting and using literature to teach mathematical concepts and a section on how children can construct meaning for mathematics as they read literature.

Rationale

Trade books afford opportunities for children to see mathematics in multiple contexts, including the world outside the classroom, and to make connections with ideas and their own experiences. Trade books can support students' learning beyond what core curricular materials provide. Jennings, Jennings, Richey, and Dixon-Krauss (1992), for example, found in their research study that using children's literature to teach mathematics increased mathematics achievement, mathematics vocabulary, and interest in mathematics. Others (Columba, Kim, & Moe, 2005; Roth McDuffie & Young, 2003) suggest that using literature to develop mathematical ideas should be encouraged because it has the potential to

- Humanize mathematics in the eyes of children and parents;
- Challenge the stereotype of mathematics as a sterile, noncreative subject that is unrelated to life;
- Build on the positive reaction that most children have to hearing and reading both familiar and new stories;
- Integrate learning in a variety of curriculum areas;
- Provide an alternative medium for communicating about mathematics; and
- Stimulate mathematical interest, enjoyment, and confidence in children.

It seems apparent that both narrative and expository texts "provide contexts in which mathematics concepts can be presented together with opportunities to think critically, solve problems, and make connections to students' knowledge about the world" (Columba et al., p. 16).

Roles of Literature in Learning Mathematics

Based on our review of articles related to literature's potential in mathematics learning, and our examination of children's trade books, we identified four different roles for literature in mathematical learning. Table 5.1 illustrates those roles and provides samples of children's books to support each role.

For each category, we listed several books that serve the role indicated. To clarify how books can achieve the purposes described, we will discuss one book from each category. Indeed many books could be placed in more than one category. Our intention is not to create discrete and distinct categories for purposes

Table 5.1: Roles of Literature in Mathematical Learning

Role and Description	Examples of Texts
1. Provide context for problem solving: • Engages students in mathematical thinking through rich literature (as compared to books that pose as literature but lack key elements) • Invites and motivates students to connect and apply mathematics in real-world situations or in a story's context—the story generates new ideas and/or mathematical connections • Exposes students to aspects of the world that are unfamiliar to students • Introduces students to contexts in which mathematics is useful and helps students see the value of mathematics in their lives • Connects students' experiences to important mathematical concepts and/or procedures (i.e., making mathematics visible) • Connects students' mathematical work to mathematics in professions	• *The Wishing Club: A Story about Fractions* (Napoli, 2007) • *Neil's Numberless World* (Coats, 2000) • *The Greedy Triangle* (Burns, 1995) • *The Great Divide: A Mathematical Marathon* (Dodds, 2005) • *Inchworm and a Half* (Pinczes, 2003)
2. Model problem solving and reasoning processes such as: • Identifying and isolating the problem • Developing a plan for a solution • Applying logic and reasoning to solve a problem • Achieving a solution that is convincing	• *One Riddle, One Answer* (Thompson, 2007) • *Betcha! Estimating* (Murphy, 1999) • *Great Estimations* (Goldstone, 2006) • *Greater Estimations* (Goldstone, 2008) • *Spaghetti and Meatballs for All* (Burns, 1997)
3. Provide direct sources for mathematical investigations (Note: Elements/pages of the book can be directly used for inquiry, as compared to generating ideas for problems in the first category): • Provides data or other information that can be used for students to pursue or create a question/problem • Provides data, graphs, or other representations for students to analyze and interpret • Inspires students to apply mathematics to verify/check whether claims are reasonable (i.e., fact check)	• *Tiger Math: Learning How to Graph from a Baby Tiger* (Nagda & Bickel, 2000) • *Measuring Penny* (Leedy, 1998) • *How Much Is a Million* (Schwarz, 1985) • *If You Made a Million* (Schwarz, 1994) • *How Much, How Many, How Far, How Heavy, How Long, How Tall Is 1000?* (Nolan, 2001)
4. Provide opportunities for practicing and solidifying procedural skills and to see a variety of contexts and ways the skills can be applied (Note: In some cases, these books pose as literature, but the contexts/photos/images are appealing and invite children to apply or practice mathematics).	• *The M & M's Brand Counting Book* (McGrath, 1994) • *The Hershey's Kisses Subtraction Book* (Pallotta, 2002) • *The Best of Times* (Tang, 2002) • *Mission Addition* (Leedy, 1999)

that books might serve, but rather to feature ways to apply books to mathematics teaching and learning. Not only can practicing teachers use these roles and examples to inform their classroom instruction, but professors can share these ideas with their own students.

Our first book exemplifies how a book could align with more than one category. In regard to *providing a context for problem solving*, children's literature affords opportunities to connect a story to mathematics that inspires students to create and solve problems and see the usefulness of mathematics in their lives. In *The Wishing Club* (Napoli, 2007), four children, ranging in age from two to eight years old, wish on a star night after night. Readers follow the children's experiences as they discover a pattern: the star grants only a fraction of each of their wishes. The fraction is determined by their age (e.g., the two-year-old receives half of a cookie, the four-year-old receives one quarter of a dollar, and the eight-year-old twins each receive one eighth of a bag of marbles). The granted wishes are represented by pictures, fraction symbols, and equations. The book concludes as the children develop a wishing strategy to receive a "whole pig" for their family.

Teachers can build a discussion focused on developing students' understandings of landmark unit fractions (i.e., ½, ¼, and ⅛), the pattern of repeatedly taking half, and exploring other number patterns. After reading about the first two nights of wishing, teachers can ask students to make conjectures about the wishing pattern with questions such as, "How is the star responding to the children's wishes?" To extend the pattern, teachers can ask, "What if a 10-year-old child joined the group?" Teachers can ask students to explain what they have observed, why they believe their prediction will happen, and whether they could think of other patterns that a different star might use.

The Wishing Club also serves as an example of a book in Categories 2 and 3. By following the characters' thinking and reasoning process as they predict what the star will do next, students see the characters' *reasoning and problem solving process* (Category 2). In addition, if a teacher elects to use the story's context to pose the question, "What will happen next?" (after the second night), the book would fit in Category 3 *providing a direct source for a mathematical investigation*.

To illustrate the second category, *One Riddle, One Answer* (Thompson, 2001) *models reasoning processes*, including flawed reasoning, as the characters work to generate a convincing solution to a riddle (the problem). The book introduces a Persian princess, Aziza, with a passion for numbers. When it comes time for Aziza to marry, she poses a riddle for her suitors to solve. The riddle is: "Placed above, it makes greater things small. Placed beside, it makes small things greater. In matters that count, it always comes first; where others increase, it keeps all things the same. What is it?"

The story depicts various suitors' conjectures and reasoning as they attempt to solve Aziza's riddle. Each of the failed suitors addresses one aspect of the riddle, but does not attend to the other parts. For example, the first suitor, an astronomer, proposes the sun as an answer. He states that when the sun is overhead, it makes greater things small in the shadows cast. Finally, the winning suitor discovers that Aziza's riddle deals with number properties for the number one. This savvy suitor explains how: one placed above a number (as a numerator in a fraction) makes the number small; one placed beside a number makes it larger (place value notions); one is the first number in counting; and one multiplied by any number does not change its value (the identity property for multiplication). At the end of the book Thompson presents a discussion of these number properties, the suitors' reasoning, and the Arabic number system.

Just after the riddle is presented in the book, teachers can ask students to develop solutions to the riddle and convince the class of their solutions. Then, the class can read the rest of the book and evaluate the reasoning processes used by the suitors. This book affords opportunities to discuss problem solving and reasoning processes and focus on issues such as considering all constraints on reasoning through problems and the need to justify answers.

Tiger Math (Nagda & Bickel, 2000), the life story of T. J., a Siberian tiger born at the Denver Zoo, *provides many opportunities for students to analyze data and graphs*, as described by Category 3. The right-hand pages describe T. J.'s story from birth to four years old, detailing his experiences growing up in the zoo. The left-hand pages show several representations of data and graphs (including circle graphs, bar graphs, and line graphs) that depict the tiger's weight at various points in time, the food he eats, and the population of tigers around the world. By selecting a page, for example, a bar graph of age in weeks versus weight in pounds on page 14, a student can generate and find answers to questions such as, "How many pounds did T. J. gain from birth to 6 weeks? How much did he weigh after 10 weeks?"

The M & M's Brand Counting Book (McGrath, 1994) is a well-known book that exemplifies Category 4 books. Although this book does not represent quality children's literature, children can relate easily to the illustrations and then create their own representations to match what they see (with tasty M & M's for manipulatives), subsequently counting and seeing each quantity. This book provides an engaging *opportunity for students to practice* and strengthen their counting skills, an essential skill that requires many opportunities for practice.

Teaching Mathematics with Quality Literature

Teaching mathematics with trade books has emerged as a strong instructional trend. Indeed, *Teaching Children Mathematics*, a prominent journal for elementary teachers, regularly includes articles about using children's literature to promote students' learning (e.g., Forbringer, 2004; Jenner & Anderson, 2000; Roth McDuffie & Young, 2003; Whitin, 2002; Wilburne, Napoli, Keat, Dile, Trout, &

Decker, 2007). These articles help teachers and professors who train them recognize that effective lessons derive from quality literature and sound instructional planning.

In her presentation at the Master Class, Austin (1998b) cited notable examples of quality literature frequently used in teaching about mathematics. For instance, the text of Demi's *One Grain of Rice: A Mathematical Folktale* (1997) creates a sense of wonder while also reading smoothly and effortlessly. In *How Much Is a Million?*, David Schwartz's (1985) text and Steven Kellogg's illustrations team up to use real-world math to help kids understand otherwise abstract number concepts.

On the other hand, some books may potentially damage students' interest in reading and math. Books that fail to meet the criteria for good literature are often didactic and contrived, described by Austin (1998a) as merely "lavishly illustrated, expensive, overproduced workbooks presenting the message math is boring and must be embedded in something in order to be meaningful (p. 121)." She suggested educators use the following criteria to determine whether books "measure up." Quality literature to promote mathematical thinking should

- contain layers of meaning;
- enable natural connections to mathematics;
- provide opportunities for the reader to use math for authentic purposes;
- convey delight in mathematical inquiry;
- make use of readers' repertoires of knowledge;
- invite the readers to learn something new and enable discovery;
- generate a sense of wonder and encourage readers' curiosity;
- employ a humorous or conversational tone;
- stimulate and engage the reader;
- have a defined logical structure, either expository or narrative;
- include a plot that grows naturally from the character's actions when in narrative form; and
- make use of natural rhythm and rhyme when in poetic form. (Austin, 1998a, p. 121)

A Scale for Selecting Quality Trade Books

With a five-criteria scale to evaluate math trade books, Hellwig, Monroe, and Jacobs's (2000) article is helpful in selecting high quality trade books. Their scale considers accuracy, text and visual appeal, connections, audience, and a "wow" factor. We build on their ideas by considering an overarching criterion to discern further which books demonstrate the most promise for conceptual learning: a book's *potential for use* in a learning environment that focuses on students making sense of mathematics.

To describe environments that focus on students' sense making, we applied Tarr et al.'s (2008) construct for a *standards-based learning environment* (SBLE). Tarr et al. observed classrooms for features that embodied tenets of the National Council of Teachers of Mathematics (NCTM) standards (National Council of Teachers of Mathematics, 2000) and classified SBLEs based on opportunities for teaching and learning in the classroom environment. Teacher-based opportunities focused on the extent to which the teacher used students' statements about mathematics to build discussion toward shared understandings for the class. Student-based opportunities included evidence that students' work was aimed at (1) developing conceptual understandings; (2) making conjectures about mathematical ideas; (3) explaining responses or strategies; and (4) sharing and valuing multiple perspectives or strategies. These characteristics served as the basis for our evaluation of trade books under the *potential for use* criterion. Using a traffic light scale for analyzing trade books (see Figure 5.1), we illustrate the evaluation process with three recently published books that focus on number and operation, a focal point throughout the elementary curriculum (National Council of Teachers of Mathematics, 2006). While this scale is intended to serve

STOP: Consider whether this book will contribute to students' learning. The book (as published) does not afford opportunities for sense making in mathematics.

CAUTION: Proceed with care. This book may have value with substantial teacher adaptations and/or carefully selected pages or sections of the book might be useful.

GO: Feel confident in using this book. It shows strong potential for use with deliberate teacher planning. The book affords opportunities for a teacher to pose higher-level questions and/or high cognitive demand problems. Students working with the book can develop conceptual understandings, make conjectures, explain their thinking, and/or value others' perspectives or strategies.

Figure 5.1: Scale evaluating a book's potential for teachers' use in a standards-based learning environment that focuses on students making sense of mathematics.

as a tool for determining a book's potential to support learning, ultimately teachers' deliberate planning and lesson facilitation are crucial—even with books that seem to have the greatest potential.

Considering the "Potential for Use" Criterion with Recently Published Books

Green Light Example

Although a green light book on its own does not ensure learning, the book's content and presentation afford abundant teaching and learning opportunities in an SBLE. *The Wishing Club*, described earlier, offers strong potential for teachers to build a discussion focused on developing students' understandings of landmark unit fractions (i.e., ½, ¼, and ⅛) and exploring number patterns. The book affords opportunities for multiple perspectives and strategies as students connect to the pictorial representations and/or the symbolic expressions. Teachers could support learning further by providing concrete objects for the pictorial representations (such as paper cookies, coins, marbles, or chips) for students to use as they investigate the children's wishing experiences in the story. Through discussion and sharing predictions, teachers can help students make meaning for fractions and the fraction pattern. Conceptual understandings for fractions are developed by connecting fractions to different meaningful contexts (money, cookie, marbles, and a pig) so that children understand how parts and wholes relate and how to combine fractional parts to make a whole (especially at the end of the book when the children form their strategy for wishing for a whole pig). The author presents wholes as a single object (a dollar, a cookie, a pig) and as a set of objects (a bag of marbles), and understanding different forms of a whole is an important part of learning about fractions (NCTM, 2006).

In addition to meeting our criteria as a green light book, *The Wishing Club* earns high scores for all aspects of Hellwig et al.'s (2000) scale as well, including the "wow" factor. With deliberate planning to develop fractions concepts and conjectures about number patterns, this book exhibits a strong potential to promote learning in an SBLE.

Yellow Light Example

Many of the books we considered for this chapter had some promising features but also many limitations that teachers would need to overcome if choosing to use them for instructional purposes. *Cheetah Math: Learning about Division from*

Baby Cheetahs (Nagda, 2007), an example of a yellow light book, is a nonfiction book that follows two cheetah cubs as they are raised at the San Diego Zoo. The reading level is K–3, and the mathematics content aligns with third to fourth grade (NCTM, 2006). As indicated in the title, the authors draw connections between aspects of raising cheetahs and division. For example, one left-hand page shows two rows of nine bottles (with each bottle representing one ounce of milk) and the explanation, "18 ounces [of milk] can be divided into 2 equal shares of 9 ounces each" (p. 8). On another page readers are asked, "How many weeks old were the cubs at 49 days?" (p. 12). Just below this question appears a seven by seven array, and to the right of each row is an equation that corresponds to that row (e.g., $7 \times 1 = 7$ is to the right of the first row, $7 \times 2 = 14$ is to the right of the second row, etc.). Later, division is represented as repeated subtraction and another problem is solved through a multiply up strategy. Pictorial representations illustrate the mathematical computations.

Although the narrative provides a rich context for mathematics applications, many of the problems are forced and/or superficial connections and afford few opportunities to problem solve. Teachers essentially would need to present problems to students without showing the book (e.g., writing each problem on flip chart), ask students to work on the problem, and then facilitate a discussion that allows students to share various strategies. This format of immediately presenting solutions and telling students how to solve problems occurs throughout this book.

In regard to Hellwig et al.'s (2000) scale, this book has both strengths and weaknesses. Our primary concern relates to the book's accuracy in how mathematics is represented. Another concern is that for some problems, division seems forced on the context. For example, later in the book, the cubs are paired with dogs that serve as companions, and the following problem is posed:

> [The cubs] weighed about 16 pounds each when they met their dogs....The dogs were a few months older and weighed about 49 pounds each. How many times bigger were the dogs than the cheetahs?

In other words, how much is 49 pounds divided by 16 pounds (p. 16)? Following this statement, the author shows a repeated subtraction method for calculating the answer (i.e., $49 - 16 = 33$; $33 - 16 = 17$; etc.). Not only does this problem statement take away some of the problem-solving process from students by telling them to use division, it pushes the use of division for a context in which many students are likely to think about multiplication first (Carpenter, Fennema, Franke, Levi, & Empson, 1999). Once again, the problem itself is worthwhile, but the author's connection to mathematics is not well considered.

Correspondingly, teachers might opt to ignore the left page, but use the problem. In the hands of teachers anticipating the book's limitations, it has potential for connections and audience.

The appeal of the book's beautiful photographs and engaging narrative draws readers into the cubs' lives and serves as a positive aspect on Hellwig et al.'s (2000) scale. On the surface, this book has considerable "wow" factor; however, deliberate planning is needed to capitalize on the book's strengths. The engaging story has the potential for students to see how mathematics is useful in the world around them, but we recommend using only the problem statements and then working with students to develop and share their approaches to solving the problems.

Red Light Example

Math at the Store (Weiss, 2008) shows mathematics in everyday life and uses many photographs from a grocery store as examples. Although the book is aimed at first- and second-grade readers with its mathematics content aligned primarily with kindergarten to first grade, it also contains references to money (coins, rate-based prices) and units of measure (quart, gallon), topics more appropriate for higher grades (NCTM, 2006). The left-side pages contain a brief narrative and end with a question, and the right-side pages show a photograph from a grocery store. For instance, on pages 8 and 9, the left side reads, "The store has lots of fruit for sale. Yum those oranges look good! How many should we buy?" The corresponding right page shows fruit displayed in bins at a grocery store with several signs naming fruit and prices (e.g., "Navel Oranges 8/$2.00"). Although this question does not represent a problem (students simply name quantities of fruit to purchase), other pages present questions that call for a calculation.

This book has little use in an SBLE because it does not present situations that would be mathematically problematic for most students. For example, asking "How many should we buy?" is not a problem because any quantity is acceptable; the question contains no constraints. For other questions, the solution appears on the adjacent page. At best, teachers could cover the right-side page to allow students to solve the problem before seeing the answer. Perhaps an even more pronounced limitation is the book's lack of focus by including a range of mathematics topics from kindergarten (counting and basic decreasing number patterns) to second or third grade (finding a total value for coins and comparing with the cost of an item, using standard units of measure for volume), while maintaining a reading level of ½. The book fails to present genuine problems or provide opportunities to delve deeply into mathematics concepts.

Using Hellwig et al.'s (2000) scale, this book receives mixed ratings. The mathematics is accurate. While the photographs are appealing, the book reads much like a textbook. Although the book attempts to make connections between mathematics and everyday life, the superficial attention to mathematics problems does not lead to strong connections. Given that the book contains mathematics appropriate for a range of grades and abilities, it seems to rank high for Hellwig et al.'s scale for audience; however, this wide range would limit its use. Finally, on first glance, the book's photographs of mathematics in real life contribute to the "wow" factor, but the "wow" fades quickly after noticing its textbookish appearance.

The idea of capturing mathematics in the community is worth pursuing further. Photographs from the produce section with signs that included rate-based prices provide rich contexts for creating problems. However, even if teachers decided to pursue a lesson around mathematics in the grocery store, students might connect more strongly with photographs from a store in their community or advertisements from their newspaper. Thus, we find little value in the book in regard to supporting an SBLE.

Responding to Books Mathematically

Teachers, professors who work with and train teachers, and librarians who recommend books to teachers and students should consider students' mathematical responses to literature. We will discuss research on this topic and then recommend some recent books that lend themselves to mathematical response. In the Master Class, Giorgis discussed two action research studies conducted with a Tucson colleague, Gloria Kauffman. In the first study, Kauffman read *The Giver* (Lowry, 1993) to her students as part of a unit on Decision Making and Taking Action. Together, Giorgis and Kauffman identified portions of the book they thought would help students relate to the literature through math. They noted page numbers and excerpts to read to students, wrote questions, and found picture books relating to the math concepts in *The Giver*. Even though the teachers generated math activities for the students, they found that the students rejected their ideas and made their own relevant, personal mathematical connections. Realizing they imposed their responses on the students, they planned a second study the following year that would not violate their beliefs about inquiry and response.

The following year Kauffman read Tom Birdseye's *Tarantula Shoes* (1995) to her students. This time the students determined questions and categories of interest they wished to investigate for their own mini-inquiries. Their responses were related to their own lives and realms of experience. For example, one group investigated the main character's trip from Arizona to Kentucky and determined the amount of gas needed for the family station wagon. Another examined the effect of shoe brands and types on jumping and making baskets. In these mini-inquiries the students not only studied shoes and maps but also used them as tools for exploring distance. Similarly, we know of a fifth-grade student who created scale maps of Denmark and Washington State to better understand and appreciate the Danish resistance of the Nazi occupation of their country in Lois Lowry's *Number the Stars* (1989).

As a result of their studies, Giorgis and Kauffman became convinced that mathematical connections should emerge naturally from literature and be placed within a context where students can draw on their own experiences to make meaning. According to Giorgis, "Literature shouldn't be used to teach math, but should support the math that emerges from students understandings." Likewise, she suggested that professors and teachers of children's literature should do the following:

1. Recognize that mathematical connections can be found in most pieces of literature.

2. Encourage teachers and preservice teachers to allow those mathematical connections to emerge naturally from children's literature rather than impose them on the literature.

3. Listen to students' discussion and connections to literature. Once we begin to listen for those mathematical connections we will realize that they can and will emerge naturally and in turn be more meaningful for children and relevant to their lives.

Teachers may want to consider the utility of recently published children's books that can encourage mathematical response. These books span several content areas while being notable for their real-world mathematics content, their appeal, and their place in a social studies or science curriculum as well. For instance, the stunningly photographed and engagingly written *What the World Eats* (D'Aluisio, 2008) takes readers on an all-you-can-eat visual tour of 25 families in 21 different countries across the globe. Readers can use mathematics to create the family recipes provided as well as the statistics listed about the families' disparate caloric consumption, varying widely from country to country. Because the author lists all the foods eaten by a family each week, there is a visual record of how much is eaten, which varies widely from family to family. Although the author has done much of the math for the reader—for instance, providing the amount of money it costs for each family's subsistence—there are numerous possibilities for comparison. Students will be able to draw their own conclusions about the impact of fast food products on family health and a family's budget by using the tables and charts provided.

Additionally, wonderful books such as *One Well: The Story of Water on Earth* (Strauss, 2007) and *If America Were a Village: A Book about the People of the United States* (Smith, 2009) are filled with interesting mathematical facts that allow children to apply their math knowledge. For instance, Strauss includes snippets about how many gallons of water it took to make a bicycle, affording children the chance to figure out the cost in water for the products they need or think they need. The highly readable text is a primer on the concept of finiteness since, as the author points out, the amount of water is not going to increase. As the world's population grows, the available water supply may be stretched to the breaking point. Smith's book echoes his earlier volume *If the World Were a Village: A Book about the World's People* (2002) in reducing the enormous numbers of Earth's citizens to 100, a number that children can handle in a way that they cannot handle millions and billions. As the book uses the number 100 to stand for much larger numbers, students can solve problems relating to where America's citizens now live, the size and composition of families, and the health conditions of its citizens.

Reflections on Teaching and Learning with Trade Books

Aligning children's literature and math has the potential to help children better understand and appreciate both literature and mathematics. When the focus is on using trade books to foster students' learning in mathematics, the yellow light and red light books provide examples of books whose visual and/or verbal appeal may actually mask the books' limitations. Similarly, just setting books in real contexts fails to ensure that all of the connections between mathematics and the world were mathematically robust.

The criterion for accuracy is particularly important for selecting books. Not unexpectedly, green light books were the most challenging to find. However, even if a book's potential for use is not high, teachers can consider adaptations or selecting specific pages or sections of books to develop into effective lessons. Regardless of the book, the teacher's role in facilitating problem solving, explorations, and discussions is paramount. Giorgis's description of the current trend of imposing "'cute' math activities on a piece of literature that emphasizes the teaching of basic math concepts" has little relevance to students' lives and experiences. Reminding us about how important quality literature is to helping kids connect with math, and how we must "not destroy literature or math in the process," Austin (1998b) cautions that as inferior books rapidly proliferate, there will be a great deal to consider when incorporating mathematics and children's literature.

Works Cited

Austin, P. (1998a). Math books as literature: Which ones measure up? *The New Advocate, 11*, 119–133.

Austin, P. (1998b, November). *Mathematics and literature: Publishers' responses to our interest in integration.* Paper presented at the annual meeting of the National Council of Teachers of English, Nashville, TN.

Carpenter, T. P., Fennema, E., Franke, M. L., Levi, L., & Empson, S. B. (1999). *Children's mathematics: Cognitively guided instruction.* Portsmouth, NH: Heinemann and Reston, VA: National Council of Teachers of Mathematics.

Columba, L., Kim, C. Y., & Moe, A. J. (2005). *The power of picture books in teaching math and science: Grades pre-k–8.* Scottsdale, AZ: Holcomb Hathaway.

Forbringer, L. L. (2004). The thirteen days of Halloween: Using children's literature to differentiate instruction in the mathematics classroom. *Teaching Children Mathematics, 11*, 82–90.

Giorgis, C. (1998, November). *Mathematical concepts emerging naturally from children's literature.* Paper presented at the annual meeting of the National Council of Teachers of English, Nashville, TN.

Hellwig, S. J., Monroe, E. E., & Jacobs, J. S. (2000). Making informed choices: Selecting children's trade books for mathematics instruction. *Teaching Children Mathematics, 7*, 138–143.

Jenner, D., & Anderson, A. (2000). Experiencing mathematics through literature: The story of Neil. *Teaching Children Mathematics, 6*, 554–547.

Jennings, C. M., Jennings, J. E., Richey, J., & Dixon-Krauss, L. (1992). Increasing interest and achievement in mathematics through children's literature. *Early Childhood Research Quarterly, 7*, 263–276.

National Council of Teachers of Mathematics. (2000). *Principles and standards for school mathematics.* Reston, VA: Author.

National Council of Teachers of Mathematics. (2006). *Curriculum focal points for prekindergarten through grade 8 mathematics.* Reston, VA: Author.

Roth McDuffie, A., & Young, T. A. (2003). Promoting mathematical discourse through children's literature. *Teaching Children Mathematics, 9*, 385–389.

Tarr, J. E., Reys, R. E., Reys, B. J., Chávez, O., Shih, J., & Osterlind, S. J. (2008). The impact of middle-grades mathematics curricula and the classroom learning environment on student achievement. *Journal for Research in Mathematics Education, 39*, 247–280.

Whitin, D. J. (2002). The potentials and pitfalls of integrating literature into the mathematics program. *Teaching Children Mathematics, 8*, 503–504.

Wilburne, J. M., Napoli, M., Keat, J., Dile, K., Trout, M., & Decker, S. (2007). Journeying into mathematics through storybooks: A kindergarten story. *Teaching Children Mathematics, 14,* 232–237.

Children's Books Cited

Birdseye, T. (1995). *Tarantula shoes.* New York: Holiday House.

Burns, M. (1995). *The greedy triangle* (G. Silveria, Illus.). New York: Scholastic.

Burns, M. (1997). *Spaghetti and meatballs for all* (D. Tilley, Illus.). New York: Scholastic.

Coats, L. (2000). *Neil's numberless world* (N. Layton, Illus.). New York: DK.

D'Aluisio, F. (2008). *What the world eats* (P. Menzel, Illus.). Berkeley, CA: Tricycle Press.

Demi. (1997). *One grain of rice: A mathematical folktale.* New York: Scholastic.

Dodds, D. A. (2005). *The great divide: A mathematical marathon* (T. Mitchell, Illus.). Cambridge, MA: Candlewick Press.

Goldstone, B. (2006). *Great estimations.* New York: Henry Holt.

Goldstone, B. (2008). *Greater estimations.* New York: Henry Holt.

Leedy, L. (1998). *Measuring Penny.* New York: Henry Holt.

Leedy, L. (1999). *Mission addition.* New York: Holiday House.

Lowry, L. (1989). *Number the stars.* Boston: Houghton Mifflin.

Lowry, L. (1993). *The giver.* Boston: Houghton Mifflin.

McGrath, B. B. (1994). *The M & M's brand counting book* (R. Glass, Illus.). Watertown, MA: Charlesbridge.

Murphy, S. J. (1999). *Betcha! Estimating* (S. D. Schindler, Illus.). Austin, TX: Steck-Vaughn.

Nagda, A. W. (2007). *Cheetah math: Learning about division from baby cheetahs.* New York: Henry Holt.

Nagda, A. W., & Bickel, C. (2000). *Tiger math: Learning how to graph from a baby tiger.* New York: Henry Holt.

Napoli, D. J. (2007). *The wishing club: A story about fractions* (A. Currey, Illus.). New York: Henry Holt.

Nolan, H. (2001). *How much, how many, how far, how heavy, how long, how tall is 1000?* (T. Walker, Illus.). Toronto, ON, Canada: Kids Can Press.

Pallotta, J. (2002). *The Hershey's Kisses subtraction book* (R. Bolster, Illus.). New York: Cartwheel.

Pinczes, E. J. (2003). *Inchworm and a half* (R. Enos, Illus.). New York: Sandpiper.

Schwartz, D. M. (1985). *How much is a million?* (S. Kellogg, Illus.). New York: Lothrop, Lee and Shepard.

Schwartz, D. M. (1994). *If you made a million* (S. Kellogg, Illus.). New York: HarperCollins.

Smith, D. J. (2002). *If the world were a village: A book about the world's people* (S. Armstrong, Illus.). Toronto, ON, Canada: Kids Can Press.

Smith, D. J. (2009). *If America were a village: A book about the people of the United States* (S. Armstrong, Illus.). Toronto, ON, Canada: Kids Can Press.

Strauss, R. (2007). *One well: The story of water on Earth* (R. Woods, Illus.). Toronto, ON, Canada: Kids Can Press.

Tang, G. (2002). *The best of times* (H. Briggs, Illus.). New York: Scholastic.

Thompson, L. (2001). *One riddle, one answer* (L. S. Wingerter, Illus.). New York: Scholastic.

Weiss, E. (2008). *Math at the store.* New York: Children's Press.

6

Multicultural Literature

Reading and Responding within Contemporary Contexts

JANELLE B. MATHIS, *University of North Texas*

Multicultural literature today is characterized by authentic stories about cultures told through rich language and captivating illustrations across all genres. Never before have so many cultural and ethnic insights, topics, and issues been available in books that share the diversity of both local and global societies as well as validate the life experiences of readers. Although at times it has been a struggle to convince readers, authors, and publishers of the need for such titles, advocates have gained many victories in the past several decades, and the field continues to become more refined. Today, the topic of multicultural literature is just as important for educators as it was at the 2007 Master Class in Teaching Children's Literature.

Definitions of multicultural literature vary and can be as simple as that provided by the Cooperative Children's Book Center (CCBC) at the University of Wisconsin–Madison, who do not claim any single definition of multicultural literature but say "we use the term to mean books by and about people of color. All children deserve books in which they can see themselves and the world in which they live reflected" (2009, para. 1 and 2). Definitions can also be quite complex, and Cai (2006) notes that the term means different things to different people as he reminds readers that the debate is concerned with "fundamental issues of a sociopolitical nature" (p. 3). Thus, the direction for the choice and use of multicultural literature reflects different stances. Despite the differences in how it is described, Cai states that the category of "multicultural literature" is needed until the field becomes one of "democratic pluralism" (p. 11). Generally speaking, however, a recent study found that many individuals define multicultural literature something like this:

Literature published in the United States that portrays diverse American cultures. Typically related to the major cultural groups in the USA: African American, Asian

American, Hispanic American, and Native American. Some definitions suggest the author needs to be an insider; other definitions don't require this; still other definitions address diversity in respects to religion, ethnicity, socioeconomic status, language, and ability. (Johnson, Freedman, Martens, Mathis, & Moreillion, 2009)

As this body of literature steadily increases, its potential for empowering readers and teachers lies in the hands of those who are aware of the titles, authors, and topics related to the curricular needs of today's learners. However, just as contemporary literacy contexts are changing in this era of technology and increased national and global diversity, so the role of multicultural literature continues to evolve. The goal of this chapter is to identify and elaborate on several topics that support an answer to the question: What is the role of multicultural literature within the instructional contexts of today's classrooms?

Following a brief review of the appearance of multicultural literature into the field of children's and adolescent literature, I discuss four issues surrounding the topic: authenticity, critical literacy, expanding notions of culture, and "new literacies." These issues have appeared frequently in recent years in the professional literature as well as in multicultural literature for young readers. I hope this chapter will create an awareness of the continued evolving field of multicultural literature and its potential to support contemporary instructional contexts.

Reflecting on the Emergence of Multicultural Literature

In most discussions of the beginnings of multicultural children's literature, scholars note Nancy Larrick's (1965) article in *Saturday Review* entitled "The All-White World of Children's Books," based on Larrick's five-year study of more than 5,000 children's books. In this groundbreaking piece, the lack of literature reflecting people of color was problematized in an impressive way by the finding that less than 1 percent of books reflected the African American child. One noted book in these earlier years was *The Snowy Day* by Ezra Jack Keats (1962) since, while it did not show ethnically specific characteristics, its main character had brown skin. African American literature of an authentic nature appeared along with the writings of such significant scholars as Rudine Sims (1983) who addressed the critical need for readers to see themselves represented in literature while also seeing the cultures of others different than themselves—the mirrors and windows metaphor that she made familiar to all interested in the field.

Viola Florez-Tighe (1983) was an early educator who advocated using multi-cultural literature in the classroom. In the 1960s, authors such as Virginia Hamilton, Jerry Pinkney, Walter Dean Myers, and others began to produce literature representative of children whose faces and voices were not formerly seen in many books. In 1983, Sims wrote for *Phi Delta Kappan* that, thanks to a small but prolific group of African American authors, the situation was improved although the number of books about African American culture was nowhere near where it should be. Other ethnic groups were also becoming evident in literature in the 1980s through writers such as Lawrence Yep, Virginia Driving Hawk Sneve, and Gary Soto.

In 1992, Kathryn Meyer Reimer noted that of the total books published in earlier years, less than 10 percent of them were about the four underrepresented cultural groups in the United States (African American, Asian American, Hispanic, and Native American), and the group least represented was the Hispanic culture. Pat Mora (1998) noted later in a significant article in *The New Advocate* that these potential writers must feel their stories and voices are important before more literature from this culture will appear. Multicultural children's literature in the 1990s was characterized by continuous improved representation, as noted by the CCBC. Furthermore, following the establishment of the Coretta Scott King Award created by the American Library Association (ALA) in 1969, there were ongoing creations of various awards for books representative of different ethnic and cultural groups. Small presses continued to be formed to publish multicultural books with one of the earliest being Children's Book Press in 1975, and larger publishing companies recognized the need and demand for multicultural literature. As this resource grew in numbers and in cultures represented, the professional literature reflected its use in classrooms although many teachers claimed still to be unsure as to what was "correct" to use.

Current Issues Around and Involving Multicultural Literature

In recent years, multicultural children's literature is found across genre and content areas, though it frequently reflects social insights and issues as it is a vehicle and voice for topics and multiple perspectives that previously were not deemed significant for readers. The topics chosen here represent those frequently found in the current professional literature and those that dominated the responses of colleagues who informally replied to an inquiry about what first comes to mind with the term *multicultural literature*. The information here is but a highlight of each of four areas that might invite readers into further exploration and realization of the evolving role of this significant body of literature. These highlights include attention to particular books and their creators and the strategies used by educators, since both well-crafted texts and response-based engagements are critical to experiencing multicultural literature that can potentially nurture and/or transform thinking.

Authenticity—Greater Insight into the Complexity of the Notion

While in past years the consideration of authenticity, accuracy, and objectivity were important in identifying excellence in children's literature, few people had a strong sense of the criteria to judge this literature. For many, just having diversity in books was quite the classroom resource, so realizing sources to help identify accurate literature was not always possible or a comfortable experience. At times, people turned to books such as Slapin and Seale's (1996) *Through Indian Eyes* or to other scholars to provide a sense of how to judge cultures not familiar to them.

Recent considerations about authenticity, however, are set apart from those of the past by the realization of the complexity of "authenticity." In *Stories Matter: The Complexity of Cultural Authenticity in Children's Literature* (Fox & Short, 2003), the editors of this significant collection of scholarly essays describe their efforts to provide contemporary insight into the complexity of the issue from the perspectives of scholars, authors, illustrators, and readers, "through a range of voices that provide a sense of history, a broad understanding of the current issues and debates, and a glimpse of possible new conversations and questions" (p. 4). They describe the chapters in this book as showing new paths as they reflect on topics such as the social responsibility of authors, the role of imagination and the experience in writing for young people, cultural sensitivity and values, authenticity of content and images, and authorial freedom. This complexity leaves these editors without a specific definition but noting that one of the key issues under debate is that of defining cultural authenticity. As mentioned earlier, different stances are revealed in different definitions (Cai, 2006), and this can result in "different courses of actions that change what happens in classrooms and in children's lives" (Fox & Short, p. 9).

Art, text, characters, and the situations surrounding the characters within multicultural books are scrutinized more and more by those who realize these books bear messages about the lifestyles and experiences of others. The many layers adding to this complexity include what may be authentic for one individual or group within a culture may not be authentic for others; who can write about what culture—insider versus outside perspectives; and the relationship of accuracy to authenticity. In addition to the book *Stories Matter*, the website for Worlds of Words provides guidelines for contemplating authenticity for reviewers of books that appear on *WOW Review*, one of the publications of this site. These guidelines and their application provide teachers and readers greater insight into making decisions about the authenticity of books they are reading. Application of these criteria can be seen in the numerous multicultural books reviewed.

A parallel issue to the notion of authenticity is that of the need for multiple perspectives, since one perspective does not necessarily stand for all within a culture, nor does one culture's insight, however accurate, represent the complete picture of any situation or event. While this topic flows into the topic of critical literacy discussed below, the notion of perspective and the life experiences that provide one's own perspective is part of the discussion around the complexity of authenticity.

Yet another aspect of authenticity that one might consider is that of language use and, in many cases, bilingual texts for all readers. While bilingual texts made their focused entry into the field in the 1990s, this first decade of the twenty-first century finds bilingual texts highly sought with attention given to the translation at hand. The literature itself provides a basis for thinking about authenticity and its current role. Bilingual books and language identity are often topics of children's multicultural literature. Pat Mora has written numerous bilingual texts, a most recent one being *Book Fiesta! Celebrate Children's Day/Book Day; Celebremos El día de los niños/El día de los labors* (2009). A few other suggested titles that authentically create a story in two languages are *My Diary from Here to There* by Amada Irma Pérez (2002) and *Iguanas in the Snow and other Winter Poems* by Franciso Alarcón (2001). Alma Flor Ada is also well known for her work as an author of bilingual children's books as well as her advocacy for their use. *I Love Saturdays y Domingos* (2001) is a favorite title she has written that tells of a child with two culturally different grandparents.

Many creators of multicultural literature are highly revered today, especially in light of the tasks they undertake to shed light on the unproclaimed histories and heroes of diverse cultures. Among these are Marilyn Nelson and Jerry Pinkney who created *Sweethearts of Rhythm: The Story of the Greatest All-Girl Swing Band in the World* (2009). Through precise, rich poetic phrases and warm, invigorating images, Nelson and Pinkney have told not only the story of this swing band during World War II, but they also share the role of music in creating resiliency for a nation at war and healing for a nation that is struggling amid prejudice and racism. Nikki Grimes, in rich poetic language, has re-created for readers both realistic worlds such as in *My Man Blue* (1999) and historical figures such as Bessie Coleman in *Talkin' about Bessie* (2002b). She gave authenticity and validity to an inner-city group of teens discovering poetry in *Bronx Masquerade* (2002a), as did Sharon Flake in *Who Am I without Him? Short Stories about Girls and the Boys in Their Lives* (2004) and *Money Hungry* (2001). Flake's novels create realistic images to which both girls and boys connect personally. Additionally, Jacqueline Woodson's *Locomotion* (2003), *Feathers* (2007), and *After Tupac and D Foster* (2008) present stories of young people discovering more about themselves as they face unique and challenging situations. Sherman Alexie has brought attention to the contemporary Native American in his book *The Absolutely True Diary of a Part-Time Indian* (2007), and Tony Johnston in *Any Small Goodness: A Novel of the Barrio* (2001) tells of Arturo and his life in the barrio of Los Angeles.

In addition to text, illustrations that authentically represent cultures draw readers into stories and contexts with each turn of the page. *A Place Where Sunflowers Grow* (Lee-Tai, 2006) tells of a young Japanese American girl's sadness when forced to leave her home to live with her family and other people of her culture in the Topaz Internment Camp. Based on a relative's story, both author and illustrator share realistic images along with the Japanese language in telling this story. E. B. Lewis shares the detail of the story in his expressive watercolors, and in *The Negro Speaks of Rivers* (Hughes, 2009) he provides authentic images in response to his reading of Langston Hughes's poetry. Kadir Nelson captures the warmth of humanity in his illustrations, and *We Are the Ship* (2008) glows with lifelike images of the faces of baseball and the African American players. With a similar glow about his work, Cuban-born Thomas Gonzalez painted the faces of the Maasai tribe in *14 Cows for America* (Deedy & Naiyomah, 2009). Yuyi Morales captures the colorful, festive glow of her Mexican culture in *Just in Case: A Trickster Tale and Spanish Alphabet Book* (2008) complete with traditional symbols that help to tell this tale.

Each of these books takes readers into well-crafted stories that provide authentic insight to particular characters at particular times. These books do not claim to represent all but to realistically capture those possible moments to which readers can connect as they learn more about themselves and others with whom they share society. Strategies to help readers delve into the issue of authenticity might include pairing books to note similarities and/or differences. Creating text sets in which each book represents a sound but differing opinion of a topic can point to authentic perspectives as students discuss why each point of view is valid. Using the Internet for inquiry to explore a topic further and seeking original artifacts and voices to support what particular books are telling us help readers confirm authenticity in light of their own research and comparison of information—a life task needed to develop critically thinking citizens. Sharing diverse texts with students and family members of particular cultures can bridge home connections and send messages that home cultures are valued and that the integrity of each culture is important as readers seek to validate information they read.

Social Justice and the Creation of Democratic Classrooms through Critical Literacy

> The function of multicultural literature is to ensure that students have the opportunity to reflect on it in all its rich diversity, to prompt them to ask questions about who we are now as a society and how we arrived at our present state, and to inspire them to actions that will create and maintain social justice. (McGinnis, 2006, p. 25)

Thus, this belief, held by many, puts children's literature at the forefront of the current focus on critical literacy.

Like other sociocultural notions, critical literacy has numerous definitions and uses. It consists of identifying multiple voices in texts, recognizing the dominant cultural discourse, engaging in multiple possible readings of texts to identifying sources of authority, and critiquing and producing a wide range of texts. Its purposes include having students examine the power relationships inherent in language use, recognize that language is not neutral, and confront their own values in the production and reception of language (Behrman, 2006).

Behrman (2006) did a critical review of the instructional and research articles pertaining to critical literacy and in each case, reading text, writing text, or comparing texts was at the heart of the critical literacy classroom practices described: reading supplementary texts, reading multiple texts, and reading from a resistant perspective; producing counter texts; conducting student-choice research projects; and taking social action. Literature can draw a reader into its events and help outsiders become part of contexts that speak to social injustice—as well as social justice. It is through multicultural literature that portrays the role of social justice and invites young readers to participate in making society more democratic that such critical literacy experiences have their roots and their wings.

Recent literature provides both stories of social justice within a single text as well as the description of events that invite a critical perspective through the instructional approaches described above. Nikki Giovanni's *Rosa* (2007) tells the deliberate actions of Rosa Parks as she took a stand for equality in not giving up her bus seat. *Miss Crandall's School for Young Ladies and Little Misses of Color* (Alexander & Nelson, 2007) tells in rich poetic format about the efforts in 1833–34 of Prudence Crandall to educate young African American women who, despite opposition, continued to pursue her goal. *Remember, the Journey to School*

Integration (Morrison, 2004) uses photographs to tell of the numerous individual and collective struggles for social justice in the civil rights era. *Crossing Bok Chito* (Tingle, 2006) is the story of how Native Americans helped slaves escape to freedom by cleverly deceiving the slave owners. Carmen Tafolla and Sharyll Tenayuca's (2007) *That's Not Fair!/No Es Justo!: Emma Tenayuca's Struggle for Justice/La lucha de Emma Tenayuca por la justicia* is the story of one young girl who decided to work to help pecan factory workers have equal rights. *Ryan and Jimmie: And the Well in Africa That Brought Them Together* (Shoveller, 2006) shows how powerful one young person can be as Ryan takes action to provide a well for a village in Africa. And, one among several stories of his life, *Harvesting Hope, the Story of Cesar Chavez* (Krull, 2003) helps young readers ponder the role of those working for social change.

Titles that share stories and historical events to provoke critical thought about social issues and democracy abound as well. *Sweetgrass Basket* (Carvell, 2005) tells in a poetic prose through the alternating voices of two Indian sisters sent to a Bureau of Indian Affairs school the unjust treatment of these children. In an effort to remove their "Indianness," the sisters were forced to work, removed from anything representing their heritage, and punished for the slightest actions deemed as disrespect by the Caucasian women running the school. This particular historical happening has only been recently brought to life for young readers to discuss and consider the injustice carried out toward this culture and these young people. *A Wreath for Emmet Till* (Nelson, 2005) tells the story of the young African American boy who was lynched when accused of whistling at a white woman in the 1960s. Marilyn Nelson's eloquent sonnet form gives dignity to this young life lost and moves readers to understand the injustices of this era.

Such books often require readers to enter into the text—to become even for a short while a participant in the events of the story. As they take on the emotions and sense of justice that they use to navigate their own world, they are forced to consider difficult situations, problematic decisions, and how to work for a difference in the realities of their own world. Drama approaches to text can help create this experience as young readers improvise situations, write inside the text as if they were in the minds of different characters, physically position themselves in the midst of a dangerous or emotional scene, consider whose voices are heard or not heard, and whether in such situations they are perpetrators, bystanders, or community members actively making a difference.

Louise M. Rosenblatt's work in developing and expanding the transactional theory of reader response continues to dominate much of the theoretical perspectives on using literature. Of her many perspectives one appropriate statement supports this current role of literature:

I am not under the illusion that the schools alone can change society. However, I can reaffirm the belief uttered so many years ago: We teachers of language and literature have a crucial role to play as educators and citizens. We phrase our goals as fostering the growth of the capacity for personally meaningful, self-critical literary experiences. The educational process that achieves this aim most effectively will serve a broader purpose, the nurturing of men and women capable of building a fully democratic society. The prospect is invigorating! (Rosenblatt, 1990, p. 107)

Expanding Notions of Culture

While multicultural literature was initially focused on representing the four major underrepresented groups recognized in the twentieth century, the twenty-first century has brought an awareness that other groups within this country have been underrepresented in the literature, such as people with a variety of physical, mental, or emotional challenges or Middle Eastern people from countries such as Pakistan, India, and Iran. Awareness continues to grow that within these generalized group titles, such as Latino or Asian, there are many different cultural representations of those who came to the United States from numerous countries. Greater insight into the global society has expanded multicultural literature to be more aware and inclusive of multiple nationalities.

Among the rich examples of Middle Eastern cultures in multicultural literature is Mitali Perkins's (2009) *Secret Keeper*, which tells the story of a young girl whose father comes to the United States in the 1970s while she is left with an uncle in Calcutta. At a time when she is expected to assume cultural habits of an Indian woman, she is becoming more aware of her own identity. *Four Feet, Two Sandals* (Williams & Mohammed, 2007) is the story of two young Pakistani girls in a refugee camp who become friends while waiting to be taken to America. While the story doesn't necessarily focus on their heritage, it does relate a situation that the authors are quite familiar with since they work with newly arrived refugees. *Koyal Dark, Mango Sweet* (Sheth, 2008) provides a contemporary look at young people in India and the custom of arranged marriages. Such books help others to understand this custom, which is important because it is also often a part of the cultural traditions of Indian people who now reside in the United States.

While global literature is covered elsewhere in this book, its role in consideration of multicultural literature is significant here in light of the current efforts to create a more personal connection between the cultures of the United States and those of other countries—to be inclusive of the United States and other countries in the term *global literature*. Immigration literature can be considered one way to bridge international and multicultural literature as the stories are told of those individuals bringing their varied cultures to a new homeland. In *Ask Me No Questions* (Budhos, 2006), Nadira and her sister leave Bangladesh to come to the United States but the trip is one of disappointment and fear due to September 11, 2001. *First Crossing* (Gallo, 2004) is a collection of stories told by teenage immigrants from a diversity of countries who, along with normal teenage challenges of identity development, must deal with prejudice and language barriers. *The Tequila Worm* (Canales, 2005) adds a bit of humor to a young girl leaving her home barrio to attend a boarding school. *La Linea* (Jaramillo, 2006) shares the all-too-often true tale of a 15-year-old illegally crossing the Mexican border to America and what he must unexpectedly endure after his funds for the trip are stolen. *The Dream on Bianca's Wall* (Medina, 2004) shares in poetry the hopes of an immigrant family's young daughter to be a teacher.

In addition to immigration literature, there is yet another recently recognized form of diverse literature as we find individuals whose life events have made them part of two cultures. Frequently, through blended family scenarios, we find stories of children who are living in families with two distinct cultures and who often find themselves not viewed or accepted as part of any one culture. *Mexican White Boy* (de la Peña, 2008) is always an outsider, and this book tells the story of many young people dealing with their biracial heritage. This theme of accepting one's identity and race is pertinent not only to bicultural families, but also to those who struggle with their physical appearance in light of the cultures with whom they identify, as in *American Born Chinese* (Yang, 2007).

Yet, another multicultural literature topic recognized anew in recent years is that of people who deal with challenges—physical, mental, and emotional. This focus has helped to improve the image of these individuals as functioning community members. Myron Uhlberg (2005) has provided a historical account of a young boy and his deaf father and their experiences with prejudice at the time of the emergence of the great Jackie Robinson. *Dad, Jackie, and Me* has autobiographical elements and is simply but sensitively told. *Ballerina Dreams* (Thompson, 2007) is a photographic essay about five little girls who wanted to dance and the ballet teacher who patiently helped them learn despite their cerebral palsy and other physical challenges. Another story, *The Hickory Chair* (Fraustino, 2001), tells of a young African American boy who is blind. He is not pitied and participates fully in life despite what might be perceived as a physical limitation. A more recent story also tells of a blind African American boy—*Piano Starts Here: The Young Art Tatum* (Parker, 2008). In a book for older readers, a young teen comes to grips with his inherited Tourette's syndrome in *Jerk, California* (Friesen, 2008). Contemporary books of this nature provide positive, realistic events that authentically break stereotypes of challenged individuals. Additionally, the

Schneider Family Award has been established to acknowledge literature that embodies an artistic expression of the disability experience for child and adolescent audiences. The latter two titles mentioned are recent winners of this award.

Literature, Technology, and the "New Literacies" of Adolescence

At the beginning of the twenty-first century, discussions were ongoing about the role of technology and literature—Would the latter succumb to the highly digital world forecast for the future? It is obvious that young people of all ages are intrigued by their ability to connect to others through e-sources and that the literature world is also making headway into this realm with books online, downloaded texts into Kindles, and digital soft-covered books for the young. The possibilities of book formats are not the issue here, but acknowledging technology as a resource to support multicultural literature is most definitely a worthy consideration. To build on the previous issues discussed here—notions of authenticity, social justice, an expanded perception of the notion of cultural diversity—technology offers immediate perspectives on almost any topic, event, individual, or geographical location presented in literature. While the Internet itself must be used with great care as to accuracy and reliability, it affords alternative perspectives on topics that can support issues or frame them as problematic. Trusted Internet sites are frequently used to further tell a story, describe a context, or invite readers to dig deeper into a historical or cultural event. *Ain't Nothing but a Man: My Quest to Find the Real John Henry* (Nelson & Aronson, 2007) sends readers to the Internet as they seek further information about this mystery in song that one man set out to solve. *Sweethearts of Rhythm* (Nelson, 2009), mentioned earlier, is typical of many books that provide Internet resources at the end of the text for further reading—including a video clip of the Sweethearts themselves singing. In a similar vein, *14 Cows for America* (Deedy & Naiyomah, 2009) sends readers to the Internet to discover more about this impressive gift from the Masaai people to the United States following the events of September 11, 2001. Often, students can take a virtual tour of a geographic area, museum, or historical trail.

Yet another way that technology supports readers is through book lists, book reviews, and actual books in digital libraries, such as at the ICDL, or International Children's Digital Library. Book lists available online include the various award-winning books from ALA, such as the Coretta Scott King Award Books or the Pura Belpré Award list. The Children's Literature Special Interest Group of the International Reading Association selects through a committee a group of books entitled the Notable Books for a Global Society. The website Worlds of Words provides a list of culturally authentic books as well as two publications,

WOW Stories and *WOW Review*. The former contains articles in which teachers are using multicultural and international literature in classes, and the latter contains reviews of numerous picture and chapter books that focus on issues of authenticity as well as excellence in the literary qualities of each title. Such resources are invaluable for those hoping to use multicultural literature in powerful ways in their classrooms. The US section of the International Board on Books for Young People (USBBY/IBBY) also offer an International Children's Book list of multicultural books that share global stories and are published in English. This list is selected by knowledgeable readers and scholars and provides yet another resource in the multicultural field.

Blogs, wikis, and certain social networking sites, such as Goodreads, invite readers to participate in book sharings and potentially rich discussions led by experts in the field or by others who just love books and reading. They can be used to show students the insights that others have from books and that differing perspectives are useful and informative.

As we consider the authenticity of particular authors and look to their background for insight into their books, writing process, and personal life experiences, author websites offer insights and afford these creators of books the opportunity to talk about their writing, characters, intent, background, and research. Nikki Grimes, Jacqueline Woodson, Jerry Pinkney, Pat Mora, Pam Muñoz Ryan, Janet Wong, Joseph Bruchac, Kahmira Sheth, and Patricia Polacco are but a few authors whose websites are rich with cultural insights to which readers can personally relate. The potential of these author connections to enhance the power of multicultural literature can be found in the authenticity authors can personally add to their published work.

In addition to authors' websites, interviews that one might not ordinarily find are available by merely searching with a viable topic. For example, *Why I Write Multicultural Books* by Cynthia Chin-Lee (2006) offers firsthand insights that are useful for many ages of readers. Or "Straight Talk on Race: Challenging the Stereotypes in Kids' Books" by Mitali Perkins (2009) begins with an insider's story of being from a nonmainstream culture in the United States. What a great article for older readers to enjoy but to put to task as they investigate multicultural literature for younger readers. Indeed, this age of technology and new literacies has much to offer the field of multicultural children's literature.

The Ultimate Role of Multicultural Literature: Has It Changed?

Returning to the question asked in the introduction to this chapter, "What is the role of multicultural literature within an instructional context characterized by technology, greater insight into global issues, and the 'new literacies' that are often used to characterize adolescents?" Perhaps a most meaningful response is one that is not new but persists in the transaction between reader and text—that is part of the ongoing identity development of young readers. In 2007, Sharon Flake, adolescent and young adult author who creates stories about African American youth, and E. B. Lewis, illustrator, spoke to the Children's Literature Assembly Master Class with a focus on multicultural literature in this age of technology and new literacies. These individuals are highly regarded in the literature field as well as with the readers, young and old, who engage with their text and illustrations. During her talk, Sharon reminded listeners that there is still a huge void in classrooms of books that represent diverse students. She hopes that her readers might realize, as in the case of many, it is okay to be "young, Black, and from the Inner City." She also hopes to inspire young readers to tell their stories as writers. In an article entitled "Who Says Black Boys Won't Read?," Flake (2007) describes the need for literature that reflects the lives of these boys and says, "the author and the reader are one and the same—bookends—both necessary for literature to be all that it must" (p. 13). Literature as a reflection of one's own life is still a powerful role of multicultural literature.

Additionally, E. B. Lewis shared that through his strong human interest stories, he hopes young readers might see that difference is good—"to see the world in a different light than we do" (Ernst & Mathis, 2008, p. 11). As technology, insight into the global community, and a variety of unique literacy forms emerge with the young people who are part of the contemporary reading scene, a key role of multicultural literature remains that of being a mirror to one's own life experiences and a window to the lives of others. The new issues around this body of literature still serve the same purpose. Today's multicultural literature provides uniquely refined story contexts that identify the complexity of understanding self and others in light of the communities in which we live.

Works Cited

Behrman, E. H. (2006). Teaching about language, power, and text: A review of classroom practices that support critical literacy. *Journal of Adolescent and Adult Literacy, 49,* 490–498.

Cai, M. (2006). *Multicultural literature for children and young adults: Reflections on critical issues.* Charlotte, NC: Information Age Publishing.

Chin-Lee, C. (2006). *Why I write multicultural books.* Retrieved from http://www.paper tigers.org/personalViews/archiveViews/ChinLee.html#

Cooperative Children's Book Center. (2009). *Multicutural literature*. Retrieved from http://www.education.wisc.edu/ccbc/books/multicultural.asp

Ernst, S. B., & Mathis, J. B. (2008). Multicultural literature: Reading, writing, and responding within a "new" literacy context. *Journal of Children's Literature, 34*(1), 10–12.

Flake, S. G. (2007). Who says black boys won't read? *Journal of Children's Literature, 34*(1), 13–14.

Florez-Tighe, V. (1983). Multiethnic literature: Supplements for basal readers (ERIC Document Reproduction Service No. ED246391).

Fox, D. L., & Short, K. G. (2003). *Stories matter: The complexity of cultural authenticity in children's literature*. Urbana, IL: National Council of Teachers of English.

Johnson, H., Freedman, L., Mathis, J., Martens, P., & Moreillion, J. (2009). *The language of "cultural" literature: What does it mean?* Retrieved from http://mclitresearch.wiki spaces.com/

Larrick, N. (1965) The all-white world of children's books. *Saturday Review, 48*, 63–65.

McGinnis, T. (2006). Considering the possibilities: Using multicultural literature to transform practice. *Voices from the Middle, 13*(3), 23–26.

Mora, P. (1998). Confessions of a Latina author. *The New Advocate, 11*, 279–290.

Perkins, M. (2009). Straight talk on race: Challenging the stereotypes in kids' books. *School Library Journal*. Retrieved from http://www.schoollibraryjournal.com/article/CA6647713.html

Reimer, K. M. (1992). Multiethnic literature: Holding fast to dreams. *Language Arts, 69*, 14–21.

Rosenblatt, L. M. (1990). Retrospect. In E. J. Farrell & J. R. Squire (Eds.), *Transactions with literature: A fifty-year perspective: For Louise Rosenblatt* (pp. 97–107). Urbana, IL: National Council of Teachers of English.

Sims, R. (1983). What has happened to the "all-white" world of children's books? *Phi Delta Kappan, 64*, 650–653.

Slapin, B., & Seale, D. (1996). *Through Indian eyes: The native experience in books for children*. Philadelphia: New Society.

Children's Books Cited

Ada, A. F. (2002). *I love Saturdays y Domingos* (E. Savadier, Illus.). New York: Atheneum.

Alarcón, F. X. (2001). *Iguanas in the snow and other winter poems* (M. C. Gonzalez, Illus.). San Francisco: Children's Book Press.

Alexander, E., & Nelson, M. (2007). *Miss Crandall's school for young ladies and little misses of color* (F. Cooper, Illus.). Honesdale, PA: Wordsong.

Alexie, S. (2007). *The absolutely true diary of a part-time Indian* (E. Forney, Illus.). Boston: Little, Brown.

Budhos, M. T. (2006). *Ask me no questions*. New York: Atheneum.

Canales, V. (2005). *The tequila worm*. New York: Wendy Lamb Books.

Carvell, M. (2005). *Sweetgrass basket*. New York: Dutton.

de la Peña, M. (2008). *Mexican white boy*. New York: Delacorte Press.

Deedy, C. A. (with Naiyomah, W. K.). (2009). *14 Cows for America* (T. Gonzalez, Illus.). Atlanta, GA: Peachtree.

Flake, S. (2001). *Money hungry*. New York: Hyperion.

Flake, S. (2004). *Who am I without him? Short stories about girls and the boys in their lives*. New York: Hyperion.

Fraustino, L. R. (2001). *The hickory chair* (B. Andrews, Illus.). New York: Arthur A. Levine/Scholastic.

Friesen, J. (2008). *Jerk, California*. New York: Speak/Penguin.

Gallo, D. R. (2004). *First crossing: Stories about teen immigrants*. Cambridge, MA: Candlewick Press.

Giovanni, N. (2007). *Rosa* (B. Collier, Illus.). New York: Square Fish.

Grimes, N. (1999). *My man Blue* (J. Lagarrigue, Illus.). New York: Penguin.

Grimes, N. (2002a). *Bronx masquerade*. New York: Penguin.

Grimes, N. (2002b). *Talkin' about Bessie: The story of aviator Elizabeth Coleman* (E. B. Lewis, Illus.). New York: Scholastic.

Hughes, L. (2009). *The Negro speaks of rivers* (E. B. Lewis, Illus.). New York: Hyperion.

Jaramillo, A. (2006). *La línea*. New York: Roaring Brook Press.

Johnston, T. (2001). *Any small goodness: A novel of the barrio* (R. Colón, Illus.). New York: Scholastic.

Keats, E. J. (1962). *The snowy day*. New York: Viking.

Krull, K. (2003). *Harvesting hope, the story of Cesar Chavez* (Y. Morales, Illus.). New York: Harcourt.

Lee-Tai, A. (2006). *A place where sunflowers grow* (F. Hoshino, Illus.). San Francisco: Children's Book Press.

Medina, J. (2004). *The dream on Blanca's wall/El sueño pegado en la pared de Blanca: Poems in English and Spanish/Poemas en Ingles y Espanol* (R. Casilla, Illus.). Honesdale, PA: Wordsong.

Mora, P. (2009). *Book fiesta! Celebrate children's day/book day; Celebremos El día de los niños/El día de los libros* (R. López, Illus.). New York: Harper Collins.

Morales, Y. (2008). *Just in case: A trickster tale and Spanish alphabet book*. New York: Roaring Brook Press.

Morrison, T. (2004). *Remember: The journey to school integration*. New York: Houghton Mifflin.

Nelson, K. (2008). *We are the ship: The story of Negro league baseball*. New York: Hyperion.

Nelson, M. (2005). *A wreath for Emmet Till* (P. Lardy, Illus.). New York: Houghton.

Nelson, M. (2009). *Sweethearts of rhythm: The story of the greatest all-girl band in the world* (J. Pinkney, Illus.). New York: Dial.

Nelson, S. R. (with Aronson, M.). (2007). *Ain't nothing but a man: My quest to find the real John Henry*. Washington, DC: National Geographic.

Parker, R. A. (2008). *Piano starts here: The young Art Tatum*. New York: Random House.

Pérez, A. I. (2002). *My diary from here to there* (M. C. Gonzalez, Illus.). San Francisco: Children's Book Press.

Perkins, M. (2009). *Secret keeper*. New York: Delacorte Press.

Sheth, K. (2006). *Koyal dark, mango sweet*. New York: Hyperion.

Shoveller, H. (2006). *Ryan and Jimmy: And the well in Africa that brought them together*. Toronto, ON, Canada: Kids Can Press.

Tafolla, C., & Teneyuca. S. (2007). *That's not fair! Emma Tenayuca's struggle for justice/¡No Es Justo!: La lucha de Emma Tenayuca por la justicia* (T. Ybáñez, Illus.). San Antonio, TX: Wings Press.

Tingle, T. (2006). *Crossing Bok Chito: A Choctaw tale of friendship and freedom* (J. R. Bridges, Illus.). El Paso, TX: Cinco Puntos Press.

Thompson, L. (2007). *Ballerina dreams*. New York: Feiwal and Friends.

Uhlberg, M. (2005). *Dad, Jackie, and me* (Bootman, C., Illus.). Atlanta, GA: Peachtree.

Williams, K. L., & Mohammed, K. (2007). *Four feet, two sandals* (D. Chayka, Illus.). Grand Rapids, MI: Eerdmans.

Woodson, J. (2003). *Locomotion*. New York: G. P. Putnam's Sons.

Woodson, J. (2007). *Feathers*. New York: New York: G. P. Putnam's Sons.

Woodson, J. (2008). *After Tupac and D Foster*. New York: G. P. Putnam's Sons.

Yang, G. L. (2006). *American born Chinese*. New York: First Second.

7

Nurturing Acceptance of Gender Diversity

APRIL WHATLEY BEDFORD, *University of New Orleans*

As chair of the Master Class in Teaching Children's Literature in 2005, I proposed a topic with which I had struggled for years: how to introduce children's books with gay and lesbian characters to preservice and practicing teachers. Invariably when I shared books such as *Heather Has Two Mommies* (Newman, 1989/2000) in my college classes, at least a few students would voice their strenuous objections to the mere existence of such books and especially to the idea of including these books in elementary and middle school classrooms. For several years, I had asked colleagues across the country what their experiences had been with sharing gay and lesbian children's literature. A few responded that their students were open to discussion of this literature, while most described experiences similar to my own. Some even said that they avoided sharing this literature altogether because they didn't want to endure the likely discomfort such discussions would prompt. Based on these informal conversations, I knew the topic of books written for children dealing with sexual orientation needed further exploration.

According to recent estimates, approximately 10 percent of the population does not identify as heterosexual (Schneider, 1988). While estimates differ about the number of children being raised in families headed by gay, lesbian, bisexual, or transgender parents—due in large part to fear of reporting because of resistance to gay and lesbian rights—one 1995 survey found that up to nine million children in America have gay or lesbian parents (Committee on Psychosocial Aspects of Child and Family Health, 2002). Additionally, according to the 2000 US Census, lesbian and gay families live in 99.3 percent of all US counties (Smith & Gates, 2001). In spite of these statistics, acceptance of gender diversity is far from the norm.

Children and adolescents who do not conform to traditional gendered behaviors are frequently the victims of name-calling and bullying and, in extreme cases, hate crimes. Due to their feelings of isolation and stigmatization, students who identify as being lesbian, gay, bisexual, transgender, or questioning/queer (LGBTQ), or those who are suspected by their classmates of being LGBTQ, often exhibit depression and anxiety, experience academic problems, become runaways, or, most tragically, commit suicide (Marinoble, 1998). Schools may be particularly dangerous places for LGBTQ students because of a "pervasive climate of fear and harassment for students and teachers" surrounding sexual orientation (Hermann-Wilmarth, 2007). Thirty-three percent of students responding to a national survey (Kosciw & Diaz, 2006) reported that they have been harassed at school because of their *actual* or *perceived* orientation; they also report that teachers rarely protect them from such harassment. Teachers repeatedly fail to disrupt the homophobic speech of students and sometimes even make derogatory remarks related to sexual orientation themselves (Kosciw & Diaz). Allowing such comments and behavior to continue unchecked affects the overall climate of a school.

Disrupting Heteronormativity through Children's Literature

One of my paramount goals as a teacher educator in children's literature is to introduce students to books that serve as both mirror and window (Bishop, 1990), helping all children see themselves reflected in books they find in their classrooms as well as to better understand their peers and the world around them through literature. At the CLA Master Class in Teaching Children's Literature in 2005, children's and young adult author Nancy Garden discussed the growing number of YA books addressing sexual orientation that are being published, with more than 100 young adult books with major gay, lesbian, bisexual, transgender, or questioning characters being published between 1990 and 2005 (Albright & Bedford, 2006). Unfortunately, the same cannot be said for children's books (those published for readers birth through eighth grade), although those numbers, too, are growing. Linda Lamme (2008), also a speaker at the 2005 Master Class, noted that picture books with LGBTQ content are still uncommon enough that every one is important regardless of quality.

The first place that prospective or practicing teachers might be introduced to children's books with LGBTQ characters is in undergraduate or graduate courses in teacher education. This, however, is likely not happening. While teacher preparation programs undoubtedly help shape teachers' beliefs as well as classroom practices, studies report that 44.4 percent of elementary and 40 percent of secondary teacher preparation programs in the United States "fail to include sexual orientation topics within program curriculum endorsed by faculty" (Macgillivray & Jennings, 2008, p. 176). Researchers posit that this exclusion may be unintentional, or it might be intentional because teacher educators are (1) unsure of *how* to discuss issues of sexual orientation; (2) unaware of whether they are *permitted* to discuss such issues; or (3) because of their own antigay beliefs (Macgillivray & Jennings).

Because textbooks often become the "defacto curriculum" for any college course (Macgillivray & Jennings, 2008), my colleague Pat Austin, from the University of New Orleans, examined inclusion of topics of sexual orientation in 15 children's literature textbooks commonly used in introductory college courses on children's literature. She found that five of the 15 did not mention LGBTQ content at all and two addressed it in only a cursory way (Albright & Bedford, 2006). Given these and similar findings by Hermann-Wilmarth (2007), it is likely that sexual orientation is not being discussed at all in some children's literature courses designed for preservice teachers. When the topic is addressed, Austin found that many textbooks do so under the heading of censorship, prompting students to view books with LGBTQ content as "dangerous."

In a course on feminist children's literature that my colleague Pat Austin and I co-designed and taught in 2001, when discussing books such as *William's Doll* (Zolotow, 1972) and other examples of literature that might encourage boys to behave in caring and compassionate ways, several students appeared uncomfortable. One woman said, "I don't want my boy to act like that. I want him to be *all boy*." Educators and researchers who have broached topics of gender diversity directly with elementary and middle school students have reported similarly disturbing findings. In their study of children's responses to picture books in which characters were portrayed in nontraditional gender roles, Anderson and Many (1992) found that both boys and girls responded negatively to a male character acting in stereotypically "feminine" ways.

In one of the few published studies of elementary teachers introducing picture books with gay and lesbian characters to their students, Schall and Kauffmann (2003) described reading aloud *King and King* (de Haan & Nijland, 2000) to Kauffmann's fourth- and fifth-grade multiage class. In this Cinderella variant, the handsome prince rejects all the princesses presented to him as potential mates in favor of another handsome prince. Students' first responses were silence, shock, and comments such as, "That's so gross." Over time, as students were given uninterrupted reading time to interact independently with several other books the researchers had chosen and to share their comments with their teacher and classmates, Schall and Kauffmann came to the conclusion that "students wanted to understand all kinds of relationships, including the relationships they saw in these books" (p. 40).

Fostering an Acceptance of a Range of Behaviors

In an effort to increase awareness of books that will help young readers "understand all kinds of relationships," a number of authors and educators (Chick, 2008; Gilmore, 2006; Herbeck, 2005; Lamme, 2008) have compiled lists of children's and young adult books with LGBTQ characters, and lists of recommended titles are easily accessible on several websites (American Library Association [ALA], 2010; Betts, 2009; Sarles, 2009; Wind, 2010). I have compiled all of these lists for further discussion. While I completely agree with Linda Lamme that children's books with LGBTQ characters are still too rare, and therefore every book matters, happily I can also report that since 2008, enough books have been written that it is no longer necessary nor feasible for me to try to highlight all of them in this chapter.

Instead, I will focus on books that meet one of three major purposes for introducing literature with LGBTQ characters to preservice and practicing teachers and librarians: (1) raising awareness of books about LGBTQ family members that will help readers see themselves and their families represented in literature; (2) promoting books that foster acceptance of a range of gendered behaviors; and (3) helping older readers answer questions about sexual identity. In the following sections I will discuss only a few of the books that are aligned with these purposes in hopes that readers will be prompted to search for these and other books with similar themes. Additionally, the books I will discuss are, with the exception of one, either picture books or novels for upper elementary and middle school students; a number of high-quality nonfiction books about LGBTQ topics have been produced, and those titles can be found on the referenced book lists but tend to fall outside the scope of this chapter.

Books Depicting LGBTQ Families

A growing number of children's books portraying gay and lesbian families are being published. These include books about same-sex parents; books that show a variety of family structures; and books in which children have LGBTQ family members other than parents. These books help all children to understand and become comfortable with a variety of family structures. As Lamme (2008) has already pointed out, the quality of these books varies wildly, with older books and books by small presses often being less visually appealing and frequently of lesser literary value than more recent books published by larger, mainstream publishers.

Same-Sex Parents

Books from small presses such as Alyson Wonderland, Hundredth Munchy Publications, and Nickname Press were all produced by earnest publishers attempting to fill a gap in the literature about same-sex parents available to children. According to the author/publisher's website (www.AppreciateDiversity.com), "Hundredth Munchy Publications believes that *Tolerant Toddlers Become Tolerant Teens* and is dedicated to providing gay-friendly children's books, a long-overdue resource for parents and teachers, both gay and straight." Alyson Wonderland is "an imprint dedicated to providing children of gay and lesbian parents books that reflect the reality of their lives" (www.jacketflap.com). Canadian-based author and publisher Heather Jopling created Nickname Press after discovering the dearth of "diversity-friendly" children's books while she was pregnant as a surrogate mother for a gay family (www.nicknamepress.com). All of these publishers are driven by laudable purposes; unfortunately, they lack the financial resources to produce books of high quality. Additionally, books from these publishers have other flaws not related to production quality. They tend to be message-driven, typically focusing more on making a point than on telling a good story.

Recently published picture books featuring same-sex parents indicate the beginnings of a hopeful trend among larger, mainstream publishers, however. These include *Molly's Family* by the renowned Nancy Garden (2004), published by Farrar, Straus and Giroux; *In Our Mothers' House* by beloved children's author/illustrator Patricia Polacco (2009), published by Philomel Books, a division of Penguin Young Readers Group; and two board books for very young children, *Mommy, Mama, and Me* (Newman, 2009b) and *Daddy, Papa, and Me* (Newman, 2009a) from Tricycle Press. The production value of all of these books is high, and they all received positive reviews based on literary quality. Tricycle Press was acquired by publishing giant Random House in 2009, and the publication of the two Newman books provides promising evidence that Random House plans to continue publishing books that further the original mission of Tricycle Press to "create books that inspire readers to see the world in different ways" (www.randomhouse.com/crown/tricycle). Similar books indicate that other mainstream publishers are following suit.

Compiling the book lists referenced previously, I identified a total of 49 picture books about same-sex parents. Of these, 11 titles were about families with two dads while the remaining 38 were about families headed by two moms. *Heather Has Two Mommies* (Newman, 1989/2000), considered a landmark book because it was the first picture book written showing a child being raised by two mothers, was heavily criticized because it graphically illustrated the story of Heather's conception through artificial insemination. In the tenth anniversary re-issue, Newman deleted those scenes. Since then, stories of how families are created by same-sex parents are not always included in picture books on that topic. For example, of the 11 books portraying families with two male parents, six depict a child engaged in daily life with both parents without making explicit how these families came to be. *Daddy's Roommate* (Wilhoite, 1990) and the follow-up *Daddy's Wedding* (Wilhoite, 1996), both considered groundbreaking books, detail how the father of the young boy who is the protagonist divorced the boy's mother and later married a man. *Daddy, Papa, and Me: How My Family Came to Be* (Aldrich, 2003) includes a description of how an African American boy was adopted by two Caucasian fathers. I would argue that there is a happy medium between leaving out the genesis of a family entirely and including graphic details about a child's conception in a picture book. Since a family created by two parents of the same sex can be formed in a variety of ways, it is important that literature for children reflect these various realities in age-appropriate contexts, and it is important for teachers and librarians to be aware of which types of family structures are included in children's books, which are left out, and what the criticisms as well as the accolades for such books have been.

Perhaps the most controversial picture book about same-sex parents to date, *And Tango Makes Three* (Richardson & Parnell, 2005), is not about two male human parents but is instead based on the true story of two male penguins living in New York's Central Park Zoo who were attracted to each other instead of female penguins, built a nest, hatched a fertilized egg, and cared for the baby, Tango, that emerged. Although it received starred reviews from *School Library Journal* and *Booklist*, in addition to much critical acclaim, it also received as much, if not more, vitriol from adult readers. The American Library Association reported that it was the most challenged book of 2006, 2007, and 2008 and the most banned book of 2009 (American Library Association, 2009). An appropriate discussion for college children's literature classes would focus on why adults might object even more strenuously to a book portraying animals of the same sex acting as co-parents than two male or female human parents.

While I initially thought that picture books featuring same-sex parents would be less prevalent than novels for children in grades 3 through 8, I actually found the opposite. A literature search of novels for middle grade readers with same-sex parents revealed only eight examples (although I can't unequivocally say that others don't exist). One of the eight was recommended for grades 3–6; the remainder were all recommended for grades 5 or above. Admittedly, a far greater number of young adult novels featuring all types of LGBTQ characters including parents exist than either picture books or novels for readers in eighth grade or below. My initial criterion for considering a book to be at the eighth-grade level was that the main character not be older than 14, but because so few books met this criterion, I broadened my search to include books recommended by publishers or reviewers for grades 7 or 8 even if the protagonists are slightly older; I then examined these books to see if the content would be considered more "children's" or more "young adult."

The novels I found including gay or lesbian parents for third- through eighth-grade readers tend to be more "problem-centered" than picture books about same-sex parents—and I found none in either genre including bisexual, transgender, or questioning parents. For example, both *Holly's Secret* by Nancy Garden (2000; recommended for grades 5 and up) and *From the Notebooks of Melanin Sun* by Jacqueline Woodson (1995; recommended for grades 6 and up) focus on the protagonists' anger and embarrassment because they have lesbian mothers. Two other novels deal with the outcomes of parental separation or divorce, both those that are common for all children, and those that are unique to the experiences of children of lesbian parents. In *Between Mom and Jo* by Julie Ann Peters (2006; recommended for grades 7 and up) 14-year-old Nick experiences great pain because of the separation of his mom and her long-term partner, Jo, who has no legal visitation rights with Nick because she was never married to Nick's mother.

Three of the novels I found include characters with gay or lesbian parents but have central conflicts that are unrelated to this fact. *Girl, Nearly 16: Absolute Torture* by Sue Limb (2005; recommended for grades 7 and up) recounts the humorous ups and downs of British teenager Jess; during a summer visit to her dad, she discovers that the reason her parents divorced is because her dad is gay, and she meets his new partner. Jess isn't overly upset by this discovery but must give up her dream that her parents will reunite. In *Newsgirl* (Ketchum, 2009; recommended for grades 5 and up), a recently published historical fiction novel, 12-year-old Amelia moves from Boston to San Francisco with her mother and her mother's female partner in 1851. Although the treatment of the two women is portrayed realistically, the plot revolves around Amelia's disguising herself as a boy to sell newspapers. The final book in this group, *The Case of the Stolen Scarab* (Garden, 2004a), should appeal to readers in third or fourth grade. Siblings Nikki and Taylor move with their two moms to an inn in Vermont and encounter an unexpected mystery they attempt to solve. Again, the focus is on the mystery rather than the children's lesbian moms. All three of these books received positive reviews and offer the encouraging possibility that more books for young readers will be published in which the inclusion of LGBTQ parents is simply present in the context of another story, rather than always being foregrounded as a source of disturbance or heartbreak.

Alternative Family Structures

I identified 15 picture books portraying a broad spectrum of family structures published over the past three decades. Again, they vary in quality but all serve a purpose. *Families* (Tax, 1981), published by The Feminist Press, is narrated by six-year-old Angie who tells readers everything she knows about families by describing the diverse human and animal families with which she is familiar. This includes Susie who "lives with her mother and her godmother" but doesn't have a father (p. 26). The book received positive reviews from *School Library Journal*, *Publishers Weekly*, and *Kirkus* when it was published nearly 30 years ago, and it is still relevant and appealing today. More recent books that contain this same message—it is love that makes a family—include *The White Swan Express: A Story about Adoption* (Okimoto, 2002) featuring four sets of North American parents who travel to China to adopt baby girls; the whimsically illustrated *The Family Book* by Todd Parr (2003); and the nonfiction *Families*, written and photographed by Susan Kuklin (2006), which received a starred review from *School Library Journal*. Each of these books presents at least one family with same-sex parents, and these families are simply included as one of a variety of family constellations rather than being singled out as unique.

LGBTQ Family Members

In addition to picture books written to help children see and accept same-sex parents and diverse family structures, more picture books are being published that tell family stories including gay and lesbian characters. Three of the earliest picture books about gay family members, published between 1989 and 1995, told stories of gay uncles dying of AIDS. Fortunately, the need for large numbers of current picture books about AIDS—particularly as a "gay disease"—no longer exists. More recent picture books about gay and lesbian relatives deal with more light-hearted themes. Some feature animal characters behaving as humans—a universal characteristic of picture books—and others depict human children and the adult relatives who are special to them. Of the picture books I reviewed about LGBTQ relatives, one was about a lesbian aunt (Hamlin, 2007), one was about a lesbian grandmother (Arnold, 1996), and five were about gay uncles (in addition to the three about uncles dying of AIDS), making uncles the most common family member found in picture books about LGBTQ relatives.

Prompting almost as many outcries for censorship as *And Tango Makes Three* (Richardson & Parnell, 2005) is the 2008 publication, *Uncle Bobby's Wedding* (Brannen, 2008), the story of a family of guinea pigs. When Chloe's favorite uncle decides to marry, she's afraid he doesn't love her anymore. The fact that Uncle Bobby is marrying his boyfriend Jamie is presented matter-of-factly; Chloe's love for her uncle and jealousy toward Jamie have nothing to do with their gender orientation, thus making this a family story with universal appeal for children. Although *And Tango Makes Three* remained at the top of the list for challenged books, *Uncle Bobby's Wedding* made the list of "Top Ten Challenged Books" the year following its publication (ALA, 2009). It also spawned a heated online debate when librarian Jamie Larue blogged about a library patron lodging a complaint about the book. Larue posted his lengthy and thoughtful response to the patron that sparked reader responses resulting in more than 60 printed pages (Larue, 2008).

Interestingly, a book with a similar theme to *Uncle Bobby's Wedding*, but published earlier, did not receive the same kind of opposition from censors. *Mini Mia and Her Darling Uncle* (Lindenbaum) was published in 2007 and tells the story of Ella, affectionately called Mini Mia by her adoring Uncle Tommy, in reference to her favorite soccer player. Like Chloe the guinea pig, Ella becomes jealous when Uncle Tommy's new friend, Fergus, begins spending time with the little girl and her uncle. Both books are resolved by the child characters discovering that their uncles don't love them any less simply because they are in loving relationships with (male) partners and that the partners offer even more fun and love for the nieces to experience.

I only found five novels for third- through eighth-grade readers portraying family members, other than parents, who are LGBTQ. These books are certainly more difficult to find in an electronic search because an LGBTQ relative of a protagonist might not be central to the description of a text. The five that I found ranged from humor to mystery to tragedy, and were rated as appropriate for fourth, fifth, sixth, or seventh graders or higher. In *A Clear Spring* (Wilson, 2002), 11-year-old Willa is reluctant to spend the summer with her two aunts in Seattle, but upon arrival she quickly becomes drawn into an "eco-mystery" that she and her cousins solve. While the aunts are primary characters, readers will be most drawn to this book because of the mystery. Likewise, *The Skull of Truth* (Coville, 1997) is a hilarious but poignant mystery about an 11-year-old boy, Charlie, a chronic liar who steals a skull from a magic shop and is compelled to tell only the truth while the skull is in his possession. He also discovers unexpected truths about family members, including the fact that his uncle's "roommate" is actually his lover.

Two other novels about gay uncles, for sixth- or seventh-grade readers, respectively, or older, include K. L. Going's (2009) *King of the Screw-ups* and Gregory Maguire's (1996) *Oasis*. *King of the Screw-ups*, which received starred reviews from both *Publishers Weekly* and *School Library Journal*, is both funny and heart-rending and tells the story of high school student Liam who is kicked out of his home by his impossible-to-please father and moves in with his gay, glam rocker uncle, "Aunt Pete." *Oasis* is a much tougher read about 13-year-old Hand, who is dealing with the death of his father, the return of the mother who abandoned him three years earlier, and the discovery that his Uncle Wolfgang is gay and dying of AIDS. This book, too, received excellent reviews and could easily be paired with other books about the death of a parent written for this age group. Jacqueline Woodson (2008) included a secondary but memorable character, a gay brother, in her Newbery Honor–winning portrait of female friendship, *After Tupac and D Foster*, a character not currently found in picture books about LGBTQ relatives.

Accepting a Range of Gendered Behaviors

One of my major goals as a professor of children's literature is to raise students' awareness of books that describe a range of gendered behaviors and to facilitate discussions about these books to foster acceptance of such behaviors. In her thought-provoking essay in *Horn Book*, Kathleen Horning (2005) described how, as an 11-year-old child questioning her sexual identity in the 1970s, there were no books in which she could specifically see herself reflected; instead, she had to "read between the lines" to find aspects of books that affirmed her developing sense of identity. Although I would argue that child readers should be given more opportunities to see themselves and their families explicitly represented in books (as the books I have already discussed do), Horning adds, "Not every young reader is ready for overt self-examination; some may prefer to find themselves in books that don't explicitly deal with gay themes but that may strike a chord nonetheless" (p. 52). As a children's literature instructor, I search for books that will stimulate conversations about gendered behavior that may not explicitly "deal with gay themes" but that would likely be questioned by readers.

Picture Books about Gender Difference

When selecting picture books to foster discussions about characters' gender and behavior, I look for books that include girls engaging in typically "masculine" behaviors and books that show boys engaging in typically "feminine" behaviors. As Tunks and McGee (2006) point out, there are currently many more picture books readily available to children that show strong, independent female characters participating in hobbies or vocations or displaying emotions or behaviors that have traditionally been associated with males than there are picture books depicting male characters behaving in ways that are typically associated with females. Additionally, when either of these types of books is shared with children, they tend to react more positively to the former and negatively to the latter (Anderson & Many, 1992; Rice, 2002; Tunks & McGee, 2006). I have found this to be true of adult readers' responses as well.

Although girls expressing a wide range of emotions and behaviors is now more acceptable in both literature and life than it once was, I would argue that girls who behave in "overly masculine" ways would likely still be teased or bullied in real life whether or not they are in books. For example, a young girl who is a soccer star but occasionally wears dresses or plays with dolls would likely be admired by both peers and adults whereas a young girl who hopes to be a football star and dresses and cuts her hair like most of the boys her age would probably be ridiculed at school and maybe even at home. Picture books such as *Horace and Morris but Mostly Dolores* by James Howe (1999) and *Betty Lou Blue* (Crocker, 2006) about atypical female characters provide a venue for open discussion of such scenarios. Both Dolores and Betty Lou have characteristics and demonstrate behaviors typically viewed as masculine, but a skillful teacher or librarian can lead young readers in a discussion about how these characters provide role models for boys and girls alike.

Picture books in which boys engage in "feminine" behavior are both harder to find and more difficult for readers to accept. Interestingly, many of the books that do exist are decades old, such as the now-classic *The Story of Ferdinand* (Leaf, 1936), *William's Doll* (Zolotow, 1972), and *Oliver Button Is a Sissy* (dePaola, 1979). In spite of this rather discouraging fact, I am continually on the lookout for recent picture books in which male characters behave in ways typically associated with females. Such behaviors range from subtle to overt and usually result in a male character being teased or bullied, but not always.

Some of the subtle "feminine" behaviors exhibited by boys in picture books include crying, showing affection, and caring for others. In *Tough Boris* (Fox, 1994), about a pirate who cries when his beloved parrot dies, and *Wilfrid Gordon McDonald Partridge* (Fox, 1985), about a young boy who helps his elderly friend restore her memory, author Mem Fox "embedded countersexist attitudes intentionally" (1993, p. 155). Neither of these characters is teased for having or showing emotions, but they can prompt discussions about how children might actually be treated if they behaved in the same ways.

Boys who participate in the arts are a frequent target for teasing in picture books and in life. Again, sharing books in which male characters are artists, musicians, or dancers and discussing how they are treated by others can lead to positive changes in the ways children actually treat one another. In the previously mentioned *Oliver Button Is a Sissy* (dePaola, 1979), the title character is ridiculed for wanting to tap dance. Other picture books that feature male characters dancing—such as *Max* (Isadora, 1976), *Song and Dance Man* (Ackerman, 1988), and *Lili at Ballet* (Isadora, 1993)—do not include teasing or bullying but are instead a celebration of dancing for both males and females. Such books will surely prompt discussions by children about expectations for gendered behavior if allowed.

In *The Bat Boy and His Violin* (Curtis, 1998), young Reginald is a gifted violinist but his love for music is discouraged by his father, a baseball coach, who would much rather see Reginald excel as an athlete. Set in the 1940s, this historical fiction picture book about the Negro National League will prompt children to discuss how views about gender may (and may not) have changed over time. James Rumsford's beautifully rendered *Silent Music: A Story of Baghdad* (2008) shows how a young Iraqi boy uses his love of calligraphy to cope with his fears of war. Both of these books could evoke inquiry into numerous social justice issues, including gender expectations across cultures and time periods, because of their multiple layers.

While boys showing emotion or those who long to express themselves through the arts may cause some level of discomfort among some readers, those who engage in overtly "feminine" behaviors—such as playing with dolls or wearing dresses—are likely to provoke stronger negative reactions. This has been the case with *William's Doll* (Zolotow) since its publication in 1972. The more recent *Silly Billy* (Brown, 2006) portrays a young boy weighted down with fears about all kinds of imagined possibilities whose grandma gives him Guatemalan worry dolls on whom to cast his worries. At first, this is a perfect solution for Billy, but then he begins to worry about bestowing such a great burden on the dolls, so he makes tiny worry dolls for them to share their burdens and eventually makes dolls for all his friends. This gem of a book about a boy who is a worrier (likely common but certainly seen as less than masculine) who also sleeps with and creates dolls could lead to valuable discussions. Marcus Ewert's *10,000 Dresses* (2008), about a boy who sees himself as a girl and wants to both wear and design dresses, will probably lead to even more uncomfortable but equally important debates.

Finally, in this category, I'd like to mention picture books in which characters behave in such outrageous, over-the-top ways that they might be referred to as "gay" by child (or adult) readers although this is never made explicit in the books themselves. Examples include *The Sissy Duckling* (Fierstein, 2002) and *The Boy Who Cried Fabulous* (Newman, 2004). Both of these books would fit Horning's description of books in which readers might "read between the lines" to make judgments about gender-appropriate behavior, and all could prompt discussions interrogating the language—such as "sissy"—we use to describe people whose behaviors make us uncomfortable.

Novels about Gender Difference

Novels about behavioral expectations based on gender written for readers in grades 4 through 8 focus on the "Q" in LGBTQ content, encompassing both *questioning* and *queer*. I have divided these books into two broad categories: those in which *others* question a character's behavior related to gender, and those in which a character questions *his or her own* gender orientation or comes to terms with his or her own queer identity. As mentioned before, more YA novels can be found that deal with these topics, but I will highlight books intended for readers in the 9–14 age group.

Others Questioning a Character's Gender

In a number of books for this age range, characters are condemned by others for "acting gay," even when they may be secure in their own heterosexual identities; this is also the reality for youth at this age. A tragic sequence of events ensues in *Burn* (Phillips, 2008) when high school ninth grader Cameron is teased and ostracized for being gay (although he is not). Eventually, both his peers and Cameron become violent, first when Cameron is assaulted in the locker room at school and afterwards when his acute humiliation results in him killing a witness to the assault. This book, while painful to read, is ripe with opportunities for discussing the behaviors of the characters who are portrayed as victims, as bullies, and as bystanders (Entenman, Murnen, & Hendricks, 2005/2006).

Sometimes bystanders do nothing at all, and sometimes they take positive action. In the next group of novels, main characters discover that friends their own age are gay or lesbian. In each case, they continue to develop these friendships, and in some cases, they stand up for their friends who are treated badly by others. Examples include *The Method* (Walker, 1990); *Face the Dragon* (Sweeney, 1992); and *Alice on the Outside* (Naylor, 1999). While their years of publication might indicate that such books are not being published currently, they are difficult to locate, so I remain hopeful that more exist and that they will continue to be published in greater numbers. One book I particularly want to recommend in this category is *The Misfits* by James Howe (2001), a book about four friends in seventh grade, each of whom is an outsider in some way, who lead a campaign for "No Name Calling Week" in their school. Although fictional, this book inspired the advent of the actual No Name Calling Week, created by GLSEN and Simon & Schuster, and occurring annually in schools across the United States since 2004.

Other books in this category include novels in which the main character is positively influenced by an adult LGBTQ character. These titles include *No Castles Here* (Bauer, 2007), about 11-year-old Augie who is dealing with many struggles in his young life, assisted by a gay "Big Brother"; *The Manny Files* (Burch, 2006), about a family whose lives are enriched by a gay male nanny (both books recommended for ages 9–13); and *Bait* (Sanchez, 2009), about a sexually abused boy whose relationship with the probation office he discovers is gay is one of the most positive experiences of his life (recommended for ages 12 and up). A final book I want to mention in this group will be of particular interest to educators. Ellen Jaffe McClain's *No Big Deal* (1994) is about a junior high school student, Janice, who takes a stand when her favorite teacher is persecuted because he is gay.

While the three preceding titles are all contemporary realistic fiction, *Hitler's Canary* (Toksvig, 2005) is a middle grades historical fiction novel about the Nazi occupation of Denmark. This remarkable book includes a secondary character, Thomas, the "dresser" for the actress mother of the nine-year-old male protagonist. While never overtly identified as gay, both Thomas's behavior and the derogatory way in which another adult male character describes him imply that he is. *Hitler's Canary* differs from the other novels discussed not only because of genre but also because Thomas is a secondary character. His creativity and bravery make him extremely admirable; I am continually searching for other books in which secondary LGBTQ characters exhibit positive traits or behaviors.

Characters Questioning Their Own Sexual Identity

While young adult books featuring characters questioning their own sexuality abound, similar books are less prevalent for elementary and middle grade readers. This is as it should be, since middle school and beyond is when most individuals likely begin to address issues related to their own sexual orientation. However, I have heard adults express the fact that they were aware of their homosexuality as early as five years old; moreover, children begin to tease their peers based on their perceived sexuality at early ages. Both of these situations might make adults uncomfortable, but they create a need for high-quality children's books that address issues of sexuality with children directly.

As I found to be true of most children's novels with LGBTQ content, fewer books exist about self-identified lesbians than gay males. One beautiful example is *The House You Pass on the Way* by Jacqueline Woodson (1997), about self-named Staggerlee, a 14-year-old of mixed racial heritage whose sexuality is only one aspect of her identity that she questions. An example of a book with a gay adolescent protagonist that I particularly like is *Totally Joe* (Howe, 2005), the sequel to *The Misfits*, in which readers learn much more about the lovable

Joe—a boy who is confident in his identity as a gay seventh grader, due in large part to his supportive family and friends—as he writes the "alphabiography" assigned by his language arts teacher. Other novels about boys questioning their sexual orientation include the humorous *Absolutely, Positively Not* (LaRochelle, 2005) and *My Most Excellent Year: A Novel of Love, Mary Poppins, and Fenway Park* (Kluger, 2008); the engaging *In Mike We Trust* (Ryan, 2009); and the darkly dramatic *Swimming in the Monsoon Sea* (Selvadurai, 2005), set in India in 1980. All of these novels are recommended for grades 7 and up.

Even more difficult to find are books for this age group in which the protagonists *might* be bisexual or transgender. Titles worth exploring for middle school readers include *Boy2Girl* (Blacker, 2005); *Blue Boy* (Satyal, 2009); and *The Boy in the Dress* (Walliams, 2009). Because questioning related to sexual identity is common to all young adolescents, we need more novels in which characters are supported in their questioning by supportive peers and adults and in which they ultimately become comfortable with whatever their sexual identity might be.

Teaching Strategies

While the intended audience for all the books I have discussed is children in kindergarten through eighth grade, it is vitally important that the adults who work with children in this age group be made aware of the existence of such books, given opportunities to confront their feelings about these books openly and honestly, and guided in how to introduce these books to the audience for whom they were intended. The work of instructors of children's literature at the university level is crucial for preservice and practicing teachers and librarians to make informed choices about book selection and sharing. My first step as a children's literature professor is to make sure that I continue to add to my own collection of books that fall within each category that I have identified and to look for books in each category that include as many genres, time periods, and cultures as possible so that the potential for discussion surrounding the books is rich and complex.

Pat Austin recommends finding multiple "entry points," such as studies about family or biography, for presenting and discussing children's books with gay and lesbian characters. One entry point for introducing books with LGBTQ themes to adult students is to gather a selection that varies in quality. Exploring issues of quality with my students, we begin by considering what makes a high-quality book within the genre we are investigating; then, we apply those criteria to books with LGBTQ content and discuss why many of the books might be of poorer quality than books dealing with less controversial subject matter. We discuss these issues within a context of social justice while considering literature as both mirror and window for readers. To supplement these discussions, I have students read reviews of the books to analyze what critics say about the quality of particular children's books with LGBTQ themes and to note which books were not reviewed by major reviewers such as *Kirkus, Publishers Weekly, School Library Journal,* and *Horn Book* (Lamme, 2008).

Within this framework, we also discuss students' personal responses to books, both orally and in writing. These discussions are tricky; I want everyone to feel comfortable enough to share their honest reactions, but I also want them to be sensitive to the fact that a range of views is likely present in any given class. Questions I use to prompt these discussions are, *Would you share this book in your elementary/middle school classroom? Why or why not? If yes, when and how would you introduce it?* During these discussions, I ask students to read informal reviews of the books we are considering on Amazon and Google Books—some of which are almost always present whether or not a book has been formally reviewed—to obtain a sense of what readers find both beneficial and objectionable. This is often an eye-opening experience.

Author studies provide another entry point for discussing books with LGBTQ characters. Authors such as Phil Bildner, Nancy Garden, James Howe, Julie Ann Peters, Robert Sabuda, Brian Selznick, and Jacqueline Woodson openly acknowledge being gay or lesbian. Most, but not all, of these authors have written at least one book with LGBTQ themes. However, readers cannot assume that because an author or illustrator creates a book with LGBTQ content, that author necessarily identifies as LGBTQ; conversely, not all LGBTQ authors or illustrators who create books for children choose to include LGBTQ content in their books.

I urge students who have already begun to develop children's literature libraries to research the backgrounds of the authors and illustrators in their collections; to examine family books for portrayals of diverse families; to scrutinize gendered behaviors of characters in books; and to identify gaps in their collections that they need to fill. Together, we read and discuss articles that provide detailed classroom studies of children's responses to books that deal with gender including those by Anderson and Many (1992); Rice (2002); and Schall and Kauffmann (2003) as well as instructional strategies recommended by Tunks and McGee (2006). All of these studies include thorough explanations that would allow them to be replicated and focus on honoring children's responses while gently expanding their views through a variety of activities. We discuss how teachers might adapt them in their own classrooms using different or more recent books.

When working with children, I encourage teachers to begin with children's aesthetic and emotional responses to a book before moving on to issues of quality. Questions to ask children might include: *Did you like this book? Why or why not? What makes it a good book? What makes it a not-so-good book?* While I see an important goal of sharing books with children as developing understanding and appreciation of what makes quality literature, I believe that children forming personally meaningful connections with books is what matters most in ensuring that reading plays a key role in their lives. A book that might not be of the highest quality might nevertheless be the book that appeals to a particular child, helps that child see himself or herself reflected within its pages, or awakens the empathy that helps a child better understand a classmate, a family member, or a current event.

Specifically, I hope that teachers will share books with children that will lead to discussions about incidents where they have felt victimized in some way, where they have been the perpetrators of teasing or bullying against others, or where they have been bystanders who have simply done nothing or who have intervened on behalf of others who need their help. I truly believe that literature can develop compassion and initiate social change in even our youngest readers, and those changes in attitudes and actions often begin with the adults who introduce children to the books that can change lives. Reading, thinking, and talking about books with LGBTQ content is uncomfortable for many adults whose careers involve children, but I strongly believe that those of us in positions to influence teachers and librarians must be willing to endure the discomfort that can lead to a more just and equitable society for all.

Works Cited

Albright, L. K., & Bedford, A. W. (2006). Master Class in Teaching Children's Literature: From resistance to acceptance—introducing books with gay and lesbian characters. *Journal of Children's Literature, 32*(1), 9–15.

American Library Association. (2009). *Attempts to remove children's book on male penguin couple parenting chick continue.* Retrieved from http://www.ala.org/ala/newspress center/news/pressreleases2009/april2009/nlw08bbtopten.cfm

American Library Association. (2010). *ALA Rainbow Project: Recommended GLBTQ books for young readers.* Retrieved from http://rainbowlist.wordpress.com/

Anderson, D. D., & Many, J. E. (1992). An analysis of children's responses to storybook characters in non-traditional roles. *Reading Horizons, 33,* 95–107.

Betts, W. E. (2009). *Rainbow reading: Gay and lesbian characters and themes in children's books.* Retrieved from http://www.windowsill.net/gaybooks.html

Bishop, R. S. (1990). Mirrors, windows, and sliding glass doors. *Perspectives: Choosing and Using Books for the Classroom, 6*(3), ix–xi.

Chick, K. (2008). Fostering appreciation for all kinds of families: Picturebooks with gay and lesbian themes. *Book Bird, 46*(1), 15–22.

Committee on Psychosocial Aspects of Child and Family Health. (2002). Coparent or second-parent adoption by same-sex parents. *Pediatrics, 109*, 339–340.

Entenman, J., Murnen, T. J., & Hendricks, C. (2005–2006). Victims, bullies, and bystanders in K–3 literature. *The Reading Teacher, 59*, 352–364.

Fox, M. (1993). *Radical reflections: Passionate opinions on teaching, learning, and living.* San Diego: Harcourt Brace.

Gilmore, D. P. (2006). Not quite out of the closet: Using children's picture books featuring gay and lesbian parents/characters. *The Dragon Lode, 25*(1), 31–39.

Herbeck, J. (2005). Creating a safe learning environment: Books for young people about homosexuality. *Book Links, 14*, 30–38.

Hermann-Wilmarth, J. M. (2007). Full inclusion: Understanding the role of gay and lesbian texts and films in teacher education classrooms. *Language Arts, 84*, 347–356.

Horning, K. T. (2005 January/February). On spies and purple socks and such. *The Horn Book Magazine, 81*, 49–67.

Kosciw, J. G., & Diaz, E. M. (2006). *The 2005 National School Climate Survey: The experiences of lesbian, gay, bisexual and transgender youth in our nation's schools.* New York: Gay, Lesbian and Straight Education Network.

Lamme, L. L. (2008). Literature about lesbian, gay, bisexual, and transgender people and their families. In S. S. Lehr (Ed.), *Shattering the looking glass: Challenge, risk, and controversy in children's literature* (pp. 209–233). Norwood, MA: Christopher-Gordon.

Larue, J. (2008). Uncle Bobby's wedding. *Myliblog.* Retrieved from http://jaslarue. blogspot.com/2008/07/uncle-bobbys-wedding.html

Macgillivray, I. K., & Jennings, T. (2008). A content analysis exploring lesbian, gay, bisexual, and transgender topics in foundations of education textbooks. *Journal of Teacher Education, 59*, 170–188.

Marinoble, R. M. (1998). Homosexuality: A blind spot in the school mirror. *Professional School Counseling, 1*(3), 4–7.

Rice, P. S. (2002). Creating spaces for boys and girls to expand their definitions of masculinity and femininity through children's literature. *Journal of Children's Literature, 28*(2), 33–42.

Sarles, P. (2009). *Gay-themed picture books for children.* Retrieved from http://booksfor kidsingayfamilies.blogspot.com

Schall, J., & Kauffmann, G. (2003). Exploring literature with gay and lesbian characters in the elementary school. *Journal of Children's Literature, 29*(1), 36–45.

Schneider, M. (1988). *Often invisible: Counseling gay and lesbian youth.* Toronto, ON, Canada: Central Toronto Youth Services.

Smith, D. M., & Gates, G. J. (2001). *Gay and Lesbian families in the United States: Same-sex unmarried partner households*. Retrieved from http://www.urban.org/Uploaded-PDF/1000491_gl_partner_households.pdf

Tunks, K. W., & McGee, J. (2006). Embracing William, Oliver Button, and Tough Boris: Learning acceptance from characters in children's literature. *Childhood Education, 82*, 213–218.

Wind, L. (2010). *I'm here. I'm queer. What the hell do I read?* Retrieved from http://www.leewind.org/

Children's Books Cited

Ackerman, K. (1988). *Song and dance man* (S. Gammell, Illus.). New York: Knopf.

Aldrich, A. R. (2003). *Daddy, Papa, and Me: How my family came to be* (M. Motz, Illus.). Oakland, CA: New Family Press.

Arnold, J. (1996). *Amy asks a question—Grandma, what's a lesbian?* (B. Lindquist, Illus.). Racine, WI: Mother Courage Press.

Bauer, A. C. E. (2007). *No castles here*. New York: Random House.

Blacker, T. (2005). *Boy2Girl*. New York: Farrar, Straus and Giroux.

Brannen, S. S. (2008). *Uncle Bobby's wedding*. New York: G. P. Putnam's, Sons.

Brown, A. (2006). *Silly Billy*. Cambridge, MA: Candlewick Press.

Burch, C. (2006). *The manny files*. New York: Atheneum.

Coville, B. (2007). *The skull of truth* (G. A. Lippincott, Illus.). San Diego: Harcourt.

Crocker, N. (2006). *Betty Lou Blue* (B. Kulikov, Illus.). New York: Dial.

Curtis, G. (1998). *The Bat Boy and his violin* (E. B. Lewis, Illus.). New York: Simon and Schuster.

de Haan, L., & Nijland, S. (2000). *King and king*. Berkeley, CA: Tricycle Press.

dePaola, T. (1979). *Oliver Button is a sissy*. San Diego: Harcourt Brace.

Ewert, M. (2008). *10,000 Dresses* (R. Ray, Illus.). New York: Seven Stories Press.

Fierstein, H. (2002). *The sissy duckling* (H. Cole, Illus.). New York: Simon and Schuster.

Fox, M. (1985). *Wilfrid Gordon McDonald Partridge* (J. Vivas, Illus.). San Diego: Kane/Miller.

Fox, M. (1994). *Tough Boris* (K. Brown, Illus.). San Diego: Harcourt Brace.

Garden, N. (2000). *Holly's secret*. New York: Farrar, Straus and Giroux.

Garden, N. (2004a). *The case of the stolen scarab*. Ridley Park, PA: Two Lives Publishing.

Garden, N. (2004b). *Molly's family*. New York: Farrar, Straus and Giroux.

Going, K. L. (2009). *King of the screw-ups*. New York: Harcourt.

Hamlin, A. (2007). *Anna's aunts get married*. New York: Bank Street College of Education.

Howe, J. (1999). *Horace and Morris but mostly Dolores* (A. Walrod, Illus.). New York: Atheneum.

Howe, J. (2001). *The misfits*. New York: Atheneum.

Howe, J. (2005). *Totally Joe*. New York: Atheneum.

Isadora, R. (1976). *Max*. New York: Macmillan.

Isadora, R. (1993). *Lili at ballet*. New York: G. P. Putnam's, Sons.

Ketchum, L. (2009). *Newsgirl*. New York: Viking/Penguin.

Kluger, S. (2008). *My most excellent year: A novel of love, Mary Poppins, and Fenway Park*. New York: Dial Books.

Kuklin, S. (2006). *Families*. New York: Hyperion.

LaRochelle, D. (2005). *Absolutely, positively not*. New York: Arthur A. Levine/Scholastic.

Leaf, M. (1936). *The story of Ferdinand* (R. Lawson, Illus.). New York: Viking.

Limb, S. (2005). *Girl, nearly 16: Absolute torture*. New York: Delacorte Press.

Lindenbaum, P. (2007). *Mini Mia and her darling uncle* (E. K. Dyssegaard, Trans.). Stockholm, Sweden: R and S Books.

Maguire, G. (1996). *Oasis*. New York: Clarion Books.

McClain, E. J. (1994). *No big deal*. New York: Lodestar.

Naylor, P. R. (1999). *Alice on the outside*. New York: Atheneum.

Newman, L. (1989/2000). *Heather has two mommies* (D. Souza, Illus.). Boston: Alyson Wonderland.

Newman, L. (2004). *The boy who cried fabulous* (P. Ferguson, Illus.). Berkeley, CA: Tricycle Press.

Newman, L. (2009a). *Daddy, Papa, and me* (C. Thompson, Illus.). Berkeley, CA: Tricycle Press.

Newman, L. (2009b). *Mommy, Mama, and me* (C. Thompson, Illus.). Berkeley, CA: Tricycle Press.

Okimoto, J. D. (2002). *The White Swan Express: A story about adoption* (E. M. Aoki, Illus.). New York: Clarion Books.

Parr, T. (2003). *The family book*. New York: Little, Brown.

Peters, J. A. (2006). *Between Mom and Jo*. New York: Little, Brown.

Phillips, S. (2008). *Burn*. New York: Little, Brown.

Polacco, P. (2009). *In our mothers' house*. New York: Philomel Books.

Richardson, J., & Parnell, P. (2005). *And Tango makes three* (H. Cole, Illus.). New York: Simon and Schuster.

Rumsford, J. (2008). *Silent music: A story of Baghdad*. New York: Roaring Brook Press.

Ryan, P. E. (2009). *In Mike we trust*. New York: HarperTeen.

Sanchez, A. (2009). *Bait*. New York: Simon and Schuster.

Satyal, R. (2009). *Blue boy*. New York: Kensington.

Selvadurai, S. (2005). *Swimming in the monsoon sea*. Toronto, ON, Canada: Tundra Books.

Sweeney, J. (1992). *Face the dragon*. New York: Delacorte Press.

Tax, M. (1981). *Families* (M. Hafner, Illus.). New York: Feminist Press.

Toksvig, S. (2005). *Hitler's canary*. New Milford, CT: Roaring Brook Press.

Walker, P. R. (1990). *The method*. San Diego: Harcourt.

Walliams, D. (2009). *The boy in the dress*. New York: Razorbill/Penguin.

Wilhoite, M. (1994). *Daddy's roommate*. Boston: Alyson Wonderland.

Wilhoite, M. (2000). *Daddy's wedding*. Boston: Alyson Wonderland.

Wilson, B. (2002). *A clear spring*. New York: Feminist Press at CUNY.

Woodson, J. (1995). *From the notebooks of Melanin Sun*. New York: Scholastic.

Woodson, J. (1997). *The house you pass on the way*. New York: Delacorte Press.

Woodson, J. (2008). *After Tupac and D Foster*. New York: G. P. Putnam's, Sons.

Zolotow, C. (1972). *William's doll* (W. P. Du Bois, Illus.). New York: Harper and Row.

8

Building Bridges of Understanding through International Literature

KATHY G. SHORT, *University of Arizona*

One of the trends in the field of children's and adolescent literature is the increasing availability of international books, the topic of the 2002 Master Class in Teaching Children's Literature. Many of these books come from other English-speaking countries, particularly England and Australia, an indication that the field still has a long way to go in opening up the world through literature. Small steps matter, however, and it is clear that gradually more books about a range of global cultures are becoming available.

These books are important because our lives are going global. Rapid economic, social, and technological changes connect us around the globe, so that knowledge of the world has become a necessity, not a luxury. The world in which children will live as adults will be fundamentally different from the world in which we grew up. The quickening pace of globalization has led to a context in which opportunities to succeed depend on global knowledge and skills, and yet many American students are ignorant of world cultures, international issues, and foreign languages. They often obtain their world knowledge through television and video games with an emphasis on conflict, catastrophe, terrorism, and war. Their understandings thus remain superficial, grounded in fear and stereotypes, leading to ethnocentrism and a lack of understanding about world cultures.

There are many ways of opening the world for children and adolescents, including technology, world language study, student exchange programs, and global studies. All of these are significant, but literature offers unique possibilities, in particular the opportunity for students to go beyond a tourist perspective of surface-level information about another culture. Literature invites readers to immerse themselves into story worlds to gain insights about how people live, feel, and think around the world—to develop emotional connections and empathy as well as knowledge. These connections go beyond the surface knowledge of food, dance, clothing, folklore, and facts about a country to the values and beliefs that lie at the core of each culture.

The goal of integrating international literature into classrooms and libraries is the same as multicultural literature—to challenge students to learn about, understand, and accept those different from themselves, thus breaking the cycles of oppression and prejudice between people of different cultures. As students read these books, they come to recognize the common feelings and needs they share with children around the world, as well as to value the unique differences that each culture adds to the richness of our world.

Literature provides a means of building bridges of understanding across countries and cultures. Through reading books from global cultures, students come to know their own culture as well as the world beyond their homes. They see how people of the world view themselves, not just how we view them. Opening the world through literature is not a new idea but has remained an elusive goal within most US schools and libraries. This chapter discusses some of the issues that have created obstacles to this goal as well as highlights, strategies, and resources for engaging teachers and students so that these books become integral to classroom life.

Challenges to the Integration of International Literature

The integration of international literature into classrooms remained an elusive goal for many years simply because there were so few books available. While international literature has always been present through well-loved characters such as Heidi, Pippi Longstocking, and Hans Brinker, their numbers were so small that they had little impact. Also, for many years, most of the books that were available about global cultures were so-called travel books, books written by Americans who traveled to a country for several weeks. These books were characterized by their superficiality and were often filled with stereotypes. Series books, for example, focused on characters such as the Bobbsie Twins who traveled to "exotic" and "primitive" countries.

This context is quickly changing as increasing numbers of books are distributed in the United States from other countries and are written and published within the United States. A lack of familiarity with these books, however, continues to be a problem because they are a recent trend, and even award-winning international books are given little attention in schools and libraries. The ALA names the Batchelder award for the most distinguished translated book at the same time as the Newbery and Caldecott awards. This award has a 40-year history and yet still remains unknown to many teachers and librarians, receiving little publicity. Other award lists, such as the Outstanding International Book list from the US section of IBBY (International Board of Books for Young People), struggle to gain recognition from publishers and educators.

Even the definition of *international literature* remains contentious. Some argue that the term should refer only to those books originally published for children in a country other than the United States in the language of that country and later republished in the United States (Tomlinson, 1999). *Global literature* is the preferred term for the broader body of books set in countries and cultures outside the United States, no matter where they were published. In this chapter, *global literature* and *international literature* will be used interchangeably to refer to the broader body of literature set in a specific global culture, no matter what the origin of the book. The origin of the book is significant to cultural authenticity; however, the increasing mobility of authors, who may live and work across several national settings, and the changing nature of the publishing industry, which leads to books being published first in the United States rather than the author's own country, have made these distinctions less useful in a global economy.

Definitions based on the origins of international literature connect to another challenge for educators about cultural authenticity of the books. Educators are often hesitant to use these books because they know that many are problematic and feel uncomfortable about their own knowledge of so many different global cultures. Examining the authorship of the broad body of international literature in the United States provides a better sense of the complexity of evaluating cultural authenticity (Fox & Short, 2003). The range of authorship includes the following:

1. Books written by authors/illustrators who are insiders to the culture they portray and who still reside within that culture. These books are typically published in the country of origin for the children of that country, and are then translated (if not written in English) and distributed in the United States. Examples are *Moribito* (Uehashi, 2008) and *Garmann's Summer* (Hole, 2008). Some translated books, however, are not from the country being portrayed, such as *The Shadows of Ghadames* (Stolz, 2005), set in Libya but written by a French journalist.

2. Books written by authors/illustrators who are insiders to the culture they are portraying, but who now reside in the United States as their primary residence even though they return regularly to their country of origin. Sometimes their work is initially published in the United States. Examples are *Inkdeath* (Funke, 2009), *Tasting the Sky* (Barakat, 2007), and *Just in Case* (Morales, 2008).

3. Books written by authors/illustrators who are immigrants to the United States and write about their country of origin. Some regularly return to their country of origin, while others left as children or young adults and rarely return, adding the complication that their writing may be based on memories of a country that no longer exists due to societal changes. Examples are *I Lost My Tooth in Africa* (Diakité, 2006), *Keeping Corner* (Sheth, 2007), and *Revolution Is Not a Dinner Party* (Compestine, 2007).

4. Books written by US authors/illustrators who draw from their family's heritage in their country of origin, but who were born and raised in the United States. These authors use family memories as well as engage in research. Examples are *When My Name Was Keoko* (Park, 2002) and *The Surrender Tree* (Engle, 2008).

5. Books written by US authors/illustrators who spend a significant period of time within a particular country, often working for some type of government or social agency or as journalists. Examples are *Colibrí* (Cameron, 2005) and *Faraway Home* (Kurtz, 2000).

6. Books written by US authors/illustrators who research a particular country and who may or may not visit that country as part of that research. Examples are *When Heaven Fell* (Marsden, 2007) and *Balarama* (Lewin & Lewin, 2009).

7. Books written by an author who is an outsider to the culture but who collaborates with an insider to strengthen authenticity. For example, Elizabeth Laird, a British author, collaborated with Sonia Nimr, a Palestinian archaeologist, storyteller, and author from Ramallah, the location of their book, *A Little Piece of Ground* (2006).

Another major challenge involves uncertainties about how to effectively use international books with students, given that many contain unfamiliar stylistic devices and terminology and the experiences and settings in the books, at first glance, seem far removed from students' lives. Students often resist narratives that have linguistic or cultural practices that are difficult for them to understand (Bond, 2006). Educators struggle with how to support students in making significant connections to these books to move their responses beyond viewing other cultures as exotic or strange. Some unintentionally adopt strategies that are tangential or even in opposition to the goals of global education by promoting we/them dualisms and highlighting superficial aspects of cultural lifestyles that reinforce rather than challenge stereotypes (Fang, Fu, & Lamme, 2003). Simply reading about the world can actually negatively influence the development of intercultural understanding (Case, 1993).

Creating Intercultural Understanding
through International Literature

Courses and workshops on international literature for teachers and librarians have become increasingly popular in recent years in response to the growing availability of these books and the emerging interest in global education. Because of the complex issues that surround these books, these courses must go beyond immersing educators in the literature. Becoming familiar with international books is a first step in a much more complicated process of challenging educators to consider issues of cultural authenticity and the types of engagements with these books that build intercultural understanding, not stereotypes.

Montero and Robertson (2006) examined the issues that inhibit and encourage teachers to use international and global children's literature in their classrooms through analysis of data from their university course. They found that teachers gained an understanding of the use of interpretive, rather than literal, translation and the resulting variation in translation quality as well as developed the ability to engage in critical analysis of cultural authenticity. Teachers came to realize the need to interrogate the stereotypes and assumptions that they bring to a text and the need to gain background information on the country, culture, perspective, and time period of a book. They also became aware that even when they considered themselves knowledgeable about a country, their perspectives as cultural outsiders often did not allow them to see the cultural nuances and richness identified by a cultural insider within a particular book. While many began the course believing they needed to gain a certain authority to teach literature in an unfamiliar culture, they gradually realized that a reader response approach and knowledge of available resources allows them to learn alongside their students. They also became aware of the significance of promoting an equity pedagogy for their classrooms.

My graduate course on international literature is structured around the same curricular framework that has emerged in my research with international literature in a K–5 elementary school that has a schoolwide focus on global inquiry through literature and the arts (Short, 2009). This framework (see Figure 8.1) highlights multiple ways of engaging with international literature to support readers' critical explorations of their own cultural identities, in-depth studies of specific cultural ways of living, the integration of diverse cultural perspectives across the curriculum, and inquiries into complex global issues.

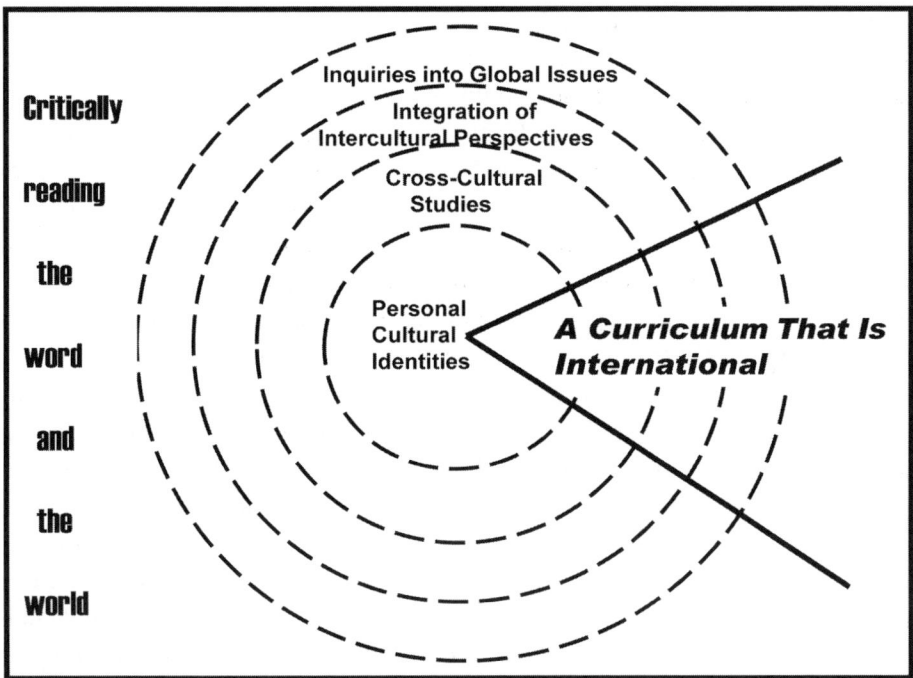

Figure 8.1: A curriculum that is international.

Exploring Personal Cultural Identities

The course begins with an exploration of our personal cultural identities to build a conceptual understanding of culture and to provide strong personal connections for the teachers and librarians in the course. Educators create identity intersections to examine the different cultural aspects of their identities, including language, religion, gender, social class, ethnicity, race, age, family structures, region and nationality, community, and education (Foss, 2002). The purpose of this engagement is to challenge teachers to consider a definition of culture that goes beyond ethnicity so that everyone sees themselves as cultural beings. If culture is only defined as ethnicity and as something only a few possess, culture becomes an "add-on" to the curriculum or something exotic, rather than integral to who we are as human beings. Geertz (1973) says that culture is "the shared patterns that set the tone, character, and quality of people's lives" (p. 216). These shared patterns go beyond external characteristics to include the values, symbols, interpretations, and perspectives held by a group of people. Culture is a way of being in the world through a design for living that involves systems of acting, believing, and valuing.

One aspect of their cultural identities that many Americans overlook or ignore is that of nationality, and, since the course focuses on international literature, we look specifically at nationality as one aspect of identity. Typically, the educators in the course are from local schools as well as other countries. Each person finds a partner from the same region in the United States or country and creates a chart where they record insider and outsider perspectives on how people within that culture look and think (see Figure 8.2). This chart creates tension-filled discussions as they wrestle with the stereotypes that others have about their nationality or region and with reducing their own sense of the diversity within their country into short phrases.

To continue their exploration of culture, I ask class members to bring to the next class session visual and symbolic representations (collages, maps, artifacts, etc.) of how they are international in their lives and identities. We share these in small groups and set up museum displays. We also discuss books where characters move across cultures, such as *Habibi* (Nye, 1999) and *Hannah's Winter* (Meehan, 2009), in small-group literature circles, focusing first on personal responses and then on how the character's identity changes in moving across global cultures and the ways in which the character is international. Other engagements that encourage educators to examine their cultural identities include cultural X-rays, cultural identity maps, and collections of artifacts that reflect the different aspects of each person's cultural identity.

These discussions lead us into a class debate about the definition of international literature and its value for readers. Small groups web their understandings of what it means to have an international perspective and then create a diamond ranking, putting internationalism at the top of their diamond and selecting eight words/characteristics they consider essential to defining internationalism. These words are arranged into a diamond shape (1, 2, 3, 2, 1) from most valued to least valued. This process takes them from thinking broadly about internationalism as they brainstorm web to debating about how to select what is of most significance for this perspective.

We then move into professional readings about internationalism and international literature using *Global Perspectives in Children's Literature* (Freeman & Lehman, 2001) and a range of articles. In my courses, I often ask students to first develop their own definitions and connections before they move into professional readings to encourage a more critical interaction with the readings and to help them uncover their current understandings and misconceptions. Another focus of the professional reading is on interculturalism as an attitude of mind, an orientation that pervades thinking so that diverse cultural perspectives are woven throughout the curriculum and school life, instead of being a special book or unit. In particular, we look at the work of European theorists such as

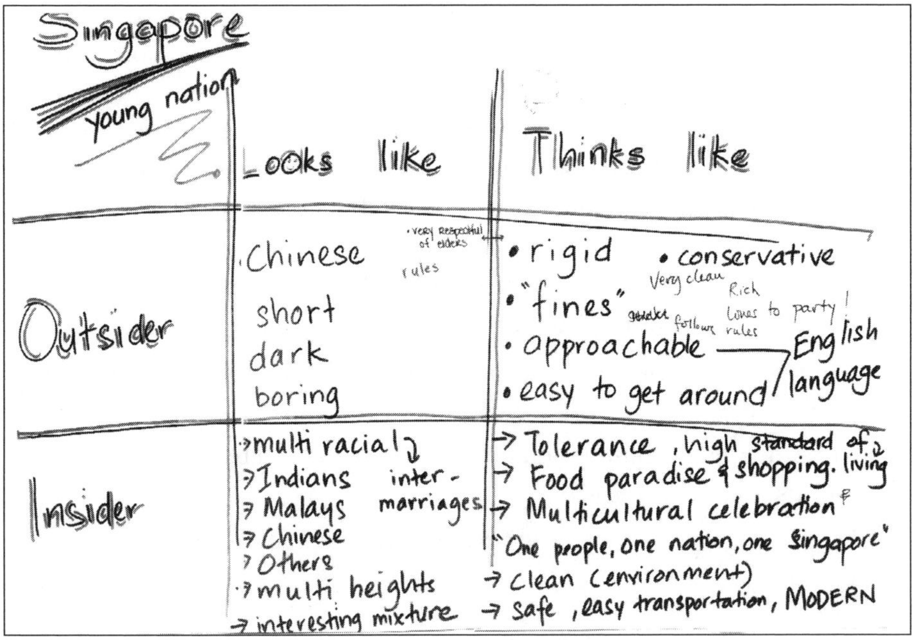

Singapore
young nation

Looks like | **Thinks like**

Outsider
- Chinese   · very respectful of elders   rules
- short
- dark
- boring

- rigid   · conservative
- "fines"   Very clean   Rich   Loves to party!   gender follows rules
- approachable — English language
- easy to get around / language

Insider
- multi racial
- Indians   inter-
- Malays   marriages
- Chinese
- Others
- multi heights
- interesting mixture

→ Tolerance, high standard of
→ Food paradise & shopping. living
→ Multicultural celebration
"One people, one nation, one Singapore"
→ Clean (environment)
→ Safe, easy transportation, MODERN

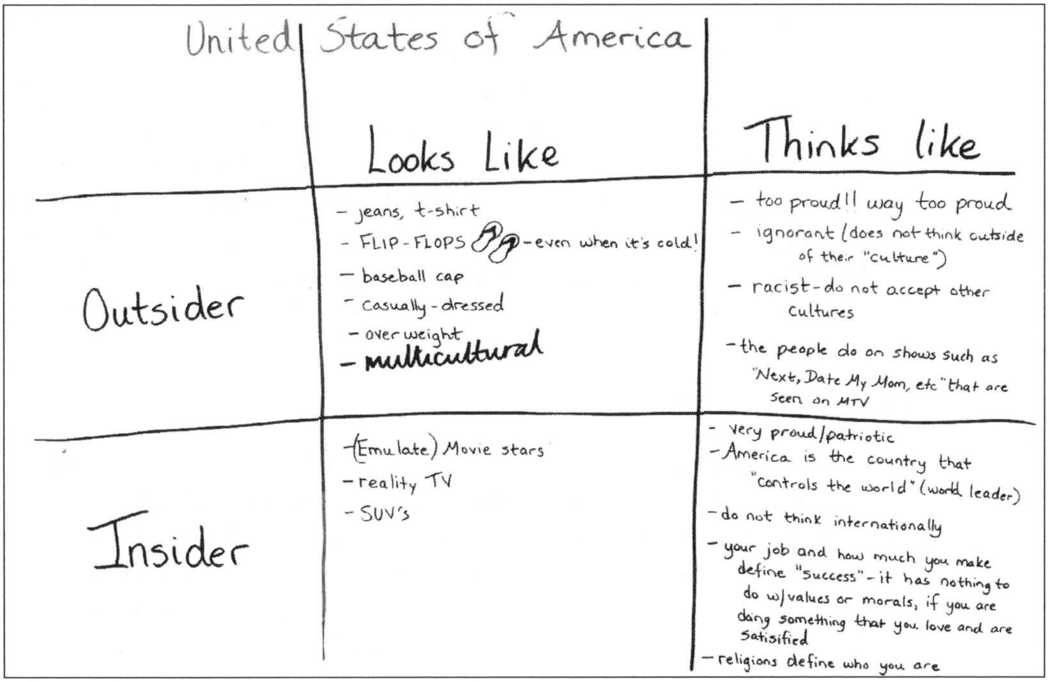

United States of America

Looks Like | **Thinks like**

Outsider
- jeans, t-shirt
- FLIP-FLOPS — even when it's cold!
- baseball cap
- casually-dressed
- over weight
- **multicultural**

- too proud!! way too proud
- ignorant (does not think outside of their "culture")
- racist- do not accept other cultures
- the people do on shows such as "Next, Date My Mom, etc" that are seen on MTV

Insider
- (Emulate) Movie stars
- reality TV
- SUV's

- very proud/patriotic
- America is the country that "controls the world" (world leader)
- do not think internationally
- your job and how much you make define "success"- it has nothing to do w/ values or morals, if you are doing something that you love and are satisfied
- religions define who you are

Figure 8.2: Charts of insider/outsider perspectives on national identities. See "Wow Stories" on the Worlds of Words website (www.wowlit.org) for other examples of classroom work.

Fennes and Hapgood (1997), Hofstede (1991), and Allan (2003) who use the term *interculturalism* to refer to understandings and relationships of diverse cultural groups that cross outside the boundaries of countries. They view *multiculturalism* as an American term referring to relationships between diverse microcultures within a county. Based on my own reading of these theorists, I have framed the course around interculturalism as an orientation that includes the following:

- Understanding one's personal cultural identity
- Building a conceptual understanding of culture and perspective
- Valuing the unique perspectives and common humanity of diverse cultural groups
- Critiquing the inequities and injustices experienced by specific cultural groups
- Developing a commitment to taking action for a more just and equitable world

We also read several novels, including recent Batchelder Award winners, in literature circles, focusing on the ways in which the character's cultural identity is revealed, such as *The Shadows of Ghadames* (Stolz, 2004), *The Crow-Girl* (Bredsdorff, 2004), *Daniel Half Human and the Good Nazi* (Chotjewitz, 2004), *Samir and Yonatan* (Carmi, 2000), and *The Friends* (Yumoto, 1996). We also create a list of issues to consider related to international literature, such as availability, authenticity, and translation. These issues cut across our readings throughout the course with the goal that class members will gradually build more complex understandings about how these issues play out in the literature, leading to a more focused examination of the issues at the end of the course.

Cross-Cultural Studies

These initial engagements provide educators with a theoretical frame on culture and interculturalism as well as a sense of their own cultural identities and the cultural ways of thinking they bring to life and to responding to literature. To encourage them to move beyond their own perspectives to consider the range of perspectives in the world, we move into an extended study of literature from a range of global cultures. Cross-cultural studies involve an in-depth study of a particular culture to gain a sense of the diversity and complexity within that culture. These studies have often taken the form of stereotypical country studies that focus on the surface aspects of culture, referred to as the 5Fs curriculum—

food, fashion, folklore, famous people, and festivals. We used an adapted version of the iceberg model of culture (Fennes & Hapgood, 1997) to uncover the ways in which this curriculum does not engage learners in the deep structure of culture—the core values and beliefs (see Figure 8.3).

The iceberg concept of culture is an important metaphor for reflecting on our responses to literature and understandings of a culture as well as for evaluating the portrayals of a culture within particular pieces of literature. The surface aspects are significant to that culture and are often an easy place to begin a cultural study but can easily lead to stereotypes unless the study moves into the deeper values and beliefs of that culture. We use blank models of the iceberg to label our current understandings of a particular culture, either individually or in small groups.

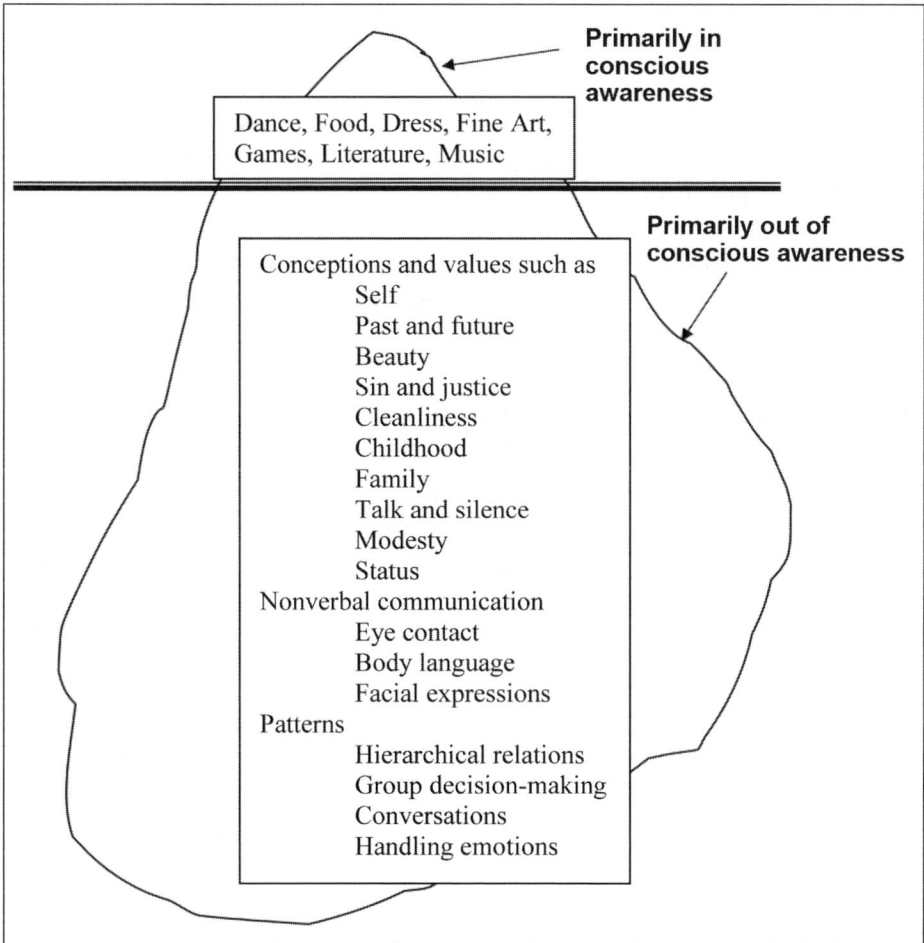

Figure 8.3: Iceberg concept of culture.

One major issue that often emerges is the need to continuously remind ourselves not to use our own cultural perspective as the "norm" against which we view and evaluate other perspectives. Educators find it relatively easy to consider and value other points of view beyond their own but fall into the trap of seeing their perspective as the "norm" instead of recognizing that their perspective is only one of many ways to view the world. The labels of "other" and "different" both assume that my view is the norm against which I judge another perspective.

The first time that I taught a course on international literature, we took on a different continent each evening, meeting in literature circles for small-group discussions of books from that part of the world and reading *Bookbird* articles written by authors from those cultures. This broad survey of literature from the world was interesting, and a range of perspectives and writing styles were evident in both the professional and children's literature. The struggle for me was the feeling that we were staying at the tip of the iceberg instead of digging more deeply.

The value of a cross-cultural study is the opportunity to focus deeply on one culture to understand its complexity and diversity, so the next time I taught the course we engaged in an in-depth study of Korean culture for several weeks. We read and discussed *When My Name Was Keoko* by Linda Sue Park (2002) about her parents' experiences during the Japanese occupation of Korea during World War II. We responded to this book in a range of ways, including creating cultural X-rays of characters to show the external features of culture that were visible to others as well as the internal values and beliefs within the heart of that person. We compared the perspectives in this book to two other books from the same time period, *So Far from the Bamboo Grove* (Watkins, 1993), a memoir by the child of a Japanese officer in Korea, and *Year of Impossible Goodbyes* (Choi, 1991), a memoir of a North Korean child. Comparing the perspectives in these three novels provided strong evidence that authors' life experiences influence the stories that they tell. In addition, we created a jackdaw—a box of information—including newspaper articles, maps, photographs, and artifacts relating to the time period and events in these books. Each person took an issue or event that intrigued him or her and did further research on the Internet to identify an artifact to share and add to our jackdaw. Jackdaws are a teaching tool that connects historical books with real events of the time through concrete objects (Lynch-Brown & Tomlinson, 2007).

We also browsed and read picture books about Korea published in the United States and compared these with picture books from South Korea. An international student from South Korea shared her collection of picture books currently being published in that country and talked about her analysis of these books and the changes in literature for children within South Korea. This experience brought to the forefront the problem of the dominance of folklore and historical fiction in books available in the United States, resulting in outdated images of life in that country, as compared to the many contemporary images of life in the South Korean books. It also led to discussions about translated books and the issue of which books are chosen for translation into English and who makes that decision.

We ended our study by looking at the Begler (1998) model, which provides a frame for examining the complex factors involved within any culture. This model indicates that all cultures exist within a historical context that shapes the cultural forms and systems, and this historical context operates within a larger geographical context that involves constant interaction and adaptation. Begler also argues that all cultures serve five basic sets of functions—economic, social, political, aesthetic, and values/beliefs. These values and beliefs shape behavioral norms and provide meaning to human activity within cultures. We made a poster-sized version of this model and recorded our current understandings about Korean culture on sticky notes, placing them on the model to gain a sense of what we understood and what was still missing from our understandings.

Class members worked with partners on their own cross-cultural studies, choosing a particular global culture to research and to gather children's and adolescent literature from both insider and outsider perspectives. Based on their reading of the literature and professional sources, they created annotated bibliographies of recommended books, which they shared with classmates. These projects were shared through displays of the books and short introductions to the displays followed by time for browsing and discussion.

Integration of Intercultural Perspectives Across the Curriculum

While the study of a specific culture can add depth to understandings about that culture, the danger still exits that international literature will be seen as restricted to special units rather than as an integral part of classroom life. Since my goal is for educators to see the value of this literature in creating an intercultural orientation, they need to explore how these books can be woven into any content area and unit of study. We particularly focus on the use of text sets, each containing 10–15 conceptually related picture books or novels reflecting a range of genres and perspectives (Short, 1993). I bring in examples of text sets around themes that contain picture books about experiences within the United States and in global contexts, such as sets on sharing family stories, dealing with death and loss, explorations of the moon, variants of Cinderella, and journeys of change. Class members browse all of the sets and then choose one set to read more closely and discuss in small groups, using graffiti boards to record their thinking as they read.

Educators then choose a theme or topic that is significant within their curriculum and puts together a text set that includes picture books from a range of global cultures. We also look at a broad concept, such as journeys, with each person reading a different novel from various cultures related to that theme. Class members come together in small groups to share and compare the types of journeys across their books. We also explore particular tools for response that are effective with text sets, including graffiti boards and comparison charts.

The focus on integration of international literature throughout the curriculum raises the issue of resources to support educators in locating high-quality literature from a range of global cultures. We take the time to closely examine resources on international literature, including annotated bibliographies from USBBY (Gebel, 2006), websites with databases such as Worlds of Words (http://wowlit.org), journals such as *Bookbird* (http://ibby.org), and annual award lists such as the USBBY Outstanding International Books (www.usbby.org) and the Batchelder (www.ala.org).

Inquires into Global Issues

James Banks (2001) argues that although racial harmony is one goal of multiculturalism, the roots of this movement are in the critique of issues of power and oppression. A critique of inequity and a call for social justice are not an add-on but central to multicultural education. Interculturalism shares this focus on critiquing the ways that power and oppression have affected various cultural groups around the world, and so global inquiries into difficult social and political issues are essential to a curriculum that is international. These issues include violence, human rights, environmental degradation, language loss, poverty, discrimination, and economic imperialism (Collins, Czarra, & Smith, 1998). The inquiries created around these global issues focus on the local and global complexity of the issue and go beyond talk about books to considering ways of taking action in the world.

Several years ago, my class engaged in a short inquiry around the global issue of genocide, using books about the Holocaust in World War II along with newspaper articles about current instances of genocide around the world. Class members browsed the collection of books and then met in small groups to discuss their experience within the context of a professional article in which a teacher reflected on her use of books about genocide (Zack, 1996). I also shared my experiences working with K–5 students on a human rights inquiry and Grade

4/5 students on an inquiry around prejudice. The use of books that raise difficult social and political issues with students prompted an intense discussion among class members and different levels of comfort in facilitating these experiences with students.

Critically Reading the Word and the World

A critical stance on issues of power, oppression, and social justice is woven through all of these curriculum components, not just our focus on the use of literature within inquiries on global issues. Without that critical stance, referred to by Freire (1970) as critically reading the word and the world, these experiences could easily become a superficial tour of culture where educators learn *about* internationalism. They might pick up information about a range of global cultures based on the view that if we just knew more about each other's culture, we would have global harmony. This approach does not consider difficult issues of inequity and social justice and does not recognize the race, class, and gender matters in how we interpret and analyze our experiences in the world as well as in the texts we read. Freire (1970) argues that a critical stance involves questioning "what is" and considering "what if" to take action.

Within this course, I see this critical stance as the continuous integration of cultural issues, such as availability, authenticity, and translation, into each set of engagements and books. We debate issues of availability, particularly which global cultures and genres are and are not well represented in the books available in the United States; translation, particularly the details of a culture that are changed or deleted during translation and the Americanization of books to make them more marketable; and cultural authenticity, particularly the types of stereotypes found in books from particular cultures and the perspectives authors bring to their work based on their life experiences. These issues are introduced early in the course and woven throughout our experiences with literature. We return to these issues from a more focused critical perspective during the last several weeks of the course through reading scholarly discussions in the professional literature. Our earlier discussions are based on observations from our browsing and literature circles, and these experiences provide a strong base from which to consider scholarly arguments about authenticity and translation. Other issues that can be discussed include the state of children's literature around the world, the process of how books get published and brought to a particular country, evaluation of international literature, and trends (Hancock, 2003).

Barbara Lehman discussed at the 2002 Master Class how she uses book pairs to highlight these issues, for example, having class members read *Nory Ryan's*

Song by Giff (2000), an American writer of Irish ancestry, along with *Under the Hawthorne Tree* by Conlon-McKenna (1990), an Irish writer, to discuss issues of insider-outsider perspectives (Hancock, 2003). Another example is pairing *Tasting the Sky*, a memoir by Ibtisam Barakat (2007) about her own childhood, with *The Sheppard's Granddaughter*, by Anne L. Carter (2008), a Canadian, to discuss Palestinian/Israeli conflicts. Montero and Robertson (2006) highlighted these same issues through a cross-cultural reader-response exchange that involved international students from the university who volunteered to join the class for this particular engagement. Novels that were set in the countries of these students were located. Each class member chose one book to read and respond to and then met with the international student who had also read that book as an insider for an in-depth discussion. Class members were asked to research the literacy education and culture of the country that was the focus of their book and to write a reflection on the cross-cultural dialogue as their culminating project for the course.

During the final class session in my course, we return to the curriculum framework and reflect on our course experiences to consider how to engage students in their classrooms and libraries. Having lived through these experiences with international literature and not just read *about* these books, class members have a strong sense of the ways in which these experiences influence understandings of interculturalism and curriculum. Particular literature engagements such as reading aloud from a picture book to establish our class focus, browsing to gain a broad sense of a particular group of books, engaging in literature discussions to deeply consider a particular novel or picture books, discussing a text set to compare perspectives, and the use of a broad range of tools for responding to literature cut across all of our class sessions. Because of my own research in classrooms, I also share examples of student artifacts and dialogue to introduce particular response strategies or literature engagements throughout the course.

What varies is the focus of our class sessions on different aspects of the curricular model including personal cultural identity, an in-depth understanding of a particular culture, the integration of a range of global perspectives, and an inquiry into a difficult global issue. These shifts create different understandings about culture, perspective, and action and result in quite different conversations. Class members gain a sense not only of the many different books available but also the need for a balance across these different ways of grouping and using literature with readers to build intercultural understanding.

The options for class members' final inquiry projects are open-ended so that they can each choose an inquiry that is compelling for them. Some choose to do an in-depth critical analysis of a particular group of books on a culture or theme, some take on a particular issue such as translation, others examine award-winning books from a range of countries or choose a particular author or illustrator for an in-depth study, and still others engage their own students in responding to a set of international books or write their own story around a specific cultural experience from their lives. Our last two class sessions usually consist of presenting these projects in displays and in conference sessions to small groups of class members.

We end the semester by returning back to our personal cultural identities. Class members create personal text sets of 5 to 10 books that reflect their intercultural connections as global citizens—their sense of place in the world. We share these through browsing all of the text sets in displays and then share more personally in small groups.

Conclusion

Engagements with international and global literature open the potential for transforming readers' perspectives through thoughtful dialogue and responses to these books. These interactions invite educators and students to reflect on their own cultural experiences and to imagine global experiences that go beyond themselves. All readers need to find their lives reflected in books, but if what they read only mirrors their own views of the world, they cannot envision alternative ways of thinking and living and are not challenged to confront global issues. Creating a curriculum that is international offers educators and students the potential to build bridges of understanding across cultures and thus transform their lives and views of the world. The challenge is to find ways to open up safe spaces that invite educators to experience the power of this literature for themselves so that they, in turn, take the risk of inviting their students to join with them in building bridges across global cultures.

Works Cited

Allan, M. (2003). Frontier crossing: Cultural dissonance, intercultural learning and the multicultural personality. *Journal of Research in International Education, 2*, 83–110.

Banks, J. A. (2001). *Cultural diversity and education: Foundations, curriculum, and teaching* (4th ed.). Boston: Allyn and Bacon.

Begler, E. (1998). Global cultures: The first steps toward understanding. *Social Education, 62*, 272–275.

Bond, E. (2006). Reading outstanding international children's books. *Journal of Children's Literature, 32*(2), 70–76.

Case, R. (1993). Key elements of a global perspective. *Social Education, 57*, 318–325.

Collins, H. T., Czarra, F. R., & Smith, A. F. (1998). Guidelines for global and international studies education: Challenges, cultures, and connections. *Social Education, 62*, 311–317.

Fang, Z, Fu, D., & Lamme, L. L. (2003). The trivialization and misuse of multicultural literature: Issues of representation and communication. In D. L. Fox & K. G. Short (Eds.), *Stories matter: The complexity of cultural authenticity in children's literature* (pp. 284–303). Urbana, IL: National Council of Teachers of English.

Fennes, H., & Hapgood, K. (1997). *Intercultural learning in the classroom: Crossing borders.* London: Cassell.

Foss, A. (2002). Peeling the onion: Teaching critical literacy with students of privilege. *Language Arts, 79*, 393–403.

Fox, D. L., & Short, K. G. (Eds.). (2003). *Stories matter: The complexity of cultural authenticity in children's literature.* Urbana, IL: National Council of Teachers of English.

Freeman, E. B., & Lehman, B. A. (2001). *Global perspectives in children's literature.* Boston: Allyn and Bacon.

Freire, P. (1970). *Pedagogy of the oppressed.* South Hadley, MA: Bergin and Garvey.

Gebel, D. (2006). (Ed.). *Crossing boundaries with children's books.* Lanham, MD: Scarecrow Press.

Geertz, C. (1973). *The interpretation of cultures.* New York: Basic Books.

Hancock, M. R. (2003). Incorporating international children's literature into college level children's literature courses: A master class in the teaching of children's literature. *Journal of Children's Literature, 29*(1), 14–19.

Hofstede, G. (1991). *Cultures and organizations: Software of the mind: Intercultural cooperation and its importance for survival.* New York: McGraw-Hill.

Lynch-Brown, C., & Tomlinson, C. M. (2007). *Essentials of children's literature* (6th ed.). Boston: Allyn and Bacon.

Montero, M. K., & Robertson, J. M. (2006). "Teachers can't teach what they don't know": Teaching teachers about international and global children's literature to facilitate culturally responsive pedagogy. *Journal of Children's Literature, 32*(2), 27–35.

Short, K. G. (1993). Making connections across literature and life. In K. E. Holland, R. A. Hungerford, & S. B. Ernst (Eds.), *Journeying: Children responding to literature* (pp. 284–301). Portsmouth, NH: Heinemann.

Short, K. G. (2009). Critically reading the word and the world: Building intercultural understanding through literature. *Bookbird: A Journal of International Children's Literature, 47*(2), 1–10.

Tomlinson, C. M. (1999). Children's books from and about other countries. *Journal of Children's Literature, 25*(1), 8–17.

Zack, V. (1996). Nightmare issues: Children's responses to racism and genocide in literature. *The New Advocate, 9*, 297–308.

Children's Books Cited

Barakat, I. (2007). *Tasting the sky: A Palestinian childhood.* New York: Farrar, Straus and Giroux.

Bredsdorff, B. (2004). *The Crow-Girl: The children of Crow Cove* (F. Ingwersen, Trans.). New York: Farrar, Straus and Giroux.

Cameron, A. (2003). *Colibrí.* New York: Farrar, Straus and Giroux.

Carmi, D. (2000). *Samir and Yonatan* (Y. Lotan, Trans.). New York: Scholastic.

Carter, A. L. (2008). *The shepherd's granddaughter.* Toronto, ON, Canada: Groundwood Books.

Choi, S. N. (1991). *Year of impossible goodbyes.* New York: Houghton Mifflin.

Chotjewitz, D. (2004). *Daniel half human and the good Nazi* (D. Orgel, Trans.). New York: Atheneum.

Compestine, Y. C. (2007). *Revolution is not a dinner party.* New York: Henry Holt.

Conlon-McKenna, M. (1990). *Under the hawthorn tree.* New York: Holiday House.

Diakité, P. (2006). *I lost my tooth in Africa* (B. W. Diakité, Illus.). New York: Scholastic.

Engle, M. (2008). *The surrender tree: Poems of Cuba's struggle for freedom.* New York: Henry Holt.

Funke, C. (2008). *Inkdeath* (A. Bell, Trans.). New York: Scholastic.

Giff, P. R. (2000). *Nory Ryan's song.* New York: Delacorte Press.

Hole, S. (2008). *Garmann's summer* (D. Bartlett, Trans.). Grand Rapids, MI: Eerdmans.

Kurtz, J. (2000). *Faraway home* (E. B. Lewis, Illus.). New York: Gulliver Books.

Laird, E., & Nimr, S. (2006). *A little piece of ground.* London, England: Haymarket Books.

Lewin, T., & Lewin, B. (2009). *Balarama: A royal elephant.* New York: Lee and Low.

Marsden, C. (2007). *When heaven fell.* Cambridge, MA: Candlewick Press.

Meehan, K. (2009). *Hannah's winter.* LaJolla, CA: Kane/Miller.

Morales, Y. (2008). *Just in case: A trickster tale and Spanish alphabet book.* New York: Roaring Brook Press.

Nye, N. S. (1997). *Habibi.* New York: Simon and Schuster.

Park, L. S. (2002). *When my name was Keoko.* New York: Clarion Books.

Rabinovici, S. (1998). *Thanks to my mother* (J. Skofield, Trans.). New York: Dial.

Sheth, K. (2007). *Keeping corner*. New York: Hyperion.

Stolz, J. (2004). *The shadows of Ghadames* (C. Temerson, Trans.). New York: Delacorte Press.

Uehashi, N. (2008). *Moribito: Guardian of the spirit* (C. Hirano, Trans.). New York: Scholastic.

Watkins, Y. K. (1993). *So far from the bamboo grove*. New York: Perfection Learning.

Yumoto, K. (1996). *The friends* (C. Hirano, Trans.). New York: Farrar, Straus and Giroux.

3

Responding to Challenges, Celebrating Possibilities

9

Children's Books as Bestsellers

Their Impact on the Field of Children's Literature

Barbara A. Lehman, *The Ohio State University*

April Whatley Bedford, *University of New Orleans*

The Harry Potter phenomenon was five years old and into its fifth book when it sparked the topic of children's books as bestsellers and their impact on the field of children's literature for the 2003 Children's Literature Assembly Master Class in the Teaching of Children's Literature. Individuals who had never paid attention to children's literature prior to that time were suddenly taking notice that young readers (and indeed readers of all ages) were enthralled by the exploits of a quidditch-playing, orphaned wizard and his friends just their age. Each of the seven titles was a huge bestseller, and every new volume was breathlessly anticipated. Publication of the final Harry Potter book, *Harry Potter and the Deathly Hallows* (Rowling, 2007), to record-breaking sales made the topic of children's literature as bestsellers more relevant than ever. Harry Potter's enormous success made his author, J. K. Rowling, a celebrity, but he also may have encouraged a related phenomenon—celebrities (actors, musicians, athletes, politicians, and the like) deciding that they, too, could write their own stories for the young and that becoming involved in the children's book business was worth their time.

While celebrity authorship and bestseller status often go hand-in-hand—children's books written by celebrities frequently become instant bestsellers because of the fame of their authors while books by less-well-known authors that appear on the bestseller lists may turn their authors into celebrities—neither part of this equation guarantees that a book will be commendable. As educators, we must ask, "What is the quality of these bestsellers?" and, "What is their impact on other authors, critics, children's literature professors, classroom teachers, parents, and children?" These are the questions that continue to be relevant when considering the role of bestsellers in the field of children's literature.

Bestselling Trends

Since the Harry Potter phenomenon generated unprecedented interest in the field of children's literature, a number of trends have emerged regarding children's literature as bestsellers. Some of these trends are welcomed by educators and children's literature scholars; others less so. On the unwelcome side, publishing practices include the proliferation of celebrity authors, as already mentioned, and movie and marketing tie-ins to children's books. Somewhat neutral trends include a focus on series fiction and the rising popularity of fantasy for young readers. An encouraging phenomenon is that of high-quality children's literature achieving bestseller status. Discussion and recommendations for addressing each of these trends follows.

Celebrity Authors

One of the earliest efforts of a celebrity authoring a children's book occurred with the 1971 publication of the novel *Mandy* (Edwards, 1971) by Julie Andrews, of *Mary Poppins* and the *Sound of Music* fame. Originally, Andrews published the book under her married name, Julie Edwards, and *Mandy* became beloved by a generation of young female readers. Since then, Andrews has published more than a dozen books, including an adult memoir and a series of picture books about Dumpy the Dumptruck, coauthored with her daughter, Emma Walton Hamilton. All of these books can be purchased at the website entitled *The Julie Andrews Collection*. This collection, as described on the website, "encompasses quality books for young readers of all ages that nurture the imagination and celebrate a sense of wonder," some of which were written by Andrews herself.

In 1993 actress Jamie Lee Curtis published her first picture book, *When I Was Little: A Four-Year-Old's Memoir of Her Youth*, illustrated by Laura Cornell. The book received much critical acclaim—it was praised by *Publishers Weekly* as a "winsome, upbeat work"—but little fanfare about its author's celebrity status. Since then, however, the author/illustrator duo has published at least seven more picture books, to mixed reviews but huge sales. Curtis also was a keynote speaker at the 2008 International Reading Association Convention in Atlanta, Georgia.

In 2000, actor John Lithgow published *The Remarkable Farkle McBride*, a picture book illustrated by C. F. Payne that achieved bestseller status. *School Library Journal* called the book "a wry and witty read aloud," and *Publishers Weekly* declared, "Lithgow's nimble verse with a limerick's beat sparkles." By 2007, Lithgow had penned additional picture books (some with coauthors) as well as a series of books and kits called "Lithgow Paloozas," designed to engage families in creating crafts together. He has also lent his name to a series of leveled readers, the Lithgow Palooza Readers.

Although celebrity-authored children's books could be found prior to 2000, the success of these authors seems to have launched the trend of celebrity authorship that has proliferated during the first decade of the new millennium. Celebrities from a variety of realms have tried their hands at writing for children, including newscasters such as Katie Couric; musicians such as country singer Leann Rimes and Spice Girl Geri Halliwell; actors such as Spike Lee, Jada Pinkett Smith, Julianne Moore, and Brooke Shields; comedians Jay Leno, Billy Crystal, Whoopie Goldberg, and Jeff Foxworthy; athletes such as professional football players and brothers Tiki and Ronde Barber; and individuals in the political realm such as Duchess of York Sarah Ferguson, former vice-presidential wife Lynne Cheney, and former presidential wife and daughter Laura and Jenna Bush.

When she published her first picture book, *The English Roses*, in 2003, Madonna claims that she was motivated to write children's books because of "how vapid and vacant and empty all the stories [I was reading to my son] were. There's, like, no lessons" (qtd. in MacPherson, 2004, p. 2). While her first book and those that followed did allow the pop star to add bestselling author to her list of accomplishments, Madonna's books are indeed didactic and did not receive the favorable reviews of her celebrity author predecessors such as Andrews, Curtis, or Lithgow. In his review for *School Library Journal* when *The English Roses* was first released, New York librarian John Peters wrote, "All in all, this overproduced episode, the first of a projected series, will have to rely on hype rather than content or presentation to find a readership." The "hype" surrounding these books seemed to do just that—attract an audience.

Whether these or other famous persons are motivated to enter the field of writing for children by the possibility that their celebrity status will ensure that their books are bestsellers and earn them a tidy sum of extra income, or even by some nobler impulses, we can't be sure. We do know that their titles almost always receive unusual publicity (for the children's book field) because of their renown and because they have access to publicity venues, such as television talk shows, which more typical authors seldom have. Publishers also may crank up the public relations machine for these books to capitalize on their authors' star status and thus generate more profit. This is money that publishers claim *can* be used to subsidize the publication of less profitable titles; whether or not that actually happens is not easy to discern.

Patricia Austin, former *Journal of Children's Literature* editor and professor of children's literature at the University of New Orleans, addressed "the celebrity factor" in children's publishing at the 2003 Master Class. Austin used Maria Shriver's bestselling *What's Wrong with Timmy?* (2001) to exemplify the problems with books written by celebrities. Citing reviews in *Booklist* and *School Library Journal*, she explained its weaknesses, including didacticism (which "cheapens that message" [Vardell, 2004, p. 13]); a style more consistent with fairy tale conventions, rather than realistic fiction (which the book is); contrived, unnatural dialogue; length (three times the amount of text in a typical picture book); and the "miraculous attitude change" (Vardell, p. 14) of the protagonist. Overall, despite its bestselling status, this book did not receive critical acclaim or even any notice by most respected review outlets and professional organizations that regularly review new children's books. This is the case, more often than not, with celebrity-authored children's books, and *didactic* is the adjective most frequently used to describe (and criticize) such books. Those "lessons" Madonna searched for in children's books are well-represented in these books.

Just as there is a range of quality in children's books created by the already rich and famous, there are also pros and cons of celebrity-authored books. Among the arguments in favor of them is that the publicity generated attracts a public who wouldn't normally buy books or read to their children. Also, the profit margins that these books generate, according to Austin, "enable a publisher to take a chance on a new, unknown author or a manuscript that may have literary merit" (Vardell, 2004, p. 14) but lack financial viability. Negative factors include the deleterious impact that didactic bestselling books may have on children's reading appetite as they tire of heavy-handed lessons and the strong possibility that the attention given to books associated with celebrities may keep better but less well-known authors from being noticed by publishers and readers alike.

How do publishers address these pros and cons? Judy O'Malley, an editor who has worked at both Houghton Mifflin and Charlesbridge, drew on her current publishing experiences and her past experiences as an editor and reviewer for *Book Links* to describe what she looks for in selecting and evaluating the best children's books to publish and promote. O'Malley has worn both hats—that of a critic and of an editor—in her work in the children's book field, and her remarks reflected the sometimes conflicting goals of those two roles. She described (Vardell, 2004) these aims by explaining that bestsellers do cause people who usually dismiss children's books as either "cute" or pedantic to take them more seriously, such as writers of books for adults, who mistakenly assume that writing books for children must be easier. The results are often not of the same caliber as their writing for adults, although if the authors are well known, publishers may accept this inferior work.

O'Malley cautioned that this is the wrong approach to writing and editing books for young readers, that writing for either audience requires different approaches but not unequal quality. When she works with prominent authors of adult literature, she demands that their writing for children be excellent and hopes that if it sells well, it enhances the stature and appeal of other juvenile literature authors. Most of all, she hopes that the books on her list are ones that endure for many generations and for "the Best to be the reason that they're Sellers" (Vardell, 2004, p. 17).

Movie and Marketing Tie-ins

Blockbusters such as Harry Potter—and likewise perhaps many celebrity-authored titles—become popular because they are so heavily publicized and marketed, including through movies and other tie-ins. For example, *Charlotte's Web* (2006) appeared on the *New York Times* bestseller list of picture books after a movie based on the book was released by Paramount Pictures in 2006 and on DVD in 2007. However, it was not the E. B. White 1952 classic, but Kate Egan's adaptation from the movie adaptation (which begins to resemble a hall of mirrors) that achieved bestselling status. Similarly, Katherine Paterson's *Bridge to Terabithia* (2006), originally written in 1977, made the paperback bestseller list in 2007, likely as a result of the Disney movie based on the book and released in February 2007. In fact, *Publishers Weekly* always includes a list of 15 of the top-selling "Children's Series and Tie-ins." Finally, Maurice Sendak's Caldecott Award–winning *Where the Wild Things Are* (1963) made the top 10 bestsellers on Amazon.com in 2009, possibly due to the release that year of the motion picture based on the book. A "movie storybook" based on the movie of the book quickly became a *New York Times* bestseller—another "hall of mirrors" example.

This is not all bad. If updated movie versions of excellent children's books can bring those books to young readers' attention, then this is a trend to be celebrated. However, if children (and their caregivers and teachers) only become familiar with a movie or an adapted written text rather than the original book on which either is based, then there is cause for alarm. Additionally, less-well-regarded books, based solely on films or television shows, also achieve bestseller status through publishing tie-ins. For example, *High School Musical* (2006), adapted by N. B. Grace from the movie, and *Jump In!* (2007) adapted by M. C. King from television movies, also have appeared on the paperback bestseller list.

Award-winning author Jane Yolen (2007) discussed the concept of *branding*, "a concept brought over from Hollywood, in which the publisher can make dozens of similar books about a particular character and so identify it to the public, that the books become their own special . . . brand" (pp. 63–64). Characters from children's books such as Clifford the Big Red Dog, Arthur the Aardvark, and Curious George have all become brands, and, according to Yolen, "Harry Potter is the ultimate brand" (p. 64). Such branding is achieved through "vertically energized synergy," which Yolen explains as multilayered corporations that also own publishing companies finding additional ways to make money from children's books by tying them to other products such as book bags, video games, movies, and children's clothing. And, Yolen believes, all of this merchandizing becomes more important than the book that spawned it. Others, like award-winning author Nancy Farmer, concur. Farmer, winner of the 2002 National Book Award for *The House of the Scorpion* (2002) and three Newbery Honors for *The Ear, the Eye and the Arm* (1994), *A Girl Named Disaster* (1996), and *The House of the Scorpion*, believes (Vardell, 2004) that all of the merchandizing and marketing hype surrounding books like Harry Potter and celebrity-authored children's books can influence book reviews, particularly if they come from a source like the *New York Times*.

Series Books

Nancy Farmer also discussed the trend of series books for children as bestsellers. According to Farmer, series books, such as Goosebumps and Disney variations of classics, while "soothing, undemanding, and short" (Vardell, 2004, p. 15), are also predictable but fleeting. However, certainly not all popular series books are short. As noted in the introduction, Harry Potter books 1 through 6 remained on the bestseller lists for well over 100 weeks. Before the publication of the final adventure of Harry, a book of predictions about the seventh Harry Potter book, *Mugglenet.com's What Will Happen in Harry Potter 7* (2006) by Ben Schoen, Emerson Spartz, Andy Gordon, Gretchen Stull, and Jamie Lawrence, surfaced on the paperback bestsellers list and received a rave review by Lee Siegel in the *New York Times Sunday Book Review* of February 11, 2007. And book 7 did indeed become a bigger phenomenon than ever with the publication of *Harry Potter and the Deathly Hallows*, released July 21, 2007, selling more than 72 million copies within the first 24 hours of its release.

Another bestselling series also appears to have reached closure (although one can never be sure) with Lemony Snicket's (aka Daniel Handler) thirteenth title in A Series of Unfortunate Events: *The End* (2006). It too remained on the *New York Times* bestseller list well into 2007. Other popular series consistently on the list have included the Magic Tree House, Junie B. Jones, and Captain Underpants titles. Two best-selling series books have recently been made into movies, contributing to the issues raised above about movie tie-ins: *Diary of a Wimpy Kid* and *Percy Jackson and the Olympiads*. Thus, as noted by Farmer, series books continue to provide some authors with strong sales.

Fantasy

The popularity of fantasy might constitute a fourth (continuing) trend. For example, Christopher Paolini, youthful author of the Inheritance trilogy, saw his first two books in this series make the *New York Times* bestseller lists: *Eldest* (2005) on the chapter books and both *Eldest* and *Eragon* (2003) on the paperback rosters. His third title, *Brisingr*, published in October 2009, may be wearing thin with reviewers, however. *Publishers Weekly* (cited on Amazon.com) calls it a "cliché journey" and hints that the "trilogy" may generate more titles yet. But the heir to the J. K. Rowling throne, at least in the young adult realm, seems to be Stephenie Meyer, author of the Twilight saga of books about a teenage girl in love with a vampire. The first book in the series, *Twilight*, published in 2005, was released as a major motion picture in 2008. The sequel, *New Moon* (2006), spent over 30 weeks at the number one position of the *New York Times* bestseller list. This book has been adapted into a movie released in 2009. *Eclipse*, the third book in the series (Meyer, 2007), had an initial print run of a million copies and sold 155,000 the first day of publication, and massive sales parties were held at book stores throughout the United States for the release of the fourth book in the series, *Breaking Dawn*, on August 2, 2008. At the time of this writing, all four books are on Amazon.com's bestsellers booklist. In an interesting trend reversal, Meyer's first novel for adults, *The Host* (published between the third and fourth *Twilight* books), was number one on the bestseller list when it was released in May 2008. And in another virtual "hall of mirrors" category, the movie version of *New Moon* has spawned a *book* companion by Mark Cotta Vaz, which itself has hit Amazon.com's bestseller list. Meyer is even extending the series into the graphic novel format, with the release of *Twilight: The Graphic Novel* in 2010.

Award-Winning Literature as Bestsellers

Author Nancy Farmer acknowledges that all authors would rejoice if their books turn into bestsellers, but many consider quality before sales. Farmer describes herself as having written bestsellers—stealth ones that sell steadily (but not spectacularly) over many years. Often award winners, which receive special promotion because of their status, these titles are ones that have enduring appeal because they are, as Ezra Pound opined, "news that *stays* news" (Vardell, 2004, p. 15). What is the secret of writing a bestseller? Farmer rejects the idea that it can be reduced to a formula or even that it can be emulated by trying to copy the style of current bestsellers. Instead, she believes that she can attribute her success to staying current with events and issues of contemporary culture, such as "clones, illegal immigration, and drug dealing" (Vardell, p. 16)—in other words, "tomorrow's news," as Farmer terms it, but which resonates far beyond today.

The bestselling status of award-winning titles, like Farmer's, constitutes the most encouraging trend related to children's literature as bestsellers. For example, shortly after the award winners were announced by the American Library Association in 2007, the Caldecott winner, *Flotsam* (2006) by David Wiesner, and two honor books—*Gone Wild* (2006) by David McLimans and *Moses: When Harriet Tubman Led Her People to Freedom* (2006) by Carole Weatherford and illustrated by Kadir Nelson—made the *New York Times* bestseller list of picture books. Likewise, the list's bestselling chapter books included the Newbery winner, *The Higher Power of Lucky* (2006) by Susan Patron, two Newbery honor books, *Hattie Big Sky* (2006) by Kirby Larson and *Penny from Heaven* (2006) by Jennifer L. Holm, and the Printz honor book, *The Book Thief* (2006) by Markus Zusak. By the beginning of April 2007, however, only *Flotsam, Moses, The Higher Power of Lucky,* and *The Book Thief* were still listed as bestsellers. This situation would seem to indicate that, while winning a prestigious award does promote a title to the bestselling ranks, such status can be relatively short-lived. The 2008 Caldecott winner, Brian Selznick's *The Invention of Hugo Cabret* (2007), and honor book *Knuffle Bunny Too: A Case of Mistaken Identity* (2007) by Mo Willems both hit the bestseller list but were off by the time of this writing in late 2009. However, Neil Gaiman's *The Graveyard Book* (2008), which won the 2009 Newbery Medal, made the list and remained there for more than a year—going against this trend and perhaps reflecting the author's adult popularity.

Finally, although bestsellers do not necessarily represent quality, recent *New York Times* bestseller lists have contained titles by highly acclaimed children's authors and illustrators, such as Mo Willems (*The Pigeon Wants a Puppy*, 2008; *Today I Will Fly!*, 2007b), David Shannon (*Pirates Don't Change Diapers* by Melinda Long, 2007), Tad Hills (*Duck, Duck, Goose*, 2007), Kate DiCamillo (*The Miraculous Journey of Edward Tulane*, 2006, and *The Magician's Elephant*, 2009), Cornelia Funke (*Inkspell*, 2005), and Gail Carson Levine (*Fairest*, 2006). In addition, the presence of so many award winners on recent lists also is heartening. Certainly, quality does not guarantee popularity, but it also does not prevent it. We can hope that children who flock to Harry Potter will become avid readers who develop appreciation for the best in children's books.

Preparing Teachers to Evaluate Bestselling Children's Literature: Barbara Lehman Reflects

As a children's literature professor at Ohio State University and former journal editor, I have explored the place of bestsellers in children's literature courses and reflected on the impact of bestsellers on my children's literature courses at the university level. My goals for students in these courses have always included gaining knowledge of the field of children's literature and its genres, becoming familiar with a range of books, developing an appreciation for reading, and honing the ability to critically evaluate children's books. With these objectives in mind, I select—as do most children's literature instructors—some required readings that exemplify both the variety and excellence of titles in the field. I hope that by reading these books, my students will sample first-hand the range and quality of literature available for children and use this experience as a benchmark against which to judge other readings they select for themselves in the course and beyond.

As a starting point in my children's literature courses, I assess my students' prior knowledge of and experience with children's books. When I ask about their childhood memories of reading, I have been stunned to learn that most college students cannot remember specific titles beyond Dr. Seuss or the much more current Harry Potter series. More recently, I have also compared my required readings with the *New York Times* bestseller lists. The first time I did this, I discovered that the only commonality between them was the novel *Holes* (Sachar, 1998), an award winner and subsequent motion picture—both of which could contribute to its popularity.

I approach this situation—my students' limited prior knowledge and the lack of congruence between my required readings and currently popular titles—in a number of ways. These include helping students become familiar with children's reading tastes and preferences; choosing favorite authors; comparing books and the movies made from them; comparing books on similar themes that represent a range of quality; reading and writing literary critiques; and sharing my own enthusiasm and passion for children's literature. Through these experiences, I hope that my students will become teachers who can make appropriate and informed use of popular and bestselling children's books to promote and develop children's interest and taste in literature.

Exploring Children's Choices

As a starting point, adults who work with young readers need a sense of what appeals to them. I researched this issue more than 20 years ago (Lehman, 1986) and learned that certain literary qualities seemed to resonate particularly well with children. Those elements include stories with a strong plot and fast pace; themes that relate to important tasks of childhood stages (that are within the realm of their experience or imagination), such as growing up and coming of age, feeling small and powerless versus the need for recognition, the need to assert self and become independent, and good versus evil; characters with whom children can identify and their relationships with other characters; an overall hopeful tone (not to be confused with happy); and a happy ending. (I would also suggest that, with appropriate, enthusiastic adult mediation, children can gain appreciation for books to which they aren't immediately attracted.)

In addition to knowing this and other research regarding children's preferences, teachers can find out what their students like by asking them directly and observing what they choose to read voluntarily. Another useful source of information about child appeal is the Children's Choices list published each year in the October issue of *The Reading Teacher* and available on the website of the International Reading Association. This project involves 10,000 children in reading and selecting what new books they like best. Teachers particularly can promote the best quality titles on these and bestseller lists to young readers. For example, as already noted, Louis Sachar's *Holes* was both a Newbery award winner and a *New York Times* bestseller. Likewise, Cynthia Kadohata's *Kira-Kira* (2004) earned both a Newbery medal and a number one spot on the *New York Times* bestseller list. This novel for older readers, set in the 1950s, portrays a Japanese-American girl and her family who deal with racial prejudice and harsh economic conditions in Georgia, in addition to the illness and loss of Katie's older sister—issues that likely will generate lively discussions.

On the 2006 Children's Choices list appears *The First Day of Winter* by the highly regarded Denise Fleming (2005); a Lee Bennett Hopkins poetry collection with the catchy title *Oh, No! Where Are My Pants? And Other Disasters* (2005); *Sleep Tight, Little Bear* (2005), a picture book by Hans Christian Andersen Award–winning author Martin Waddell; a picture book by Newbery Award–winning author Kate DiCamillo, *Mercy Watson to the Rescue* (2005), first in the Mercy Watson series; *Walter: The Story of a Rat,* by Barbara Wersba (2005); *Each Little Bird That Sings* (2005), a National Book Award finalist by Deborah Wiles; acclaimed British author Philip Pullman's *The Scarecrow and His Servant* (2005); and another Brian Jacques title in the Redwall series, *High Rhulain* (2005). (There also can be found a celebrity-authored title by football stars Tiki and Ronde Barber [with Robert Burleigh, whose other work is acclaimed], *Game Day* [2005], so evidence that some celebrity-authored texts have child appeal exists.)

Developing Author Preferences

Any of the above works by highly acclaimed authors would also be good links to other books (including award winners) by the same writers. For example, if children chose the Kate DiCamillo titles listed above, they might also enjoy her Newbery Medal book and *New York Times* paperback bestseller, *The Tale of Despereaux* (2003). *Holes* author Louis Sachar has a sequel, *Small Steps* (2006), about another former resident of the infamous Camp Green Lake. *Hoot*, by Carl Hiaasen (2002)—a Newbery Honor book and *New York Times* paperback bestseller—also has been succeeded by another novel with environmental themes and a Florida setting: *Flush* (2005). Deborah Wiles's popularity for *Each Little Bird That Sings* might extend to her earlier Coretta Scott King award winner, *Freedom Summer* (2001a), or to *Love, Ruby Lavender* (2001b). Until his death in 2011, Brian Jacques spun 18 of his highly popular Redwall yarns. If readers are hooked on one, they might enjoy reading more of these adventurous tales. According to the official Redwall website, a new title is published each year—practically enough to satisfy the most avid fan! Like Brian Jacques, most bestselling authors have their own websites where readers may go to find out not only more about their books but also about their lives, further developing young readers' preferences for particular authors. Children who have rediscovered Katherine Paterson's *Bridge to Terabithia* via the movie version also may respond well to her numerous other titles, many of which have received awards, such as *The Great Gilly Hopkins* (1978), *Jip, His Story* (1997), and *The Same Stuff as Stars* (2002).

Comparing Books and Movies

In addition to movie tie-ins already mentioned, *Hoot* was adapted to film in 2006, and the movie version of Susan Cooper's *The Dark Is Rising* (1973, Newbery Honor 1974) appeared in 2007. In fact, the development of children's book movie adaptations seems to be a growing trend in the field of popular culture, with the release in 2005 of *The Chronicles of Narnia: The Lion, the Witch, and the Wardrobe* based on the C. S. Lewis book by that title (1950), *Zathura* from Chris Van Allsburg's picture book (2002), and *Because of Winn-Dixie* from Kate DiCamillo's award-winning novel (2000, Newbery Honor 2001). Each of these films offers an excellent opportunity to capitalize on children's interest and expose them to the books from which the motion pictures are adapted. A particularly valuable critical thinking experience can be comparing the movie versions to the original stories. How faithful to the original is the film adaptation? What is changed, and what remains the same? What effect do the changes have? Are they appropriate, and do they retain the spirit of the original work? What is the overall quality of the movie adaptation?

Comparing Books with Similar Themes

Throughout my children's literature courses, I acknowledge the appeal of bestsellers and, with my students, explore why they are attractive. I use this information to raise students' literary consciousness by having them compare critically acclaimed titles and less well-reviewed bestsellers that have similar themes or narratives to discover for themselves any difference in quality and to realize that popularity does not constitute quality. If I can teach them to think this way, I believe that they will come to understand why quality literature is important, be able to recognize it for themselves, and value lasting pleasure, not merely fleeting popularity.

Reading and Writing Reviews

Along with comparing the books themselves, students may read and compare the reviews of bestselling books and more critically acclaimed books with similar themes. While they might not always agree with the reviewers' opinions, this activity helps prospective and practicing teachers to not only become familiar with the aspects of a children's book that literary critics analyze but also to gain awareness of those review sources that are considered reputable in the field of children's literature, such as *Publishers Weekly*, *School Library Journal*, and *The Horn Book*. Comparing reviews with students' opinions often leads to lively classroom discussions, and students who participate in such discussions in their university children's literature courses might involve their own students in similar experiences. In *Writing about Reading: From Book Talk to Literary Essays, Grades 3–8*, educator Janet Angelillo (2003) gives excellent suggestions for engaging elementary and middle grades students in talking about books, reading book reviews and author interviews, and eventually writing their own reviews. This book is a helpful resource for the university instructor of children's literature as well as for classroom teachers.

Sharing Our Passion

Above all, I believe that adults who work with children need to share books enthusiastically with young readers. If we truly know and enjoy children's literature and keep abreast of children's reading interests, we often can find a match between the two. Furthermore, we can create that link if we convey our passion and pleasure with the books we share. Children respond well to enthusiasm, and one of the most natural ways to show it is by reading aloud to them frequently and expressively, making the books come alive. Another way is to "sell" books with book talks. When I piqued the curiosity of my fourth graders with such advertisements, the books I shared always were immediately claimed by readers, who, in turn, "sold" them to their peers. Finally, engaging children in animated discussions about books will generate further interest in reading and turn more books into "bestsellers" among avid readers.

Conclusion

Writing this chapter was a bit disconcerting because it felt like a moving target; that is, bestselling lists are updated weekly. Thus, anything we wrote would be highly tentative and subject to continuous change. That said, we conclude this chapter by consideration of what we mean by "bestsellers." Are they whatever books currently are on the lists? Obviously, some titles hold this status far longer than others, but to attain recognition as a bestseller for even one week is highly coveted. However, since adults purchase most books, becoming a bestseller may be more a reflection of their interests and agendas than of children's. A better measure of child appeal, as noted, might be something like the "Children's Choices" lists.

More lasting than the first definition, perhaps, is Nancy Farmer's definition of bestsellers as those books that have staying power, that sell at a stable rate for long periods of time, possibly even decades, like classics such as *Charlotte's Web* or *The Lion, the Witch and the Wardrobe*. These are books that most likely have held children's interest over the years. Significantly, they also often are titles repeatedly acclaimed by adults. In any case, we believe that the most valid measure of bestseller status is whether a book "sells" young readers on the "best" in children's literature. Ultimately, our goal is to nurture not only avid readers but also readers who appreciate literary quality. These are the titles—which hold *both* child appeal and literary merit—that comprise the heart and soul of *children's* literature.

Works Cited

Angelillo, J. (2003). *Writing about reading: From book talk to literary essays, grades 3–8*. Portsmouth, NH: Heinemann.

International Reading Association and Children's Book Council. (2010). *Children's Choices Reading List.* Retrieved from http://www.reading.org/Resources/Booklists/ChildrensChoices.aspx

Lehman, B. A. (1986). Children's choice and critical acclaim in literature for children. *Dissertation Abstracts International, 48*(05A), 1137.

MacPherson, K. (2004, November 3). Critics, authors chafe as more celebrities join ranks of children's authors. *Pittsburgh Post-Gazette.* Retrieved from http://www.post-gazette.com/pg/04308/405539-75.stm

Siegel, L. (2007, February 11). Children's books. *The New York Times Sunday Book Review.* Retrieved from http://www.nytimes.com/2007/02/11/books/review/Siegel.t.html?ex=1176609600&en=7f9eb0900bbc6c0e&ei=5070

Vardell, S. M. (2004). Children's books as best sellers: Their impact on the field of children's literature. *Journal of Children's Literature, 30*(1), 13–18.

Yolen, J. (2007). Ten things I no longer enjoy about publishing but am willing to endure. *Journal of Children's Literature, 33*(1), 62–67.

Children's Books Cited

Barber, T., & Barber, R. (with Burleigh, R.). (2005). *Game day* (B. Root, Illus.). New York: Simon and Schuster.

Cooper, S. (1973). *The dark is rising.* New York: Atheneum.

Curtis, J. L. (1993). *When I was little: A four-year-old's memoir of her youth* (L. Cornell, llus.). New York: HarperCollins.

DiCamillo, K. (2000). *Because of Winn-Dixie.* Cambridge, MA: Candlewick Press.

DiCamillo, K. (2003). *The tale of Despereaux.* Cambridge, MA: Candlewick Press.

DiCamillo, K. (2005). *Mercy Watson to the rescue* (C. Van Dusen, Illus.). Cambridge, MA: Candlewick Press.

DiCamillo, K. (2006). *The miraculous journey of Edward Tulane.* Cambridge, MA: Candlewick Press.

DiCamillo, K. (2009). *The magician's elephant* (Y. Tanaka, Illus.). Cambridge, MA: Candlewick Press.

Edwards, J. A. (1971). *Mandy* (J. G. Brown, Illus.). New York: HarperCollins.

Egan, K. (2006). *Charlotte's web: The movie storybook.* New York: HarperEntertainment.

Farmer, N. (1994). *The ear, the eye and the arm.* New York: Orchard Books.

Farmer, N. (1996). *A girl named Disaster.* New York: Orchard Books.

Farmer, N. (2002). *The house of the scorpion.* New York: Atheneum.

Fleming, D. (2005). *The first day of winter.* New York: Holt.

Funke, C. (2005). *Inkspell* (A. Bell, Trans.). New York: Chicken House/Scholastic.

Gaiman, N. (2008). *The graveyard book* (D. McKean, Illus.). New York: HarperCollins.

Grace, N. B. (2006). *High school musical: The junior novel.* New York: Disney Press.

Hiaasen, C. (2002). *Hoot.* New York: Knopf.

Hiaasen, C. (2005). *Flush.* New York: Knopf.

Hills, T. (2007). *Duck, duck, goose.* New York: Schwartz and Wade Books.

Holm, J. L. (2006). *Penny from heaven.* New York: Random House.

Hopkins, L. B. (2005). *Oh, no! Where are my pants? And other disasters* (W. Erlbruch, Illus.). New York: HarperCollins.

Jacques, B. (2005). *High Rhulain.* New York: Philomel Books.

Kadohata, C. (2004). *Kira-Kira.* New York: Atheneum.

King, M. C. (2007). *Jump in! The junior novel.* New York: Disney Press.

Larson, K. (2006). *Hattie big sky.* New York: Delacorte Press.

Levine, G. C. (2006). *Fairest.* New York: Macmillan.

Lewis, C. S. (1950). *The lion, the witch and the wardrobe.* New York: HarperCollins.

Lithgow, J. (2000). *The remarkable Farkle McBride* (C. F. Payne, Illus.). New York: Simon and Schuster.

Long, M. (2007). *Pirates don't change diapers* (D. Shannon, Illus.). San Diego: Harcourt.

Madonna. (2003). *The English roses* (J. Fulvimari, Illus.). New York: Callaway.

McLimans, D. (2006). *Gone wild: An endangered animal alphabet.* New York: Walker.

Meyer, S. (2005). *Twilight.* New York: Little, Brown.

Meyer, S. (2006). *New Moon.* New York: Little, Brown.

Meyer, S. (2007). *Eclipse.* New York: Little, Brown.

Meyer, S. (2008a). *Breaking Dawn.* New York: Little, Brown.

Meyer, S. (2008b). *The Host.* New York: Little, Brown.

Meyer, S. (2010). *Twilight: The graphic novel.* New York: Yen Press.

Paolini, C. (2003). *Eragon.* New York: Knopf.

Paolini, C. (2005). *Eldest.* New York: Knopf.

Paterson, K. (1978). *The great Gilly Hopkins.* New York: Crowell.

Paterson, K. (1997). *Jip: His story.* New York: Scholastic.

Paterson, K. (2002). *The same stuff as stars.* New York: Clarion Books.

Paterson, K. (2006). *Bridge to Terabithia.* New York: HarperEntertainment.

Patron, S. (2006). *The higher power of Lucky.* New York: Atheneum.

Pullman, P. (2005). *The scarecrow and his servant*. New York: Knopf.

Rowling, J. K. (2005). *Harry Potter and the half-blood prince*. New York: Scholastic.

Rowling, J. K. (2007). *Harry Potter and the deathly hallows*. New York: Scholastic.

Sachar, L. (1998). *Holes*. New York: Farrar, Straus and Giroux.

Sachar, L. (2006). *Small steps*. New York: Delacorte Press.

Schoen, B., Spartz, E. Gordon, A., Stull, G., & Lawrence, J. (2006). *Mugglenet.com's what will happen in Harry Potter 7: Who lives, who dies, who falls in love and how will the adventure finally end?* Berkeley, CA: Ulysses Press.

Selznick, B. (2007). *The invention of Hugo Cabret*. New York: Scholastic.

Sendak, M. (1963). *Where the wild things are*. New York: Harper and Row.

Shriver, M. (2001). *What's wrong with Timmy?* Boston: Little, Brown.

Snicket, L. (2006). *The end (a series of unfortunate events, book 13)* (B. Helquist, Illus.). New York: HarperCollins.

Van Allsburg, C. (2002). *Zathura*. Boston: Houghton Mifflin.

Waddell, M. (2005). *Sleep tight, little bear* (B. Firth, Illus.). Cambridge, MA: Candlewick Press.

Weatherford, C. B. (2006). *Moses: When Harriet Tubman led her people to freedom* (K. Nelson, Illus.). New York: Jump at the Sun/Hyperion.

Wersba, B. (2005). *Walter: The story of a rat* (D. Diamond, Illus.). Asheville, NC: Front Street.

Wiesner, D. (2006). *Flotsam*. New York: Clarion Books.

Wiles, D. (2001a). *Freedom summer* (J. Lagarrigue, Illus.). New York: Atheneum.

Wiles, D. (2001b). *Love, Ruby Lavender*. San Diego: Gulliver/Harcourt.

Wiles, D. (2005). *Each little bird that sings*. San Diego: Gulliver/Harcourt.

Willems, M. (2007a). *Knuffle Bunny Too*. New York: Hyperion.

Willems, M. (2007b). *Today I will fly! An elephant and piggie book*. New York: Hyperion.

Willems, M. (2008). *The pigeon wants a puppy*. New York: Hyperion.

Zusak, M. (2006). *The book thief*. New York: Knopf.

From *Charlotte's Web* to the World Wide Web

The Impact of the Internet on the Field of Children's Literature

Sylvia M. Vardell, *Texas Woman's University*

How has technology changed the field of children's literature? What are the questions we should be asking about the potential for technology to transform our field in the future? These were the issues that were addressed at the 2004 Master Class in the Teaching of Children's Literature. That same year, Donald Leu and his colleagues wondered about "the chapters we still have to write in our classrooms" (p. 502) about children's literature and the Internet. They proposed that, "as we begin to use the Internet for teaching and learning, we open the door for students to acquire new literacies for reading, writing, communicating, and collaborating online" (Castek, Bevens-Mangelson, & Goldstone, 2006, p. 726) and to enhance students' responses to diversity and to literature (Leu et al., 2004). Seven years after this Master Class, we find that these questions and topics are still relevant. Considering these issues from the perspectives of children's literature scholars, authors, publishers, and educators, the following themes emerge: (1) the Internet has greatly expanded access to resources in the field of children's literature; (2) the Internet creates myriad opportunities for communication among all of those who are passionate about our field; and (3) technological advances should be used to enhance learning and to promote a love of literature. Within these themes, one can find multiple suggestions and resources for everyone who works with children and literature, whether you are a college professor, librarian, teacher, or even a child yourself.

Collegiality via the Web: A Scholarly Perspective

Michael Joseph is the rare book librarian in the Rutgers University Libraries and associate director of the Youth Literature Certificate Program at Rutgers University, an online program with both continuing education and for-credit courses in children's literature. In addition, he is the founder and moderator of the highly regarded discussion list in the field of children's literature, Child_Lit. As a librarian and a children's literature scholar, Joseph believes that the Internet serves as a tool to collegialize the work that is done in the field of children's literature. In his own work experience, he has struggled with "fitting in" with other librarians and library science faculty in his own university, not always sharing similar views, often an uncomfortable position for a faculty member to inhabit. In his view, the Internet provides an avenue for professionals within the field of children's literature to establish a supportive community of colleagues across distances and across institutions. Creating such communities was his purpose for developing Child_Lit.

Child_Lit is an unmoderated, online discussion group about children's literature. Its purpose is to examine "the theory and criticism of literature for children and young adults" (*Child_Lit*). Anyone may join this discussion list, which exists to promote discussion of aspects of children's literature including "authorship, illustration, publication, promotion, readership, reception, criticism and literature's changing social functions and implications." More specifically, Child_Lit was conceived "to foster the sharing of ideas by researchers engaged in original scholarship." At times, there have been more than 1,500 subscribers to the list including librarians, K–12 teachers, college and university professors, publishers, authors, illustrators, and parents.

Child_Lit also serves additional functions. For example, a historical view of discussions that have taken place on the list can be accessed through the Child_Lit archives. The discussion list also offers subscribers an opportunity to post current events in children's literature that are happening throughout the country and throughout the world. The informal nature of the discussion group allows researchers to request favors and resources from one another. Joseph particularly sees Child_Lit as a valuable resource to assistant professors who are beginning their scholarly inquiry or developing a line of research. Electronic mailing lists and discussion lists are excellent tools for the professional who wants to be part of a greater children's literature community. One can sign up to receive communal messages via email on a daily or digest basis. Middle school librarian Donna MacKinney recommends, "Listservs are the very best way to keep abreast of the newest titles, authors, and diverse opinions on books and children's publishing. If I could only have ONE resource I'd go with listservs" (Vardell, 2008).

In addition to these functions, other resources can be found on Child_Lit under the heading of "More Useful Information." These include a link called "Child Lit and the Classroom," created and maintained by Susan Stan, which describes why and how the list might be used by college students enrolled in children's literature courses. There are also links to the Children's Literature

Association, to an e-directory of the homepages of children's literature scholars, and a list of children's literature journals compiled by Wally Hastings and annotated by Michael Joseph.

Joseph himself accesses technology in a variety of ways to study and teach the history of children's literature. Several fascinating examples of how Joseph has combined technology and children's literature are available on his website, Michael Joseph Home Page. These examples, found under the heading "My Web Exhibitions," include Illustrations to Mother Goose's Melodies, *Intersection: How to Make a Wood Engraving* by John DePol, and *The Pop-up World of Ann Montanaro*. All of these exhibits offer fascinating glimpses of the possibilities that exist for enhancing the study of children's literature through technology.

There is no question that the Internet provides the opportunity for more innovation and communication within the field of children's literature. Educators can have easy access to professional organizations through their websites, newsletters, and discussion lists. The National Council of Teachers of English, for example, offers opportunities to link with colleagues through its organizational website, through subscriptions to the *INBOX* and other regular communications, and through a variety of discussion lists for specialized teaching groups. In addition, one can order professional books, register for a conference or submit a proposal, and participate actively in the life of the professional organization—without ever leaving the comfort of home. And nearly every major organization offers similar layers of information and participation. Even print journals are available electronically to organization members, and some journals are moving entirely to an electronic or digital format. For many, it may be hard to remember a time when colleagues relied on a letter in a stamped envelope for information about committee responsibilities or the latest conference. Our collegial community has the potential to become even more cohesive with more frequent and friendly communication available to all who choose to participate.

Authors, Illustrators, and Poets on the Web: One Author's Perspective

Cynthia Leitich Smith is just one children's and young adult author who has taken full advantage of the benefits the Internet can offer writers. Leitich Smith has published a variety of children's books including the picture book *Jingle Dancer*, a novel, *Rain Is Not My Indian Name,* and a collection of short stories, *Indian Shoes*, all of which reflect contemporary Native American life. She has also authored short stories for various anthologies and a young adult gothic fantasy novel, *Tantalize*. In addition, Leitich Smith hosts a major website that features extensive children's literature resources such as reader/teacher guides for her books, stories about her writing life, a schedule of events such as school visits (both real and cyber), as well as a broad range of thematic bibliographies, an alphabetical listing of other author and illustrator websites and biographies, information about state and national book awards, and tips for aspiring writers. Her website has become so successful, it now attracts 1.2 million visitors a year.

The website created and managed by Leitich Smith contains more than 400 pages, and one of the author's main purposes for managing this site is "to spread the word that good books matter!" Among other functions, her site offers guidance to parents in choosing books for children and provides numerous literature-related resources for teachers. Two of Leitich Smith's favorite linked sites, which include innumerable resources, are fellow author Tracie Vaughn Zimmer's site (containing primarily poetry resources) and Planet Esme, the diverse site of author Esme Raji Codell.

Leitich Smith contends that the Internet fosters community, specifically community among readers and writers. In her own experience as an author, the old-fashioned image of an author working alone in a garret is completely false. "Authors," according to Leitich Smith, "are big communicators," and the Internet has vastly increased their opportunities for communication. This includes venues for communicating with other authors to find writing resources and to establish mentor/mentee relationships. Leitich Smith herself joined a discussion list of children's authors hoping to find a mentor to guide her decisions about publishing as a business, and has been fortunate to be mentored—through the Internet—by author Jane Kurtz.

In turn, Leitich Smith has mentored three authors in Texas, California, and New York via email and the World Wide Web. Electronic messaging allows her to encourage these emerging authors to "keep going" and offers Leitich Smith a chance to tell them, "I believe in you." In addition to offering encouragement, which Leitich Smith believes is crucial to authors, the Internet allows authors to critique manuscripts for one another at a rapid pace. She will sometimes review the same picture book manuscript for one of her mentees 16 or 17 times in one weekend, a feat that would simply not be possible without technology.

One of the aspects of Internet communication Leitich Smith especially appreciates as an author is the ability to correspond with readers. Specifically, she is gratified at the heartfelt responses to her work she has received from teenage girls. Not only are these young readers given an opportunity to communicate with authors—an opportunity that was limited in the past—but the author herself is easily able to validate the reactions of the reader and to tell the reader, "Thank you for reading; thank you for caring about this book."

More broadly, Leitich Smith contends that the Internet allows teachers to plan virtual visits with an author for an entire class. Through instant messaging, students are able to communicate directly with an author about his or her work and often form interpersonal, one-on-one connections with the author as result. Procedures for arranging virtual author visits can be found on Leitich Smith's website, and she believes that personal connections formed as a result of these visits help convey the message to technology-savvy but reluctant readers that technology and literature can be a cooperative venture.

In terms of her own books, Leitich Smith's young adult novel, *Rain Is Not My Indian Name*, a "crying girl's novel," is one of the first tween books that featured the Internet as a major plot component. In the novel, the main character, Rain, creates a memorial on the World Wide Web to honor her best friend, Galen, who has died. Through email, she is also able to correspond with her absent mentor/grandfather. Leitich Smith notes that portraying Internet-friendly Native American characters cuts against the false stereotype of Native people as primitives, something she also accomplishes by being a Native American author with an online presence. Leitich Smith urges educators to take advantage of the opportunities offered by technology to nurture connections among readers, writers, educators, and parents—opportunities that so many students are already pursuing. She posted a book "trailer," like a movie trailer or preview, for *Rain Is Not My Indian Name* created by a fan, Shayne Leighton. Other authors are following suit, using YouTube video booktalks to lure young audiences to reading, while teens are also experimenting with responding to their favorite works by creating graphic and video tributes posted on YouTube and elsewhere.

Many, many authors, illustrators, and poets now host their own private websites (usually labeled with their name in the URL), and they offer a variety of information geared to readers of various ages. These include the highly interactive and animated website of Harry Potter creator J. K. Rowling and the visually stunning websites of illustrators such as William Low and Kadir Nelson. Some, such as poet Kristine (O'Connell) George, have even received awards, such as her site's recognition as "An American Library Association Great Web Site for Kids." (For a full listing of author and illustrator sites receiving this recognition, go to "Great Web Sites for Kids" on the American Library Association site.) In fact, there is a growing perception that an author may be at a disadvantage *without* a website of her or his own.

Child readers are certainly attuned to searching for information on the Internet and expect to see their favorite author and illustrator "celebrities" online. Adults who study children's literature often enjoy researching the lives and works of their favorite authors and illustrators and offer their research findings on the Web as well (as "author studies," critical analyses, etc.). Subscription-based electronic databases such as Contemporary Literary Criticism, Contemporary Authors, or the Dictionary of Literary Biography make this process even easier for fans of all ages. The Children's Book Council maintains a comprehensive list of children's "Author and Illustrator Sites," and search engines such as Google provide access to anyone with a Web presence. The Society of Children's Book Writers and Illustrators offers resources for aspiring authors and artists, as well as information and links relevant to the field of children's literature in general. For information about authors, about becoming an author, and for communicating with authors, the Internet has made it possible to connect with creators of children's books in a way that was only possible for a select few in the past.

More technological innovations are on the horizon for those who create children's literature. Some are experimenting with YouTube video clips, such as young adult author John Green and his brother's Vlogbrothers on YouTube (also see his website SparksFlyUp.com), and with establishing a presence on social networking sites like author Phil Bildner's Facebook fan site. He is also on Twitter (to access, go to Bildner's website). Numerous authors, illustrators, and poets have launched their own blogs. Authors such as Newbery winner Lois Lowry ("Lowry Updates") share their musings on the writing life. Cynthia Leitich Smith's blog, "Cynsations," was recently named one of the two most read blogs in children's literature by the Society of Children's Book Writers and Illustrators (SCBWI) in its regular "To Market" column.

In fact, blogging gives anyone interested an opportunity to experience cyber-authorship, and this practice seems to be especially popular among children's literature enthusiasts. These include blogs by editors such as Roger Sutton, editor-in-chief of *Horn Book*, whose blog, "Read Roger," was the other most read blog in children's literature, according to the SCBWI; librarians such as City Public Library's Elizabeth Bird, whose blog "A Fuse #8 Production" can now be found on the *School Library Journal* website; teachers such as Monica Edinger, who blogs daily on "Educating Alice" and also launches individual blogs for each of her fourth-grade students; and parents such as the blogger who identifies herself as "Mother Reader."

Publishers on the Web: An Insider Perspective

Virtually all publishers of children's books have their own Internet presence. For example, Random House Publishing maintains a sizeable corporate website that features up-to-the-minute information about children's books, authors, and programs. Different sites are designed specifically for teachers (Teachers@ Random); librarians (Librarians@Random); parents (Parents' Guide); and children (Kids@Random).

Holiday House Books for Young People offers a monthly electronic newsletter directed to educators and librarians. To subscribe, readers send an email to marketing@holidayhouse.com with "Newsletter Sign Up" in the subject line. Having held children's marketing positions at both Random House and Holiday House, Terry Borzumato offers her perspective on how technology has enabled publishers to increase their communication with the range of readers of children's literature.

As a marketing director, one of Borzumato's key tasks has always been to communicate with teachers, librarians, children, parents, and booksellers about the books and authors her employer publishes. Before the days of the Internet, publishers created direct mailings as their primary source of communication with various audiences, but these were expensive. Technology now allows publishers to stay in touch with a much larger population for much less expense; however, websites and email simply enhance, but do not replace, personal contact. Borzumato describes how she loves to talk about books with children's literature lovers and to introduce authors personally to their readers. She believes these personal connections "will never go away."

Teachers@Random contains numerous resources that are available for anyone to log onto, at any time. As viewers enter the site, they encounter a message board, informing them about "What's New" in children's publishing at Random House including new books, new authors, and events where authors and illustrators will be appearing. Organized by grade level (K–3, 4–5, 6–8, 9–12), visitors to the site may click on covers of new books to read a summary, find out more about the author, order the book, and even read chapter excerpts of selected titles. Currently, there are approximately 88,000 page views on this site.

Under the heading "Teachers Guides and More," viewers may search the hundreds of free, printable teachers guides by title, grade level, theme, discipline, or time period, as well as peruse new guides just published. Under "Authors and Illustrators," viewers may search the alphabetical listings for biographies on the children's authors and illustrators who publish with Random House, read the "Spotlight" column on a new author, or schedule a school visit with one of the authors or illustrators. A comprehensive index of children's book awards and honors containing all winners, past and present, from Random House Children's Books, a link specifically to Newbery and Caldecott winners, and lists of books that have been named to state award nomination lists for 45 states can be found under "Awards and Honors." Annotations of books appropriate for each month of the year are included in the "Planning Calendar." Examples include suggested titles for National Poetry Month in April and Asian Heritage Month in May. Under "Resources," teachers will find extensive links to other children's literature sites.

In addition to the information always available on the website, more than 30,000 teachers subscribe to monthly online newsletters in which they receive information on new books and "interesting tidbits," such as re-issued books and new covers for old favorites. Borzumato agrees that this level of interest and communication with teachers "is so exciting for us," and she described how "email is such an important part of what we do." While she definitely sees the advantages of email in allowing publishers to bring current news to a huge audience instantly, Borzumato adds that they are careful about the number of emails they send because they do not want readers to be overwhelmed by the amount of information they receive.

A later site created by Random House is Librarians@Random. Organized much like the teacher site, librarians who visit this site are able to read at least a dozen book talks on new books each month and also subscribe to an online newsletter. Visitors to Parents' Guide on the Random House site will find not only recommended books but also advice for raising a reader. At the Listening Library link, parents and children may listen to audio clips of books available for purchase on tape or CD.

Borzumato is most enthusiastic about the way the Internet "has opened up a whole new world for kids." Kids can now publish their own reviews of books; visit the websites of authors, illustrators, and publishers to learn more about their particular reading interests; and even create their own websites to share stories about the reading life. At Kids@Random, young readers can visit links devoted to favorite characters such as Junie B. Jones and Nate the Great. They can even join the Magic Tree House Readers and Writers Club. Borzumato believes all of these innovations are helping get kids more excited about books than ever before.

Publishers, too, are moving quickly to experiment with various technologies for promoting books, authors, and reading via the Web. Many offer print, audio, and video resources for learning more about children's literature. Most publishing companies, such as Random House and HarperCollins Children's, even direct their audience to separate layers of information depending on whether users are children, parents, or educators. Others, such as Simon and Schuster (SimonSaysKids.com) appeal to children at various age levels. Each offers information as well as opportunities for interaction via games, contests, free materials, etc.

More recently, several publishers are experimenting with "multi-platform" publication, using print and other media to promote a book and provide book-connected experiences for young readers. For example, for the publication of Christopher Paolini's third book, *Brisingr*, Random House launched *Vroengard Academy, an Alternate Reality Experience* (ARE), an interactive online game that includes real-world components, with 41,000 young people signed up in the first month. Scholastic introduced its new 39 Clues 10-book series (the first book by Rick Riordan) with multimedia connections including a feature film directed by Steven Spielberg, collectible cards, and an online game that will serve as a portal as young readers try to solve a mystery for a grand prize of $10,000. And HarperCollins created The Amanda Project, an interactive, collaborative fictional mystery series for tween and teen girls, told across a variety of media including books, a website that features games and a social networking platform, a related series of blogs and satellite sites, music, and merchandise. For adults who work with children, publisher websites are helpful for keeping up with the latest books as well as for mustering creative connections and materials for motivating young readers to check out those books. Such Web-based resources can provide both commercial and pedagogical value.

Teaching via the Web: An Educator's Perspective

At the time of this writing, I have been offering children's literature coursework entirely via the Internet for more than a decade. In thinking about the evolution of my teaching of children's literature courses, I have carefully considered the pieces of technology that have revolutionized my teaching and helped me to continue to make a personal connection with students. The book review note cards I created in the 1970s have been transformed by word processing, email, the Internet, blogging, and online discussion. At any given moment, I might find the following examples of items currently in my email inbox as examples of children's literature-related technology—a notice of an author visit, email messages from colleagues, a student assignment, conference opportunities, a survey, and newsletters from both NCTE and Random House—all of which demonstrate how my professional life has been enhanced by electronic information exchange.

My foray into incorporating information obtained from the Internet began several years ago with encouraging students to research children's authors through helpful sites created by fellow professors and librarians such as the Children's Literature Web Guide created by David K. Brown in Calgary in 1998. Other sites included those of professional associations such as NCTE and CLA;

organizations such as the Academy of American Poets (Poets.org); and children's literature faculty websites. Other types of websites have also broadened the range of information available to teachers of children's literature including Booksense, the family of independent-bookseller websites; lists of award-winning books such as the Newbery and Caldecott winners found at the American Library Association website; databases such as the "Database of Award-Winning Children's Literature" created by librarian Lisa Bartle, which includes information about 57 different children's book awards; and book review sites such as Kidsreads.com and Teenreads.com where kids share their responses to literature. Fans of children's books can quickly order the latest award-winning titles from Amazon or Booksense or even online discount vendors (such as Half. com). Students can access book reviews through print or online databases such as Books in Print, or book vendors such as Follett Library Resources (via Title-wave). Or they can look up how to pronounce "Jon Scieszka" at TeachingBooks. net, a multimedia website with an online audio Author Pronunciation Guide, or listen to interviews with authors at Just One More Book!, a three-times-a-week podcast by Canadian book lovers Andrea Ross and Mark Blevins with downloadable files. The list of electronic resources in the children's literature arena grows almost daily.

Additionally, we ought to consider the somewhat controversial resources of full texts accessible electronically such as The Online Books Page, which makes available 20,000 free books on the World Wide Web; Project Gutenberg, which provides 10,000 free titles to be released on DVD; 545 picture books from all over the world, which can be viewed at the International Children's Digital Library or Lookybook, a site that features 300 picture books (and the number is growing) in their entirety—from cover to cover. Recently, I saw a page-by-page posting of the out-of-print Random House early reader *Do You Know What I'm Going to Do Next Saturday?* up for viewing on Flickr, an online photo management and sharing application usually used for sharing pictures with family and friends. That's innovative! These sites are especially helpful in providing historical works of children's literature, as well as books in a variety of languages and from a variety of countries.

Consider the handy Kindle, the wireless reading device from Amazon with over 145,000 e-books available, including professional books such as Teri Lesesne's *Naked Reading* (Stenhouse, 2006) available in a Kindle edition. Not everyone is a fan of the e-book format, but we certainly ought to be familiar with it and what it offers. This is especially true in light of Amazon.com's announcement in July 2010 that sales of electronic books had outnumbered sales of hardback books, although it is important to note that this phenomenon corresponded with a drop in the sale price of the Kindle (Amazon Media Room, 2010). I suggest we consider pairing online books or e-books with physical books for study, discussion, and comparison.

As a professor of children's literature, I, like many of my colleagues, have had to face the challenge of taking children's literature courses entirely online and teaching them from a distance via electronic platforms such as Blackboard or WebCT. I have carefully considered that teaching approaches for an online course are, in many ways, different than a traditional course (Compton, 2009). Formerly, in classroom-based courses, students would complete assignments such as written book responses, author studies, oral presentations, creative projects, field experiences, independent research, and quizzes and exams. When I moved the course to the Web, I had to consider which of these were still appropriate for the electronic learning environment and how they could be adapted or modified for distance learning. In addition, teaching online requires a great deal of writing and organization, since nearly every word you might speak or "lecture" needs to be written (or taped), representing a huge time commitment. Students, too, must spend more time writing, which I believe is a distinct advantage in online courses. There are no "shy" students, since all must participate in online "discussion" to receive credit. Overall, I believe I invest more time in dialogue and feedback and require more public sharing of students' assignments when teaching a cyber class. Specifically, I expect students to create a website or blog where they post original book reviews, author studies, and other work that may have utility to the general public. This not only allows students to demonstrate their own learning but also creates a resource for others. It also pushes them even further in their knowledge and use of technology tools. And they are so proud of their website or blog at the end of the semester. In fact, some colleagues have experimented with inviting groups (of adults or children) to contribute to the world's general knowledge by posting on Wikipedia, "the free encyclopedia" that accepts offerings from anyone, anywhere, and archives and attributes all contributions so the history of all entries is public. This may be the best example of constructivist learning ever. Other students are experimenting with the 3-D virtual world of Second Life, creating personal avatars and interacting with other students and teachers in game-like conference events.

Using the audio medium has been a staple of my teaching for many years, beginning with the old-fashioned book on cassette. But audiobooks are experiencing a resurgence of interest now that more and more people are tech-savvy, using iPods, MP3 players, and even the Kindle or the cell phone to download and listen to books (Duncan, 2010). It's a particularly popular medium with tweens, teens, and kids with special linguistic or learning needs. I encourage my adult students to listen to audiobooks as part of their "reading assignment" and offer audio clips embedded in my online course sites to give them a sampling. They can also refer to the new American Library Association Odyssey Award for the best audiobooks, to Audible.com for downloadable books, or blogs such as Audiobooker on the Booklist Online for further suggestions. Some are even turning the tables and making podcasts of their own book reviews available on our course site for others to listen to. I'm experimenting with creating original podcasts and video segments to enhance my teaching and connecting with students.

I also admit that I struggle to find a different rhythm as a teacher when teaching online. Communication is critical; developing a relationship with students is a critical factor in their completion of a course (Nagel, Blignaut, & Cronje, 2009). I check on students daily, making sure I have heard from every student over time. I also send feedback regularly to guide their learning. Thus, I am no longer teaching a Tuesday/Thursday class or a Monday night class, but rather I am checking the class site and email questions daily (even several times a day). In addition, I feel some administrative pressure to maintain and create more online classes, although some courses are more effective in the online environment than others. If I had my choice, my ideal is to teach a "hybrid" class, one that has occasional face-to-face classroom sessions and maintains ongoing communication electronically. In my opinion, this option satisfies the longing of many students as well as teachers to come together in an actual place to meet, support, and learn from one another, but offers the convenience of fewer trips to campus, parking hassles, and childcare costs, for example.

Some of the key issues related to online teaching are double-edged "swords," so to speak, with advantages and disadvantages for each issue. First is access. While distance learning allows students from all over the world to take classes— I recently taught students online who were living in Indonesia and Hawaii—the numbers of students enrolling in online courses can be huge, and professors may simply be unable to keep up with this demand. The flexibility offered by distance learning is wonderful because it allows students and teachers to work anytime, anywhere; however, such flexibility requires much self-discipline, a challenge for some students. Technology itself, while offering many advantages, creates new problems such as compatibility between platforms and equipment. I believe that learning through writing is a great benefit for teachers and students, but I also acknowledge the increased time commitment for reading and writing inherent in online courses. The fact that online courses are available to a global audience offers many practical advantages, but issues of privacy, security, and copyright also become paramount. Finally, the question of the professorial role is also important. Who owns an online course—the university or the individual professor who created the course? The Massachusetts Institute of Technology (MIT) has been particularly innovative in offering online coursework free and open to the public via its OpenCourseWare platform, and at the National Kaohsiung First University of Science and Technology in Taiwan, Dr. Chi-Fen Emily Chen offers an entire 18-week course, Children's Literature, with all course materials available free on the Web to anyone who is interested.

Will distance learning replace the face-to-face educational experience? What would bring a student to a campus or other central location to meet her or his professor and classmates? If one can arrange virtual author visits, online social networking, and audio and video links to capture voices and faces, will the need for physical contact diminish? How are ongoing mentoring relationships established if teacher and learner never meet in person? And most importantly, can a passion for literature and the love of reading be communicated without ever passing a book around the table or exclaiming out loud about a favorite passage? As a professor, I struggle with each of these concerns as I continue to welcome students into the field of children's literature.

Conclusion

Regardless of the role they play within the field of children's literature, scholars, authors, publishers, and educators all recognize the tension inherent in expanding the place of technology in the "book world." Although the advent of the World Wide Web, email, blogs, and online courses have immeasurably increased communication and access to information, technology should not replace human contact and connection. We're still social animals, after all. Undeniably, technology has forever changed—and will continue to change—the field of children's literature. More literature-related resources are available to more people than ever before and there are multiple opportunities for communicating about our reading and responding, too. In his "The Blue Skunk" blog, librarian Doug Johnson (2008) mulls over the idea of the "postliterate" person, "those who can read, but choose to meet their primary information and recreational needs through audio, video, graphics and gaming." Young people today have more choices for intellectual recreation. But Johnson goes on to say, "I would argue that postliteracy may be a return to more natural forms of communication—speaking, storytelling, dialogue, debate, and dramatization. It is just now that these modes can be captured and stored digitally as (or more) easily as writing. And information, emotion and persuasion may be even more powerfully conveyed in multi-media formats. . . . It is telling, I believe, that the human love for storytelling has just never gone away throughout history. We just have new ways to do it and preserve it." We may be experiencing a paradigm shift as our field sees the practice of reading books for pleasure and information give way to reading all kinds of things for pleasure and information, but the need for connection through story (true stories and fiction) remains unchanged. Educators can embrace the possibilities of technology for enhancing teaching and communication and use it as another tool in promoting a lifelong love of learning and reading. As Newbery Award–winning author Lois Lowry put it, "There is something about that moment, when literature becomes accessible, and a door of the world opens."

Works Cited

Amazon Media Room. (2010, July 19). *Amazon.com now selling more Kindle books than hardcover books*. Retrieved from http://phx.corporate-ir.net/phoenix.zhtml?c=17606060&p=irol-newsArticle&ID=1449176&highlight=

Castek, J., Bevens-Mangelston, J., & Goldstone, B. (2006). Reading adventures online: Five ways to introduce the new literacies of the Internet through children's literature. *The Reading Teacher, 59*, 714–728.

Child_Lit [Information Page]. Retrieved from https://email.rutgers.edu/mailman/listinfo/child_lit

Compton, L. K. L. (2009). Preparing language teachers to teach language online: A look at skills, roles, and responsibilities. *Computer Assisted Language Learning, 22*, 73–99.

Duncan, R. (2010). Ebooks and beyond: The challenge for public libraries. *APLIS, 23*, 44–45.

Johnson, D. (2008, August 13). Libraries for a post-literate society [Web log message]. Retrieved from http://doug-johnson.squarespace.com/blue-skunk-blog/2008/8/13/libraries-for-a-post-literate-society-i.html

Leu, D. J., Jr., Castek, J., Henry, L., Coiro, J., & McMullan, M. (2004). The lessons that children teach us: Integrating children's literature and the new literacies of the Internet. *The Reading Teacher, 57*, 496–503.

Nagel, L., Blignaut, A. S., & Cronje, J. C. (2009). Read-only participants: A case for student communication in online classes. *Interactive Learning Environments, 17*, 37–51.

Vardell, S. M. (2008). *Children's literature in action: A librarian's guide*. Westport, CT: Libraries Unlimited.

11

Censorship, Challenge, and Choice

LINDA M. PAVONETTI, *Oakland University*

O*nce upon a time . . .*
From the time we are toddlers we hear stories that begin this way. The story I'm about to relate is not a fairy tale. Sadly, it's true. The teacher in this story, let's call him Mr. C, is a real teacher who was teaching fifth grade in a private, parochial school. Throughout the year, one of the parents and Mr. C had been at loggerheads about his choice of required books. On the last day of school, the parent walked up to Mr. C and admitted they had experienced a tumultuous year, but that her son had learned a lot. She finished her compliment with a question. "Why do you want to make him think so much?"

Often, books that encourage children to think are the ones that are challenged. Mr. C had been fortunate. The parent had not filed a formal complaint or demanded that any books be removed from the fifth-grade reading list. Most of us who teach or who work in libraries or schools may never experience a full-blown censorship case. But we never know when a parent, community member, administrator, or coworker might challenge our choice of reading materials. How likely is it that the censor will knock at our door? I invite you to take a look at some of the startling statistics about censorship in the United States.

"More than a book a day faces expulsion from free and open public access in US schools and libraries every year" (American Library Association, 2006a). Between 1990 and 2000, the American Library Association (ALA) Office of Intellectual Freedom (OIF) reported 6,364 book challenges (ALA, 2010). The next five years saw more than 3,000 challenges (ALA, 2006b); 546 challenges in 2006 (ALA, 2007); 420 challenges reported from schools and libraries in 2007 (ALA, 2010); and 513 in 2008. In fact, ALA identifies 10,415 challenges to books in schools and libraries *reported* to the OIF in the past 18 years (ALA, 2010). However, if we consider that "research suggests that for each challenge reported there are as many as four or five that go unreported" (ALA, 2008), the number of formal challenges probably exceeded 40,000.

What do we—college professors, classroom teachers, and librarians—need to know about censorship? What proactive steps will protect us from censorship?

What Is Censorship?

Censorship is a term that is frequently misused and misunderstood. According to the *Intellectual Freedom Manual* (ALA, 2006c), censorship is "a change in the access status of material, based on the content of the work and made by a governing authority or its representatives. Such changes include exclusion, restriction, removal or age/grade level changes" (p. 495). However, it is important to understand that censorship is the final step in what is frequently a lengthy process that might conclude in a court of law. As Ginny Moore Kruse, recipient of the 1997 ALA/American Association of School Librarians (AASL) Intellectual Freedom Award and the Wisconsin Library Association's Intellectual Freedom Award, explained at the CLA Master Class on censorship (Pavonetti, 2002), there are frequently five levels or stages involved in a formal censorship case. Each level advances the debate toward more formal, and eventually legal, proceedings (see Figure 11.1).

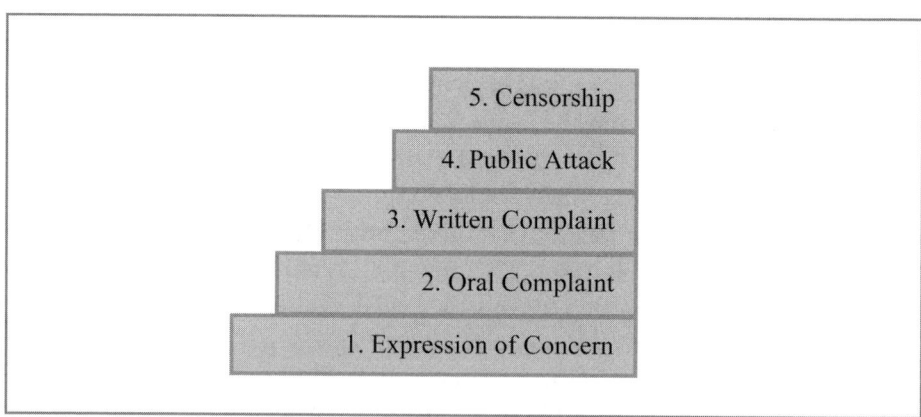

Figure 11.1: Levels of censorship complaints.

Expression of Concern

A concerned adult notices a neighborhood student carrying a book, overhears a conversation, reads an article in a newspaper, magazine, or even a school or library newsletter. Wherever or whatever it is, the book or topic generates unease in the adult. The ALA points out that even though the expression of concern is not a formal challenge, it should be taken seriously: it is "an inquiry that has *judgmental* [emphasis added] overtones" (ALA, 2006c, p. 495). At this level, the person who inquires about the book or material is usually looking for information but is not necessarily planning a formal challenge. The recommended procedure at this level, according to Kruse, is constructive dialogue so that any potential action is staved off. A conciliatory attitude—"I understand that you have concerns"—is generally more helpful than an antagonistic or threatening stance. It is imperative to discuss the expression of concern with a supervisor or administrator before the complaint proceeds to the next level (Pavonetti, 2002).

Oral Complaint

This is the second level, and somewhat more serious than the first, but it is still in the realm of an informal inquiry. This complaint is "an oral challenge to the presence and/or appropriateness of the material in question" (ALA, 2006c, p. 495). At this stage, the complaint might be in the form of an email or a note from a parent or other adult, but the protest remains informal. Once again, the recommended procedure at this level is constructive dialogue. The teacher or librarian who received the complaint should invite the person into the library or classroom to discuss the book. Many complainants simply want to be heard, and it is a lot easier to listen at this stage than when the problem escalates. If we thrust a form in the would-be censor's face, we will certainly trigger a chain reaction. It is at this level that we want to ascertain that the person has actually read the book. Frequently, complaints are registered based on hearsay or textual passages that have been misquoted or taken out of context.

Written Complaint

This is the formal challenge. The *Intellectual Freedom Manual* (ALA, 2006c) defines a challenge as "a formal, written complaint requesting that library materials be removed or restricted" (p. 495). At this point, the complainant has already "filled out *THE* form" or is ready to do so. The form referenced is a document pre-scribed by library or school district policy for book challenges or censorship cas-es. It is a formal document, usually contained in the school district or library's censorship policy (see National Council of Teachers of English Anti-Censorship Center or the American Library Association's Office for Intellectual Freedom webpages for links to additional information).

Kruse strongly emphasizes that we must be sure, at this level, to continue to *talk* to the person. If we engage the person in conversation and allow the person to vent, we still may be able to defuse the situation (Pavonetti, 2002).

Public Attack

The public attack is "a publicly disseminated statement challenging the value of the material, presented to the media and/or others outside the institutional organization in order to gain public support for further action" (ALA, 2006c, p. 495). These kinds of incidents frequently arise from the ubiquitous call-in show, letters to the editor, widespread email campaigns, and other such public forums. These tend to inflame large segments of the population and possibly lead to more formal complaints. In recent years, many of these public attacks have been well-organized efforts on a local, state, or national level, with far-reaching con-sequences. The efforts to censor J. K. Rowling's Harry Potter series and Philip Pullman's His Dark Materials trilogy (when the Pullman's movie was about to be released in 2007, almost 10 years after the first American edition appeared) are demonstrative of what organized groups of concerned adults can achieve.

Censorship

The final level is the actual removal of challenged material from the classroom or the library. At this point, access to the book is limited and, just as importantly, the students' right to read, view, listen, etc., is also constrained. This is when a book is considered "banned."

Language is powerful; there are few words that are value-free. So too with the words *censorship* and *intellectual freedom*. Censorship implies a negative situ-ation—prohibiting access or restricting a basic liberty. Intellectual freedom car-ries positive implications, both as individual words and when combined. Few Americans are anti-freedom and when pressed, even fewer object to the idea of intellectual freedom. Consequently, it is imperative for each of us who works with children to consider the words we use when we discuss students' rights to read, write, listen, and view materials that will encourage them to develop into thoughtful citizens.

Self-Censorship and Selection

Authorial Self-Censorship: Robert Cormier and Katherine Paterson

Selection, censorship, and *self-censorship* are terms that need continual clarification to understand any discussion of book selection policy. There are two principal definitions for self-censorship: a personal definition and an authorial definition. From an author's point of view, self-censorship refers to the tendency to omit possibly controversial material. Robert Cormier, author of *The Chocolate War* (1974), discussed his own writing and self-censorship.

> I have learned, astonishingly, that not all censorship is bad and that, in fact, censorship for the writer begins at home....This is what angers me most about censorship, the fact that I have already been censored—and willingly—before my manuscripts leave my house. I am that censor. (qtd. in Simmons, 1994, p. 66)

Cormier detailed his struggles in writing and publishing *The Chocolate War*. His 15-year-old daughter wanted to read his manuscript but before he gave it to her, he eliminated one chapter. When his publisher offered editorial comments on the book—including the chapter Cormier had removed for his daughter's reading—they included reservations about that same chapter (Simmons, 1994). Cormier wrote that he had been "willing to inflict that chapter on other people's 15-year-old daughters but unwilling to inflict it on my own daughter" (qtd. in Simmons, p. 68).

Like Cormier, Katherine Paterson, author of numerous award-winning books, has often come under fire for the language in *The Great Gilly Hopkins* (1978), a Newbery Honor book. She was once told that if Gilly didn't cuss, she'd be a "wonderful character" (West, 1997, p. 7). Paterson retorted, "She lies, steals, bullies. She's terribly prejudiced. She won't [*sic*] be a wonderful character if only she didn't cuss" (qtd. in West, p. 7). Reflectively, Paterson notes that her encounters with censorship have affected her writing:

> Now when I put a word in a book that I think might offend somebody, I take a second look at it. I no longer write as naïvely as I once did....I think, "Is this word or this scene absolutely necessary?" I usually keep what I wrote, but I can no longer be naïve about the possible consequences of using certain words or including certain scenes. (qtd. in West, p. 8)

What Cormier and Paterson discovered, I believe, illuminates the differences among censorship, self-censorship, and selection. If they had decided never to include sex or "language" in any future books because of the possibility that an editor, librarian, critic, parent, teacher, or reader might object, that's self-censorship. If their publishers demanded they expurgate scenes because of previous difficulties with censors—lost sales, bad reviews, lawyers' fees—it would be censorship. An author's responsibility is to create characters who speak like real people, act like real people, and negotiate true-to-life situations that may contain literarily necessary—but not gratuitous—sex, language, religion, humanism, or any number of other issues that precipitate censorship cases. In other words, authors need to be *selective* rather than *reactive* in their craft.

Personal Self-Censorship: Teachers and Librarians

Self-censorship takes on a different meaning when we look at a teacher's or librarian's role in developing a library collection or choosing books for curricular purposes. Basically, the difference lies in motivation: Selection is a positive action whereas censorship is a negative reaction. The question we need to ask ourselves is this: *Do I select books based on their overall content or theme or do I reject books based on a partial reading, i.e., limited paragraphs or passages, or other extra-textual concerns?*

> To the selector, the important thing is to find reasons to keep the book. Given such a guiding principle, the selector looks for values, for strengths, for virtues which will over shadow minor objections. For the censor, on the other hand, the important thing is to find reasons to reject the book; his guiding principle leads him to seek out the objectionable features, the weaknesses, the possibilities for misinterpretation. (Asheim, 1953, ¶ 22)

The book that has topped the most challenged lists in 2006, 2007, and 2008 is an ideal example of the contrast between teachers' and librarians' selection policies that govern book-acquisition decisions. Richardson and Parnell's *And Tango Makes Three* (2005) is a nonfiction picture storybook about two male penguins in New York's Central Park Zoo who adopt an abandoned fertilized egg, tend it until it hatches, then raise the chick as their own. Readers have had varied responses, one of which is homophobic—the male penguins must be "gay"—while another is biological—the adult penguins are ensuring the continuation of their species. According to Robert P. Doyle's (2008) annual list of challenged and banned books, a library patron in Lodi, California, objected because *Tango* is "homosexual story line that has been sugarcoated with cute penguins" (¶ 30).

The challenges that have been lodged have been based on "sexism, homosexuality, anti-family, religious viewpoint, [and that the book is] unsuited to age group" (Doyle, ¶ 12).

From a curricular point of view, this book could easily become part of a social studies unit on family or a science unit on any number of topics: egg-laying birds, reptiles, fish, mammals, etc.; penguins; habitat—captivity vs. natural; or even gendered behavior in animals. Much of this is determined by the school's curriculum: family is generally studied in the primary grades, whereas reproduction or gendered behavior would be repeated at different mastery levels from the intermediate grades through high school.

Purchasing *And Tango Makes Three*—even in multiple copies—could be easily justified based on curricular needs. However, there might be objections in a school whose district or state curriculum does not include subject matter that might be reinforced by this book. This is where teachers' book-buying decisions become problematic: If they do not purchase the book, are they reacting to censorship? In the past, their principals have unilaterally banned books from their schools. Teachers heard about the controversy on the radio and decided to protect their untenured jobs; self-censorship? The curriculum does not include penguins so *And Tango Makes Three* is not a necessary purchase; selection criteria?

All of these are common explanations for the acquisition decisions teachers make. Certainly community standards are an important factor in what books belong in a library or classroom collection. So, is censorship always wrong? Yes. But that is because when a book is censored, the censor is insisting that *no one* should *ever* read it. With self-censorship or selection—which frequently appear to be quite similar—a teacher or librarian makes a decision that a book is not appropriate in her collection for specific reasons that are contained in a *written* selection policy.

Self-censorship is a major problem according to surveys that have investigated classroom teacher behavior (Agee, 1999). "In a 1990 *Education Daily* survey, over 14% of North Carolina teachers surveyed said they sometimes suppress materials or ideas to avoid controversy" (Sipe, 1999, ¶ 15). As Cerra (1996) reported, her survey of 375 Minnesota elementary school teachers found that "self-censorship among teachers was pervasive" (as reported in Agee, 1999, p. 61). The figures were astounding: 70 percent would change text in read-aloud situations because of language; 60 percent would not purchase highly recommended books "if the books contained 'risky' subject matter" (Cerra, as cited in Agee, p. 61). Elizabeth Noll (1994) surveyed secondary teachers in seven states and reported similar levels of self-censorship.

Stealth Censorship

One topic that is seldom discussed is covert, silent, or "stealth" censorship. Librarians track how many books—and what kinds of books—disappear and never return to the collection. In some situations, these are books that patrons are embarrassed to check out, or books that might endanger juvenile patrons if a parent were informed. There may be a social stigma if a student is seen checking out or returning such titles. Books on homosexuality fit this description, and they frequently go missing.

However, there is a second reason for items disappearing from library shelves and never resurfacing. There are organized groups who target specific titles because they believe the books should not be read by anyone, i.e., the books should be censored. These include groups on both the Right and the Left, and the books targeted often reflect what the censors consider unacceptable images of family (religious Right) or undermine equality (Left). "Five of the most frequently challenged materials between 1982 and 1993 were subject to both direct-mail and newsletter campaigns by national and state-level religious-right groups" (Sipe, 1999, ¶ 6). For a variety of reasons that may include being reluctant to engage in a censorship battle, or having challenged a book and lost—which leaves it in circulation—these groups or individuals remove books without checking them out—and never return them to the library.

Silent Censorship

Teachers and librarians, as an aggregate, generally support intellectual freedom and reject censorship. There has been a tendency even among highly trained and certified librarians, media specialists, and teachers to adopt reading software that is designed to assist record-keeping and motivate readers with incentives.

Prepackaged programs or "book lot" purchases, where there is no choice except those made by the packagers, is an extremely subtle and seldom discussed form of censorship. Jim Trelease, popular motivational speaker and author of *The Read-Aloud Handbook* (2006), affirms that most librarians carefully match acquisitions with the appropriate grades and social levels of students, but then adds:

> Unfortunately, these procedures can be short-circuited when a district simply buys a prepackaged collection of books, a package that is already coded for reading levels—which saves considerable time, money, and effort but might provide [unsuitable] volumes. (Trelease, 2009, ¶ 5)

Trelease references programs such as Accelerated Reader that offer prepackaged sets of books and quizzes keyed to specific reading levels. One problem is that the books are leveled using the Flesch-Kincaid reading index that does not take into account the themes or topics of the books, as a professional librarian would. For example, Brock Cole's young adult book, *The Facts Speak for Themselves* (1997), is about a 13-year-old girl who has witnessed the murder of her best friend's father—who is also her lover. Accelerated Reader recommends it for the same reading level (3.6—third grade, sixth month) as Cynthia Rylant's picture storybook *When I Was Young in the Mountains* (1982), the author's reminiscences of her life in the mountains as a child (for a more complete discussion, see Pavonetti, Brimmer, & Cipielewski, 2002–2003). A professional librarian or a certified teacher, personally selecting books for students, would *not* recommend Cole's book to third-grade students.

Proactive Stances to Protect against Challenges

Teachers and librarians should be aware of basic preemptive measures they can establish to avoid book challenges. The most important is to have a district policy that governs the procedures for book challenges. Every school office, classroom, and library should have a copy of the policy. Each year, before classes resume, a committee of faculty members should read and, if necessary, update the policy. There should be an inservice session to acquaint new faculty and staff and remind other faculty members of the best methods of handling concerns, oral complaints, and other informal challenges. At that point, each faculty member should be encouraged to prepare a personal selection policy based on the local, district, or state curricula. There are several levels of preparation that taken together will go a long way to protect teacher choices and constitute justification that will withstand most challenges.

Preparing a Selection Policy

There are numerous factors that influence a selection policy: grade level, curriculum, demographics, community standards, existing classroom library, quality of school and neighborhood libraries, and economics. The selection policy should flow naturally from the school's Mission Statement and Educational Philosophy. The selection policy should reflect the educational, intellectual, and emotional needs of students, the educational dreams of the school board, the administration, the teachers, and the community, and our heritage of freedom to read and inquire and think. (Donelson, 1994, p. 234)

It is certainly recommended that teachers and librarians read books about selection policies as well as inquire about other schools' policies. However, each policy will be distinctive, just as the children, teachers, staff, administration, families, and neighborhoods contiguous to the school are distinctive. But there are other actions besides establishing a school or district procedure for handling challenges or formulating a school or classroom selection policy. Three methods I recommend to teachers and librarians include (a) creating good school-home communications; (b) maintaining a teacher's book log notebook; and (c) initiating multiple text options, providing alternatives for required books, and setting up book discussion groups.

Good School–Home Communications

In a 2008 report representing 10,681 children, the National Center for Education Statistics, Institute of Education Sciences, US Department of Education reported that

> about 54 percent of students in grades K through 12 had parents who reported receiving notes or e-mail from the school specifically about their child; 91 percent had parents who reported receiving newsletters, memos, or notices addressed to all parents; and 49 percent had parents who reported that the school had contacted them by telephone. (Herrold & O'Donnell, 2008, p. 3)

When schools communicate regularly and clearly, avoiding jargon and other language that might interfere with comprehension, parents are more empowered. Hoover-Dempsey and her colleagues (2005) examined school practices that supported "parents' trust in schools" (p. 117). Two methods supported by their longitudinal research, as well as by numerous other studies, include "establishing and maintaining respectful and collaborative attitudes toward families (e.g., Griffith, 1998; Lareau, 1989; Lawson, 2003) and frequent opportunities for two-way communication between parents and teachers (e.g., Adams & Christenson, 1998; Bandura, 1997; Sanders & Harvey, 2002; Scribner et al., 1999)" (Hoover-Dempsey et al., 2005, p. 117). For more than 25 years, Ken Donelson and Alleen Nilsen (1980), authors of the oldest and most respected young adult literature textbook, have exhorted teachers and librarians to establish effective communications with parents and the community: "Librarians and English teachers should work diligently to win community support for academic freedom and the right to read *before* censorship strikes" (p. 414).

There is abundant positive anecdotal evidence from teachers who inform parents—in advance—of all and any books the students will be reading. In such situations, parents sign a form agreeing to allow their students to read and participate in class discussions or they can opt to have their children read an alternate text. Donelson and Nilsen (1980) agree that program transparency is vital. "Some may argue that alerting parents to books or techniques will encourage censors to move more rapidly, but censors never need help to move [quickly]" (p. 415).

Book Logs

Over the years of working with teachers—elementary through high school—I have developed a form that enables busy educators to track the books they teach, books that are on their classroom shelves, and books they may want to add to the curriculum. There are several vital components to this book log:

1. Information about the book: *Bibliography, Genre, Global Topic/s, Theme/s,* and *Ethnic Group/s* represented. This is mostly informational material, but topic, theme, and ethnic designations can provide justification for curricular purposes.

2. *Number of Pages, Reading Level,* and *Interest Level* are indicators of what books are appropriate for what students. Books with low reading levels and high interest levels may be appropriate for reluctant readers. Books on an adult reading level and a young adult interest level might be appropriate for advanced placement high school students.

3. *Major Awards* and *Reviews*: These are two categories that are important when defending book choices to parents, community members, administrators, or other faculty members. Major book awards are one way to demonstrate a book's literary quality. Nothing is guaranteed and depending on award-winning books to protect from challenges is an iffy proposition. However, a preponderance of positive evidence from reputable reviewing sources (e.g., *Horn Book Magazine, School Library Journal, Booklist, The Bulletin of the Center for Children's Books, Voya, ALAN Review*) will build a stronger case for curricular inclusion.

4. *Warning*: This may seem like a strange category but it is important for teachers and librarians to be sensitive to language, violence, sexually explicit material, or other potentially censorable content. One method of catching such components is to take notes while reading and rereading the book. While we may gloss over objectionable content during a first read, note taking will slow the process so that we pick up on material we previously overlooked.

5. *Summary*: This is primarily to assist our sometimes sketchy memory, but it can also be used as a sales pitch—a book talk to motivate students who are looking for a good read.

The final three sections can be the most tedious but also the most important. It is not necessary to complete them immediately, but think of these spaces as a way of keeping track of good ideas.

6. *Connections* might include books by the same author or on the same theme. They might be opportunities for comparing or contrasting two authors' treatment of the same topic. There are several award-winning books about foster children that could be paired with *The Great Gilly Hopkins* (Paterson, 1978), including *The Road to Paris* (Grimes, 2006), *Locomotion* (Woodson, 2003), and *Pictures of Hollis Woods* (Giff, 2002). Having these connections at our fingertips can provide alternative texts should parents object to a required book.

7. *Activities/Extensions* is a place for ideas—as you read about them or as you generate them—about extending the learning experience beyond the text. These activities demonstrate how books stimulate cross-disciplinary thinking by students.

8. *Applicable Standards*: This section is the most important component in protecting teachers against censorship. Everyone who writes about school censorship urges teachers and librarians to know why they are using or recommending every book in their libraries. Donelson and Nilsen (1980) recommend answering these five questions:

    a. Why will the teacher use this book for this particular class?

    b. What objectives—literary, psychological, or pedagogical—does the teacher have in mind in using this book?

    c. How will the teacher use this book to achieve those objectives?

    d. What problems—stylistic, thematic, or censorial—exist in the book and how will the teacher face them?

e. Assuming the objectives are met, how will students reading the book change? (p. 415)

Multiple Texts as an Alternative for Required Books

A third proactive deterrent to censorship in the classroom is to provide a variety of texts instead of one book for all students. By utilizing book clubs in the classroom—a technique successfully employed from kindergarten through senior high—teachers are able to accommodate multiple reading levels and genres while allowing parents to voice their preference among a limited number of options. The pedagogical reasons for this technique are well established (Paratore & McCormack, 1997). Harvey Daniels (2002) and Taffy Raphael et al. (1997) offer ways of designing book clubs or literature groups (think Oprah's wildly popular book clubs) in which students read and discuss their choice of books that are thematically similar. Students are more motivated to read when they have a choice in the books they read, even if it is a limited choice (Pavonetti, 1997).

When parents come to school to challenge a book that the class is reading or the teacher is reading aloud, it is important to not only listen to the parents' objections but also to be ready to compromise. One method of selecting an alternative is to enlist the objecting parent's assistance in finding a replacement. As Nilsen and Donelson (2009) suggest, this book must not be longer or more difficult than the original assignment or the student may feel penalized. Conversely, the book should not be shorter or easier, a situation that could encourage other students to cry censorship in hopes of receiving an easier assignment. "Finding another book approximately as long and as difficult as the original choice is no easy matter, but parents who demand substitutes must help, lest the teacher offend once more" (pp. 424, 426).

Why Intellectual Freedom Is an Important Issue

What motivates a censor? Reichman (2001) attributes four motives that are seldom exclusive: (a) family values; (b) political views; (c) religion; (d) minority rights (pp. 17–19). These categories often incorporate fear of change or of other ways of life. Some are motivated by a desire to control of a small portion of their world that seems to be whirling out of control, in other words, their children. There is an adage that suggests as unemployment and inflation rise, so do the number of challenges and censorship cases.

Censorship is not a modern phenomenon. Plato argued that fiction could emotionally damage young readers in *The Republic* (approximately 360 BC). The Chinese Emperor Chi Huang Ti burned Confucius' writings (2nd century BC). During the sixteenth century, the Catholic Church published its notorious Index of Forbidden Works—which remained in effect until the mid-twentieth century (Nilsen & Donelson, 2009, p. 390). Concerned citizens have argued about the effects of the printed word, especially on young people, for thousands of years—and it's a sure bet that censorship won't disappear anytime in the near future. But as teachers and librarians we must recognize censorship for what it does to students, our patrons, classrooms, book collections, and to us.

Censorship erodes our belief in ourselves, in our judgment as educated professionals. If we are afraid for our careers, we no longer select what, in our assessment, are the best materials for teaching the individual students in our classrooms. We turn to packaged programs—basal series, anthologies, textbooks, or electronic quizzes on a preselected database of books. We surrender students' minds to lesson plans and scripted teaching based on "average" students. One size does not fit all when it comes to books or teaching.

Censorship erodes our students' potential. "Those who would restrict . . . students' reading lists are doing something even worse than denying young people information; they are preventing them from learning to think for themselves. A growing mind must be encouraged, not shackled" (West, 1997, p. xv).

Critical thinking is an important skill for a democratic society. It is not enough that students memorize words that they parrot back on standardized examinations. "The basic process of thinking—critical thinking, analytical thinking, disciplined thinking—is at the heart of every other skill students learn in school" (West, 1997, p. xv). Judith Saltman (1998) suggests that reading is the first step in acquiring those qualities on which the United States was founded: critical thinking, informed decision making, personal value systems, and empathy for others.

There are differences of opinion as to what constitutes censorship. The strict anticensorship activists condemn not only book censors but also "teachers who skip words when reading a text aloud or who skip parts of an in-class showing of a video" (McDonald, 1991, as cited in Brinkley, 1999, p. 43). This would therefore include the adults—teachers, librarians, and parents—who painted diapers on Maurice Sendak's Mickey (Sendak, 1970), or those of us who substitute *Negro* for *nigger* in Twain's books—or employ other euphemisms rather than reading the author's exact words. Each of us must set our own bar—and be ready to justify what we read in class and why we do it.

There are too many facets to censorship to discuss them all in a single chapter. But the bottom line is that each time a book is censored, even if we are not aware that it has happened, we are a bit poorer for the loss. Brinkley (1999) quotes the National PTA's position that censorship is dangerous because it "denies students the right to explore ideas and to make informed, rational judgments. In the long run, it also reduces their capacity to adjust to a changing world" (p. 46).

Oh, and by the way, the book that agitated Mr. C's parent so much? *Julie of the Wolves* (George, 1972), the 1973 Newbery Award winner and number 32 on the ALA most challenged books of the 1990s (ALA, n.d.). The parent did not want her son "thinking so much," but imagination and critical thinking are vital ingredients in education, and literature is essential to both. "The missing ingredient in the making of knowledge . . . is the power of the imagination, and literature offers a vital arena for exploring and developing [it]" (Agee, 1994, pp. 61–62). The more we allow censors to dictate what can be taught, what can be read, watched, or discussed, the more limited our students' world knowledge will be.

Conclusion

If we think positively—intellectual freedom is a right and a privilege that we must protect—we will be prepared for any situation. We will ensure that our schools and libraries have a board-approved book selection policy and if parents or community members challenge our curriculum or collections, that this policy is followed. We will prepare thoroughly and thoughtfully by writing rationales for any books in our classrooms, books we teach or read aloud. We will be prepared with multiple texts because one size seldom fits all—especially in young people. And we will remember Thomas Jefferson's words, published on the 2005 ALA's Banned Books Week poster:

"If [a] book be false in its facts, disprove them; if false in its reasoning, refute it. But, for God's sake, let us freely hear both sides, if we choose."—Thomas Jefferson to N. G. Dufief, 1814 (Coates, 2001).

Works Cited

Agee, H. (1994). Literature, intellectual freedom, and the ecology of the imagination. In J. E. Brown (Ed.), *Preserving intellectual freedom: Fighting censorship in our schools* (pp. 53–62). Urbana, IL: National Council of Teachers of English.

Agee, J. (1999). "There it was, that one sex scene": English teachers on censorship. *English Journal, 89*(2), 61–69.

American Library Association. (n.d.). *100 most frequently challenged books: 1990–1999*. Retrieved from http://www.ala.org/ala/issuesadvocacy/banned/frequentlychallenged/challengedbydecade/1990_1999/index.cfm

American Library Association. (2006a). *Banned books week 2006*. Retrieved from http://www.ala.org/ala/newspresscenter/mediapresscenter/presskits/bannedbooksweek2006/bbwpk06.cfm

American Library Association. (2006b). *Harry Potter tops list of most challenged books of 21st century*. Retrieved from http://www.ala.org/ala/newspresscenter/news/press releases2006/september2006/harrypottermostchallenge.cfm

American Library Association. (2006c). *Intellectual freedom manual* (7th ed.). Chicago: Author.

American Library Association. (2007). "And Tango makes three" *tops ALA's 2006 list of most challenged books*. Retrieved from http://www.ala.org/ala/newspresscenter/news/pressreleases2007/march2007/mc06.cfm

American Library Association. (2008, July). *Tango* tops "most challenged" list for second year. *Newsletter on Intellectual Freedom, 133*, 164–165. Retrieved from https://members.ala.org/nif/v57n4/tango.html

American Library Association. (2010). *Number of challenges by year, reason, initiator and institution (1990–2009)*. Retrieved from http://www.ala.org/ala/issuesadvocacy/banned/frequentlychallenged/challengesbytype/index.cfm

Asheim, L. (1953). *Not censorship but selection*. Retrieved from http://www.ala.org/ala/aboutala/offices/oif/basics/notcensorship.cfm

Brinkley, E. H. (1999). *Caught off guard: Teachers rethinking censorship and controversy*. Boston: Allyn and Bacon.

Coates, E. R., Sr. (Ed.). (1995). *Thomas Jefferson on politics and government: Quotations from the writings of Thomas Jefferson*. Retrieved from http://etext.virginia.edu/jefferson/quotations/index.html

Daniels, H. (2002). *Literature circles: Voice and choice in book clubs and reading groups* (2nd ed.). Portland, ME: Stenhouse.

Donelson, K. L. (1994). Ten steps toward the freedom to read. In J. S. Simmons (Ed.), *Censorship: A threat to reading, learning, thinking* (pp. 231–242). Newark, DE: International Reading Association.

Donelson, K. L., & Nilsen, A. P. (1980). *Literature for today's young adults*. Glenview, IL: Scott, Foresman.

Doyle, R. P. (2008). *Books challenged or banned in 2007–2008*. Retrieved from http://www.ala.org/ala/issuesadvocacy/banned/bannedbooksweek/ideasandresources/free_downloads/2008banned.pdf

Herrold, K., & O'Donnell, K. (2008). *Parent and family involvement in education, 2006–07 school year* (NCES 2008-050). Washington, DC: National Center for Education Statistics, Institute of Education Sciences, US Department of Education.

Hoover-Dempsey, K. V., Walker, J. M. T., Sandler, H. M., Whetsel, D., Green, C. L., Wilkins, A. S., & Closson, K. (2005). Why do parents become involved? Research findings and implications. *Elementary School Journal, 106*, 105–130.

National Council of Teachers of English. (2008). *SLATE: Support for the Learning and Teaching of English.* Retrieved from http://www.ncte.org/action/slate

Nilsen, A. P., & Donelson, K. L. (2009). *Literature for today's young adults* (8th ed.). Boston: Pearson.

Noll, E. (1994). The ripple effect of censorship: Silencing in the classroom. *English Journal, 83*(8), 59–64.

Paratore, J. R., & McCormack, R. L., (Eds.). (1997). *Peer talk in the classroom: Learning from research.* Newark, DE: International Reading Association.

Pavonetti, L. M. (1997). *The implications of culturally mediated definitions of reading on motivation and pedagogy* (Doctoral dissertation). University of Houston, Houston, TX.

Pavonetti, L. M. (2002). It seems important that we should have the right to read . . . . *Journal of Children's Literature, 28*(1), 9–15.

Pavonetti, L. M., Brimmer, K. M., & Cipielewski, J. F. (2002–2003). Accelerated Reader: What are the lasting effects on the reading habits of middle school students exposed to Accelerated Reader in elementary grades? *Journal of Adolescent and Adult Literacy, 46*, 300–311.

Raphael, T. E., Pardo, L. S., Highfield, K., & McMahon, S. I. (1997). *Book club: A literature-based curriculum.* Littleton, MA: Small Planet Communications.

Reichman, H. (2001). *Censorship and selection: Issues and answers for schools* (3rd ed.). Chicago: American Library Association.

Saltman, J. (1998). Censoring the imagination: Challenges to children's books. *Emergency Librarian, 25*(3), 8–12.

Simmons, J. S. (Ed.). (1994). *Censorship: A threat to reading, learning, thinking.* Newark, DE: International Reading Association.

Sipe, R. B. (1999). Don't confront censors, prepare for them. *Education Digest, 64*(6), 42–46.

Trelease, J. (2006). *The read-aloud handbook* (6th ed.). New York: Penguin.

Trelease, J. (2009). *Censors and children's literature: When and what is "inappropriate"?* Retrieved from http://www.trelease-on-reading.com/censor8.html#inappropriate

West, M. I. (1997). *Trust your children: Voices against censorship in children's literature* (2nd ed.). New York: Neal-Schuman.

Children's Books Cited

Cole, B. (1997). *The facts speak for themselves.* Asheville, NC: Front Street.

Cormier, R. (1974). *The chocolate war.* New York: Pantheon Books.

George, J. C. (1972). *Julie of the wolves* (J. Schoenherr, Illus.). New York: Harper and Row.

Giff, P. R. (2002). *Pictures of Hollis Woods*. New York: Random House/Wendy Lamb Books.

Grimes, N. (2006). *The road to Paris*. New York: G. P. Putnam's, Sons.

Paterson, K. (1978). *The great Gilly Hopkins*. New York: Crowell.

Richardson, J., & Parnell, P. (2005). *And Tango makes three* (H. Cole, Illus.). New York: Simon and Schuster.

Rylant, C. (1982). *When I was young in the mountains* (D. Goode, Illus.). New York: Dutton.

Sendak, M. (1970). *In the night kitchen*. New York: Harper and Row.

Woodson, J. (2003). *Locomotion*. New York: G. P. Putnam's Sons.

Keeping the Passion for Literature Alive in Today's Classrooms

12

LETTIE K. ALBRIGHT, *Texas Woman's University*

> Now I lay me down to rest,
> And hope to pass tomorrow's test,
> If I should die before I wake,
> That's one less test I have to take.

Teachers have the privilege and responsibility of helping children discover the joy of reading. Unfortunately, as teachers and librarians in this country have faced the testing demands of the No Child Left Behind Act and of their own states, they increasingly find that time spent with mandated curricular programs and test preparation replaces children's extended time with actual literature. Concerned with the trend of a lessening role of children's books in today's test-oriented classrooms, the National Council of Teachers of English adopted a proposal by CLA for a *Resolution on the Essential Roles and Value of Literature in the Curriculum* (NCTE, 2006). This position statement affirms the

- Value of reading and literature for appreciation, learning and enjoyment
- Critical need of instilling in young people a love of literature and reading for its own sake
- Important and critical roles that children's and young adult literature should play in the classroom (para. 5)

Building on this resolution, Janelle Mathis and I (2007) focused the 2006 Master Class on this essential issue. During the session, two professors, Kathy Short of the University of Arizona and Nancy Roser of University of Texas at Austin, and two children's book authors, Candace Fleming and Jim Murphy, discussed their thoughts on the current environment. In this chapter, I first provide an overview of the current issues and then share insights into theoretical and practical ideas and suggestions from the speakers and others for teachers, librarians, and college professors who want to continue using literature in classrooms dominated by testing and standards.

Standards, Tests, and Pressures

In 2001, the No Child Left Behind Act (NCLB) was established to create accountability and high standards for all schools—arguably notable goals. However, in implementation, it often resulted in a narrowing of the curriculum due to penalties for schools not meeting the requirements and to its emphasis on "scientifically based research," which directly or indirectly limited the types of materials schools could use for reading instruction. Barbara Lehman (2009) asserted that the impact has "left little room for exemplary teaching practices . . . such as literature discussions, reading aloud, response to literature, literary study, and the use of nonfiction and multicultural literature" (p. 196).

At the Master Class, Nancy Roser reminded us that current state standards across the United States reveal "evidence of value for literature instruction and for children's literary meaning-making" (Mathis & Albright, 2007, p. 3). However, she also noted a new wave of attention to and scrutiny of standards and the curriculum, which threatens extinction of standards that are not "measurable." Some critics, pundits, policymakers, and even well-meaning advocates for children are arguing that these standards contain "unclear edges." For example, standards for students in fourth through eighth grades in Texas previously were expected to "describe mental images that texts . . . evoke" and "compare text events with . . . experiences," comprehension strategies supported by research. However, in the 2009 revised standards, such strategies were placed in the appendix and addressed within the main document as a means of understanding content of particular genres. The focus and thrust of proposed revisions in some states is on the basics of spelling, grammar, punctuation, and code—lauded as measurable aims identified by "scientific evidence."

Also concerning to educators are mandates that dictate the content students are to "learn" from the children's literature used in the classroom. For example, the new Texas standards expect second-grade students to "identify moral lessons as themes in well-known fables, lessons, myths, or stories." Recently, a member of a state school board made a motion to keep Bill Martin Jr., author of *Brown Bear, Brown Bear, What Do You See?* (1967) and many other popular books, out of the third-grade social studies curriculum because she thought that Martin had written books for adults that include "very strong critiques of capitalism and the American system" (Shurley, 2010, para. 3). Not only did the board member identify the wrong man—this Bill Martin is not the same Bill Martin who wrote the adult books—but the reasoning for the removal in the first place suggests censorship of content and the implied message that children should only be exposed to particular perspectives.

Recent developments in policy and mandates will further impact the role of children's literature in the classroom in ways not yet known. The American Recovery and Reinvestment Act of 2009 has authorized the reform program Race to the Top Fund, a competitive reform program. At the time of this writing, President Obama and members of Congress are working on the reauthorization of the Elementary and Secondary Education Act (also known as NCLB). This review comes amid adamant calls for changes in its structure and after the results of the *Reading First Impact Study: Final Report* (Gamse, Jacob, Horst, Boulay, & Unlu, 2008), which shows no consistent or significant impact of the program on reading comprehension test scores. Furthermore, the *Common Core State Standards Initiative* (National Governors, 2010), led by governors and state school officers, has resulted in a national set of standards for reading and math from kindergarten through grade 12. These efforts will likely further influence classroom instruction and the role of children's literature in that instruction. Some are hopeful that future changes may further support students' engagement with authentic literature (Lehman, 2009).

Currently, however, many scholars of children's literature have expressed concern with the negative impact of NCLB and the high-stakes testing environment on the role of children's literature in classrooms (e.g., Hickman, 2008; Lehman, 2009; Lehr, 2008; Scharer, Freeman, & Lehman, 2008). During the Master Class, Kathy Short revealed that she finds herself in conversations with teachers today she has not had in 25 years—concerns about finding space for literature within mandates. During these talks, experienced teachers often express frustration at being forced to teach in ways that are not meaningful for their students, and new teachers, who have been told the basal is the way to teach reading, begin asking, "Is that all there is?"

Children's book authors also acknowledge the pressures of the changing environments of both teaching and writing literature. Even school visits may present challenges, according to Candace Fleming, author of many books, including *Clever Jack Takes the Cake* (2010), the award-winning *The Great and Only Barnum: The Tremendous, Stupendous Life of Showman P. T. Barnum* (2009), *The Lincolns: A Scrapbook Look at Abraham and Mary* (2008), and *Our Eleanor: A Scrapbook Look at Eleanor Roosevelt's Remarkable Life* (2005), as well as the beloved *Boxes for Katje* (2003) and *Muncha! Muncha! Muncha!* (2002). During the session, she shared that officials often tell her that visits cannot take place in February, since that month is dedicated to preparing for March testing. Furthermore, she often receives invitations that include specific requests to address items on state tests, such as the five-paragraph essay, the six traits of writing, Venn diagrams comparing and contrasting her stories, and story pyramids. Amazingly, Fleming shared, "More than once I was uninvited after it was determined that a visit from me would *not* reinforce learning standards." She was quick to note, "It would have, however, reinforced the joy of story, the exuberance of putting words to paper, and the thrill of using imagination" (qtd. in Mathis & Albright, 2007, p. 2).

Fleming admitted that, unfortunately, she notices the subtle effects on a writer who believes "that writing from my heart is the only way I can give something of lasting value to my reader" (qtd. in Mathis & Albright, 2007, p. 3). The current trends are raising questions as she works on a book—concerns as to the book's worth as a classroom tool, whether the school librarian will purchase it, or whether a classroom teacher will share it with a class in light of the six traits or other required writing topics. She also wonders if readers will have time to read a book that is an honest interpretation of the world and if her books will be considered "true learning." She acknowledges the need to guard against this kind of thinking—to guard against writing to the test—and to continue to acknowledge her personal need to offer something special for children.

Finally, children are also aware of the impact of these changes. Fleming's book *The Fabled Fourth Graders of Aesop Elementary School* (2007) focuses on those events most familiar to fourth graders, and, therefore, includes a short chapter on testing. When she received the poem at the beginning of this chapter from a fifth-grade fan, she worried, "When kids begin poking fun at the testing environment; when testing has passed into the folklore of childhood like school lunches and burping the alphabet, you know it's left an indelible mark. It's become part of their everyday existence" (qtd. in Mathis & Albright, 2007, p. 2).

In response to teachers' question of whether the basal is "all there is," Kathy Short replies with an adamant "no," because "we know that engagements with literature can challenge children to connect and reflect on their identities, consider new ideas, question what is, imagine what might be, and open up the world" (qtd. in Mathis & Albright, 2007, p. 4). So, as Roser asked in the Master Class session, what can we who share books with children, intent upon helping them to read, write, imagine, and take action in their world, do in light of this current situation? She reminded us that, despite the pressures of increasingly high-stakes tests, many informed teachers continue to help students achieve access to texts and make room for classroom inquiry and literary meaning-making even within the constraints of local, state, and national standards. In the following section, I share some of these ways of making children's literature an integral part of the curriculum.

Insights from Children's Literature Experts: Theory, Growth, Autonomy, and Instructional Decisions

Children's literature specialists provide many helpful suggestions for educators working in today's schools based on knowledge of theory and teaching, the current testing environment, and the field of children's literature. This volume contains a wealth of suggestions related to helping educators develop passion, connoisseurship, and generativity in their efforts to share the wonderful world of children's literature with their students. In the following section, additional suggestions are offered that specifically address the current climate of high-stakes testing and standards. These insights center on articulating a theory for the use of children's literature in today's classrooms, engaging in professional growth and autonomy, and making wise instructional decisions.

Articulating a Theory

To explain and argue for classroom and library instructional practices that ensure children's opportunities to interact with literature, educators first need to be able to express a firm theoretical foundation. Many theories have been discussed in this book and provide invaluable support for today's educators. Moreover, Barbara Lehman, in a 2009 *Language Arts* column on policy, suggested that we particularly need a strong theory in today's testing environment. She reiterated the literary framework described in her book *Children's Literature and Learning: Literary Study Across the Curriculum* (2007), in which she argued that the current focus on literacy outcomes does not exclude "literary goals and experiences"; they "are often compatible—that learning to read can (and *should*) be learned by learning to read *literarily* (Lehman, 2009, p. 198). In this framework, Lehman (2007, 2009) illustrated how literary and child development theories merge to support the incorporation of children's literature across the curriculum. She showed how teachers can use the relationships among literary and literacy concepts (for example, the literary concept of plot and the literacy concept of sequence) to help students develop "literary literacy" (Cai, as cited in Lehman, 2009, p. 198). This framework contributes important ideas to the development of a solid theoretical foundation.

We are not arguing that children's classroom interactions with literature should be relegated to strategy and skill lessons alone. As many in this volume have discussed, children need opportunities to engage with literature for purely personal enjoyment and purposes, to learn about themselves and others, to interpret and respond, to transform them, and to inspire them to work for social justice. In fact, Kathy Short reminded us that comprehension supports these experiences but is not the goal; therefore, we have to compromise some of our beliefs about the role of literature to include it in our classrooms today. Some (e.g., Cooper, 2009) argue that, in the early grades, literature should not even be used for strategy instruction. Cooper explained, however, that she is not purporting that teachers of young children "should refrain from initiating purposeful and incidental observations, conversation, comments, or questions around children's literature that serve comprehension. Young children can learn a lot from a provocative question and classroom discussion" (p. 184). As we develop a theoretical framework that will support the inclusion of children's literature in the classroom, we will need to balance these issues. Clearly, though, with the current testing pressures, we need a theory that addresses the concerns of those creating the mandates while we work with all constituencies to influence and change inappropriate policies.

What can we do next to support a theoretical framework to guarantee children's access to a literary world? Lehman (2009) suggested the following practical steps:

- Find common ground and work collaboratively among the various children's literature fields—education, English, and library and information sciences.
- Make the development of this rationale a priority among those involved.
- Communicate with and educate stakeholders by addressing their questions and issues and "ensuring that "our answers also have practical, hard-headed values underpinning them."
- Advocate by keeping current with research about children's literature and sharing it with teacher candidates, school officials, policymakers, and the general public. (p. 199)

Equipped with theory, research, and practical ideas, educators can more effectively influence the direction of policy and mandates. We can help dispel myths about the incompatibility of using children's literature in the classroom and achieving the goals of state standards and testing.

Engaging in Professional Growth and Autonomy

At the Master Class, Nancy Roser added to the conversation about educator responsibility. She challenged those who share books with children, intent upon helping them to read, write, imagine, and take action in their world, to involve themselves in three critical areas of growth and autonomy by taking the following actions:

- Continue to deepen personal understandings about what helps kids read, write, and think—and share these with others as well. For example, consider collaborating with the school librarian and other faculty members to locate resources, plan instruction, and participate in a teacher book club (Williams & Bauer, 2006).

- Reclaim *assessment* as a term belonging (and critical to) the lexicon of classroom teachers, who can, in turn, demonstrate its pervasive and central role in their instruction. Taking back the term will let educators use it to show their own evidence of children's deepening knowledge, skills, understandings, and effort.

- Teach young teachers to know books (and texts of all types), to know how children navigate their varied pathways to literacy, and to trust the power and potential of books and children in combination. Also, practicing teachers can review their own college-level children's literature courses or enroll in current courses. (Williams & Bauer)

Additionally, educators should be encouraged to become involved in professional organizations, such as NCTE, Children's Literature Assembly, and the American Library Association.

Making Instructional Decisions about Reading and Writing Instruction

Even with the constraints on curriculum that many educators face, teachers can often make varied instructional choices that allow the inclusion of literature in the daily experiences of literacy learners. At the 2006 Master Class, Kathy Short offered suggestions that focus on teaching within, beyond, and outside a traditional basal program. Author Jim Murphy revealed tips on his own writing that can be shared with students.

Outside the Basal Program

Kathy Short suggested that educators offer students alternative opportunities to engage with literature both in other content areas and within the literacy block. An initial recommendation is to find space for literature outside of the literacy block. This can include the following:

- Literature discussions around content area studies. For example, in art class, students could choose to read about artists in biography picture books, such as Jonah Winter's *Frida* (2002), his mother's *My Name Is Georgia: A Portrait by Jeanette Winter* (2003), *Michelangelo* (Stanley, 2003), *Diego: Bigger Than Life* (Bernier-Grand, 2009), *Action Jackson* (about the painter Jackson Pollack; Greenberg & Jordan, 2007), and *The Secret World of Walter Anderson* (winner of the 2010 NCTE Orbis Picture Award for Nonfiction; Bass, 2009). These authors have also written additional biographies of artists that could be included.

- Planning for both teacher read-alouds and independent student reading at other times of the day. For example, during a study of adaptation in science, teachers could read aloud selections from the book *Venom* (Singer, 2007) or include *The Evolution of Calpurnia Tate* (Kelly, 2009), a Newbery Honor Book, in the classroom library.

These ideas reflect the *Resolution on the Essential Roles and Value of Literature in the Curriculum* (NCTE, 2006) that call for a wide range of high-quality literature representing diverse experiences and perspectives integrated into all content areas.

Another approach is to substitute literature for basal stories. This strategy involves reading literature in small groups but using these stories as the basis for teaching the strategies and skills that are part of the basal program. This approach meets the recommendations of NCTE (2006) that (a) reading curricula focus on selecting, reading, responding to, and analyzing a wide range of literature, (b) students engage in deep and extended experiences with full authentic texts rather than with adaptations, and (c) students are guaranteed opportunities to select literature representing a variety of topics and degree of difficulty. This method allows teachers to directly address the components of a basal program while still offering students experiences with authentic literature.

Within the Basal Program

If the use of a basal program is required or chosen, Short reminded us that there are still potential ways of organizing the schedule around literature and the stories within the basal readers.

- While the teacher meets with reading groups, students might read literature independently in place of workbooks, centers, or other methods of keeping students busy at this time.

- The time for the basal lesson might be shortened to three or four days rather than five days, depending on the students' level of engagement with the story. By saving time, a text set of literature that relates to the basal unit can be created and woven throughout the basal unit in the forms of read-alouds, independent reading, and literature discussions. Yet another possibility, since the unit will probably end one to two weeks early, is to include literature at the end of a unit, in the form of a picture book or novel study as a class or in small groups.

- Exchange or add read-alouds to those provided with the basal program.

- Use the basal reader as an anthology or collection of stories. This might take the form of treating the stories in the basal unit as a text set where each child chooses several stories to read and then meets with others for a text set discussion. Since each child has read different stories, the focus is describing what each read and then engaging in discussion to find similarities and differences across the stories.

- In the intermediate grades, the basal readers often contain chapters taken from novels. The basal can be used as a preview source where children read the stories in the basal to decide which novel they want to select for an in-depth novel study.

- Yet another idea is to embed the basal stories in a unit. The unit can be organized around an author, illustrator, topic, genre, or theme. It can begin with a touchstone text—a key piece of children's literature—followed by students then reading widely from many different books related to the focus. The basal stories can be used to examine that focus and end with investigations that take children back to the literature for continued inquiry.

The variety of these suggestions provides educators with options they can consider to fit their many different situations and requirements.

Beyond the Basal Program

Yet another strategy is to use the basal but substitute engagements that involve children in more significant ways than might be called for by the basal program. Kathy Short offered some strategies that might be used.

- Provide a bookmark for readers to write several words that are interesting or difficult as they read. These bookmarks are then used to discuss vocabulary and problem-solve meanings from context, thus eliminating the need for preteaching vocabulary.

- In one fourth-grade basal, it is recommended that students read a story twice in round robin fashion. During the first reading, the teacher models comprehension strategies and then asks comprehension questions after the second reading. As an alternative to this procedure, the class might read the story the first time as partners engaged in the "Say Something" strategy. This could then be followed by a class discussion that results in a list of questions that students are still wondering about related to the story. The second reading of the story involves each set of partners exploring chosen questions and sharing their findings with the larger group.

- One fifth-grade teacher substitutes literature but also provides more significant engagements. He spends the first 30 minutes of the literacy time reading aloud and doing think-alouds of his reading strategies as students follow along in their own copies of the book. Students also read to pre-K children to work on fluency and to engage in reading broadly from many different types of materials. The basal reader itself is set up in a listening center.

A final suggestion is to use the basal occasionally as a source of stories. Short told about one first-grade teacher's use of the basal as a collection of stories from which the students choose to read when the teacher is called out of the room or interrupted by a visitor. Other teachers keep the basal on the bookshelf as an occasional source of short stories for independent reading or reading-strategy work. In these situations, literature is the main reading source with the basal used as a supplement.

Sharing Strategies Used by Children's Literature Authors

When students discover that authors make careful choices throughout their process of writing a book, they are introduced to authentic literacy situations they then can emulate. While acknowledging the impact of the current environment on their writing, Master Class speakers Candace Fleming and Jim Murphy both strive to engage readers by conducting thorough research, carefully considering their own writing choices, building upon students' interests, and fostering connections. Murphy is the author of many acclaimed nonfiction books, including *The Crossing: How George Washington Saved the American Revolution* (2010), *An American Plague: The True and Terrifying Story of the Yellow Fever Epidemic of 1793* (2003), and *The Great Fire* (1995). Among his many awards are the ALA 2010 Margaret A. Edwards Award for contributions to young adult literature,

Newbery Honor Book Awards, the Robert J. Sibert Informational Book Honor Award, and the NCTE Orbis Pictus for Outstanding Nonfiction for Children Awards. Educators may use ideas from this masterful writer to help foster interest in reading, writing, inquiry, and other literacy activities.

Murphy explained that his creations for children begin with research, and he contemplates just how to present interesting, shocking facts or personalized accounts he finds in primary source archives. For example, *The Long Road to Gettysburg* (1992) illustrates how his description of two young men at Gettysburg brings readers personally into the horrors of the battlefield. In *An American Plague*, Murphy uses realistic descriptions of black vomit and immense bowel movements to make readers aware of why the people involved with the yellow fever epidemic of 1793 were consumed by fear—a fear so great that all the major government figures ran away. Murphy emphasized his efforts to tell the most important elements but also to use historical contingency as a means to engage the reader: If one person had acted differently, what would this mean for history? Such a focus on "people making choices" and "choices making a difference" creates a sense of relevancy for readers and gives literature life in contemporary times. What better way of creating a love of literature and especially nonfiction!

The author also focuses on surprising the reader and bringing out those contextual facts that often lie dormant in most accounts but are interesting to readers. Furthermore, when writing, Murphy often envisions a reader who does not care about the topic. He tells himself, "Whatever you do, write visually!" and through such images, he invites readers to become part of history's context. For example, in *An American Plague*, the reader becomes part of a mysterious event unsolvable by even the best medical minds at the time. Since it is not until the last chapter that Murphy shines the light of modern knowledge on the event, the reader is part of this mystery throughout the book.

Illustrations play a major role in many works of literature; therefore, it is important to consider how students respond to them and might learn to make use of them in their own works. For example, Murphy uses illustrations in *An American Plague* that add information and call for inferences not presented in the main text. Children might be intrigued to learn that, although there were many artists in 1793, amazingly not one drawing of the disease exists since most people fled the scene; Murphy included illustrations from other epidemics and public notices. Students can learn to emulate Murphy's love of research and his focus on engaging the reader.

Murphy's delight in this work represents a significant source of connections for young readers—connections that are critical in creating and maintaining a love of literature.

Many other authors have written about their writing processes and one good resource is the website *Suffolk Web: Places for Kids and Teens: Autobiographies: Children's Authors and Illustrators*, which contains an annotated list of children's book author and illustrator autobiographies.

With collaboration, reflection, and careful decision making, educators can find ways to bring together students and children's literature. Ways of including literature in the classroom can occur outside, within, and beyond a traditional basal program. They can occur within the context of authentic literary works.

Conclusion

There are many different forces affecting what occurs in classrooms across the United States. Kathy Short presents a realistic and challenging reminder to all teachers about using literature in the classroom:

> Ironically making space for literature within mandates can make our teaching of comprehension stronger, while making true change less likely. We can teach kids how to problem-solve and work with *what is* in an effective and thoughtful manner, but what is missing is teaching kids how to ask new questions and to ask *why* things are the way they are and to imagine in order to consider new possibilities. We must be careful that in trying to cope with mandates, we fail to challenge and so eliminate the possibility of real change, both in classrooms and in the world. Our compromises should not eliminate dialogue with others around a book in order to create possibilities for transforming self and the world. (qtd. in Mathis & Albright, 2007, p. 6)

This concept of social justice underlies the ideas in this chapter and is crucial to our work with children's literature. We must help children become critical readers of texts so they themselves can strive for a better world. They should have chances to hear, read, and critique multiple perspectives, to avoid what author Chimamanda Adichie (2009) calls "the danger of a single story" about a person, place, or culture. Furthermore, professors, teachers, and librarians must also work for what is right for our children. Above all, we must remember that no curricular decisions made in light of any mandate or test can change the fact that children have a basic right to read. We must continue to advocate for this right and to fight for children's extended time with quality literature. There is renewed hope that we can foster in our children an enduring, lifelong love of literature.

Works Cited

Adichie, C. (2009, July). *Chimamanda Adichie: The danger of a single story* [Video file]. Retrieved from http://www.ted.com/talks/chimamanda_adichie_the_danger_of_a_single_story.html

Cooper, P. M. (2009). Children's literature for reading strategy instruction: Innovation or interference? *Language Arts, 86*, 178–187.

Gamse, B. C., Jacob, R. T., Horst, M., Boulay, B., & Unlu, F. (2008). *Reading first impact study: Final report* (NCEE 2009-4038). Washington, DC: National Center for Education Evaluation and Regional Assistance, Institute of Education Sciences, US Department of Education.

Hickman, J. H. (2008). Half a century of children's literature and reading. In M. J. Fresch (Ed.), *An essential history of current reading practices* (pp. 144–156). Newark, DE: International Reading Association.

Lehman, B. A. (2007). *Children's literature and learning: Literary study across the curriculum.* New York: Teachers College Press.

Lehman, B. A. (2009). Children's literature in a testing time. *Language Arts, 86*, 196–200.

Lehr, S. S. (Ed.). (2008). *Shattering the looking glass: Challenge, risk, and controversy in children's literature.* Norwood, MA: Christopher-Gordon.

Mathis, J. B., & Albright, L. K. (2007). Keeping the love of literature alive in this high-stakes testing environment. *Journal of Children's Literature, 33*(1), 14–19.

National Council of Teachers of English. (2006). *Resolution on the Essential Roles and Value of Literature in the Curriculum.* Retrieved from http://www.ncte.org/positions/statements/valueofliterature

National Governors Association Center for Best Practices & Council of Chief State School Officers (2010). *Common Core State Standards Initiative.* Retrieved from http://corestandards.org/

Scharer, P. L., Freeman, E. B., & Lehman, B. A. (2008). Children's literature in the classroom: Essential or marginal? In S. S. Lehr (Ed.), *Shattering the looking glass: Challenge, risk, and controversy in children's literature* (pp. 15–26). Norwood, MA: Christopher-Gordon.

Shurley, T. (2010, January 25). Name confusion gets kid's author banned from Texas curriculum. *Dallas Morning News.* Retrieved from http://www.dallasnews.com/sharedcontent/dws/news/texassouthwest/stories/DN-books_25tex.ART.State.Edition1.4ba2046.html

Williams, N. L., & Bauer, P. T. (2006). Pathways to affective accountability: Selecting, locating, and using children's literature in elementary school classrooms. *The Reading Teacher, 60*, 14–22.

Children's Literature Cited

Bass, H. (2009). *The secret world of Walter Anderson* (E. B. Lewis, Illus.). Cambridge, MA: Candlewick Press.

Bernier-Grand, C. T. (2009). *Diego: Bigger than life* (D. Diaz, Illus.). Tarrytown, NY: Marshall Cavendish.

Fleming, C. (2002). *Muncha! Muncha! Muncha!* (G. B. Karas, Illus.). New York: Atheneum Books.

Fleming, C. (2003). *Boxes for Katje* (S. Dressen-McQueen, Illus.). New York: Farrar, Straus and Giroux.

Fleming, C. (2005). *Our Eleanor: A scrapbook look at Eleanor Roosevelt's remarkable life*. New York: Atheneum Books.

Fleming, C. (2007). *The fabled fourth graders of Aesop Elementary School*. New York: Random House/Schwartz and Wade Books.

Fleming, C. (2008). *The Lincolns: A scrapbook look at Abraham and Mary*. New York: Random House/Schwartz and Wade Books.

Fleming, C. (2009). *The great and only Barnum: The tremendous, stupendous life of showman P. T. Barnum* (R. Fenwick, Illus.). New York: Random House/Schwartz and Wade Books.

Fleming, C. (2010). *Clever Jack takes the cake* (G. B. Karas, Illus.). New York: Random House/Schwartz & Wade.

Greenberg, J., & Jordan, S. (2007). *Action Jackson* (R. A. Parker, Illus.). New York: Macmillan/Square Fish.

Kelly, J. (2009). *The evolution of Calpurnia Tate*. New York: Holt.

Martin, B., Jr. (1967). *Brown bear, brown bear, what do you see?* (E. Carle, Illus.). New York: Holt.

Murphy, J. (1992). *The long road to Gettysburg*. New York: Clarion Books.

Murphy, J. (1995). *The great fire*. New York: Scholastic.

Murphy, J. (2003). *An American plague: The true and terrifying story of the yellow fever epidemic of 1793*. New York: Clarion Books.

Murphy, J. (2010). *The crossing: How George Washington saved the American Revolution*. New York: Scholastic.

Singer, M. (2007). *Venom*. Plain City, OH: Darby Creek.

Stanley, D. (2003). *Michelangelo*. New York: HarperCollins.

Winter, J. (2002). *Frida* (A. Juan, Illus.). New York: Scholastic.

Winter, J. (2003). *My name is Georgia*. New York: Voyager Books/Harcourt.

Conclusion

Reflecting on the Master Class
Its Impact on the Field of Children's Literature

APRIL WHATLEY BEDFORD, *University of New Orleans*

LETTIE K. ALBRIGHT, *Texas Woman's University*

In our introductory chapter, we proposed a theory about what the outcomes of children's literature learning should be: passion, connoisseurship, and generativity. This theory could be stated in a number of ways. For example, in their chapter about alternative ways to teach college children's literature courses, Martinez and Roser stated the three goals they identified from examining 55 syllabi that professors have established for their courses. These courses should

- Help teachers develop familiarity with quality children's books broadly representative of our world;
- Support teachers' deeper understandings of literary texts (e.g., texts' power to engage, their qualities and craft, their invitations to respond); and
- Guide teachers toward acquiring instructional strategies that help children to read deeply, interpretively, and joyfully.

We see these goals as aligned with our conceptual framework of passion, connoisseurship, and generativity. We believe that if teachers become highly aware of the range of children's books that are being created to serve as both window and mirror for readers, they will be capable of making productive decisions about how and when to teach with children's literature, the definition of generativity. We also believe that becoming thoroughly familiar with the ways that children's books work through literary study, teachers will develop both the appreciation for and ability to critique children's literature that defines connoisseurship. Finally, we believe that teachers who read "deeply, interpretively, and joyfully" themselves will develop such a passion for children's books that they can't help but pass that passion on to their students.

In this chapter, we will briefly revisit the themes of the previous chapters to situate them within our conceptual framework. We will also pose lingering questions that we continue to ponder as we return to these chapters. Finally, we will conclude this text with a guide to assist teachers in analyzing their own teaching to make it increasingly literature-focused.

Passion

Although all chapters touched in some way on all three strands of our conceptual framework, most focused more heavily on one or two. We do see passion for children's literature as the underlying feature that will cause teachers and librarians *to want* to share their enthusiasm with children, to gain the knowledge that is required of a connoisseur, and to apply that knowledge to making sound decisions about the place of children's literature in curriculum and instruction. We also believe that each author's passion for his or her topic can be clearly felt when reading each chapter in this volume.

Freeman identifies "reading for pleasure" as one of four main areas of concern in her chapter on uses and abuses of children's literature, and certainly reading for pleasure equates with a passion for reading. Martinez and Roser write about the importance of offering "genuine literary experiences" to children, and Hancock discusses the value of invitations for authentic, genuine responses to literature—as opposed to contrived responses such as the ubiquitous "book report"—to ignite passion in child readers.

Two other themes across chapters that relate to passion are reading to develop a sense of identity—the idea of literature as "mirror"—and reading to develop an appreciation for diversity—the idea of literature as "window." A number of chapters touch on the crucial need to make sure that school and classroom libraries include a range of literature that will serve as both mirror and window (Bishop, 1990) and that teachers and librarians incorporate this broad range of literature into their work with children. Chapters by Mathis (on multicultural literature), Bedford (on literature with LGBTQ characters), and Short (on international literature) focus heavily on notions of identity and diversity, and we strongly believe that reading for these two purposes will ignite passion for literature. Specifically, Short describes how she begins her courses in international literature with engagements that help students make personal connections to "interculturalism," and these kinds of individual connections to children's books can develop passionate readers.

The final chapter, by Albright, addresses both the importance of, and strategies for, keeping a passion for children's literature alive in the midst of high-stakes testing, narrow and scripted curricula, and skills-based standards and mandates. This brings us back full circle to the opening chapter by Martinez and Roser, who assert that inherent in the goal of children reading deeply and joyfully is that their teachers will also read joyfully. The concept of adults deriving joy from reading children's books has recently been illuminated by professors outside the field of children's literature (English, 2000; Garner, 2009; Martino, 2008). We believe that the only way that adults—teachers, librarians, even parents—can inspire a passion for literature in children is by joyfully reading children's books themselves.

Connoisseurship

Martinez and Roser cited Sebesta (2001) as saying—jokingly—that a recognized "canon" of children's literature would make the jobs of college instructors of children's literature much easier, but the authors were gratified to find in their examination of 55 syllabi that there is little overlap among the books that professors require students to read in undergraduate and graduate courses in children's literature, indicating that such a canon does not exist. The concept of a canon—as well as the fact that the rapidly expanding body of children's literature defies the existence of one—hints at our call for teachers, librarians, and children to be connoisseurs of children's literature, experts who both appreciate and are able to critique the books they read based on quality. We hope that individual readers will know enough about the literature that exists as well as the criteria for evaluating that literature that they can create their own "personal canons"—an instructional invitation April Bedford has offered to her students.

Connoisseurs must have a depth of knowledge about the range of books that have been and are being published for children, and Freeman focused on educators' knowledge of genres, in addition to how those genres are continually changing, as one of the four major areas of her chapter. Hancock further explored how readers might respond to new genres as well as to new categories of multicultural and global literature, the focus of chapters by Mathis and Short.

Giorgis, Mathis, Bedford, Short, and Lehman all surveyed existing bodies of certain types of literature in their chapters on visual literacy, multicultural literature, books with LGBTQ characters, international literature, and bestselling children's books.

Both Freeman and Lehman considered how children's books have become commodities through commercial merchandising tie-ins to bestselling children's books and television shows and movies based on children's books, among other avenues. Adult connoisseurs of children's literature know how to use this somewhat disturbing trend to their advantage by engaging children in comparing and contrasting examples of excellent literature with film versions, thus developing the skills of critique that are a hallmark of connoisseurship. Albright's chapter offers suggestions for developing connoisseurs by studying the craft and process of authors and illustrators of children's books.

Peter Appelbaum (2008) provides a model for developing connoisseurship in children's literature in *Children's Books for Grown-up Teachers: Reading and Writing Curriculum Theory*. He recommends that educators become deeply engaged with children's books, not as teachers but as readers, and that they then think deeply about how their experiences while reading can become the basis for curricular theorizing. This is different from building a curriculum based on specific texts; Applebaum's work frees teachers from always having to think about how they might "use" a particular children's book to teach specific skills or develop related concepts. Instead, teachers are urged to discuss their experiences as engaged readers of children's books and how those experiences may inform their teaching and their students' learning.

Generativity

Chapter authors touched on generativity—the ability to make productive decisions—in a variety of ways. Most of the authors referred to the theoretical underpinnings of our work in children's literature, and we firmly believe that teachers and librarians will make more productive decisions if their decisions are guided by sound theory. Louise Rosenblatt's reader response theory was the most frequently mentioned as the basis for teaching and studying children's literature; Marjorie Hancock provided a thorough review of Rosenblatt's theory and how it has informed her work in the area of responding to literature.

Rosenblatt's reader response theory has often been cited, too, as the basis for literature-based elementary and middle school classrooms (and appropriately so), but a common criticism of the way in which some teachers have interpreted this theory is that *any* connection a child makes to a book is fine, a sort of "anything goes" approach. This is not our interpretation of Rosenblatt; instead, we apply her theory by asking children to support their connections to texts by referring back to the texts themselves. Martinez and Roser argue that as college instructors of children's literature, we need to prepare teachers so that they can trust themselves and the children they teach to make astounding and *supported* observations about books.

A large component of Rosenblatt's theory involves purpose for reading, with readers sometimes assuming an *efferent* stance—reading to take away specific information—and sometimes assuming an *aesthetic* stance—reading for pure enjoyment. We believe that knowing which stance to assume during any particular reading event is another decision that generative readers are able to make with confidence. This aspect of generativity applies to both adult and child readers.

Critical theory is a second theory informing a number of chapters in this volume. Critical theory supports and is supported by reader response theory in several ways. Hancock describes Rosenblatt's belief in literature as the foundation of democratic education and her own beliefs in how reading promotes democracy, empathy, and "socially empowered response" democracy. Mathis and Short refer to these same principles in their chapters on multicultural literature and international literature, respectively, and discuss in detail how they hope that reading a diverse range of children's literature will inspire both adult and child readers to take action for social justice. CLA members Junko Yokota and Mingshui Cai, in a 2002 issue of *Language Arts*, recommended several children's books that promote critical literacy and social justice; Mathis, Bedford, and Short all include several more recent titles in their chapters. Additionally, Yokota and Cai provided information about the Jane Addams Children's Book Award that annually recognizes the best children's literature for promoting peace, equality, and social justice, more information about which can be found on the website of the Jane Addams Peace Association.

Professionals who are generative also know how to apply selection strategies to decide when and how best to use the tools that are available to help them teach with and about children's literature; which books to include in their classroom or school libraries; and how and for what purposes to share particular books with particular children. Technology has perhaps provided the greatest number of tools that have changed, and are continuing to change, the field of children's literature most rapidly. Martinez and Roser; Freeman; Hancock; and Mathis all describe a variety of ways in which technology has affected the teaching of children's literature, and Vardell's entire chapter is devoted to this topic. We realize that it is quite likely that by the time this book is in print, there will already be changes or advances in technology not familiar to these authors at the time their chapters were written.

Young, McDuffie, and Ward provide a model, specifically designed to help teachers choose books to help young readers develop mathematical concepts, that includes examples of books that are less than stellar. We believe that connoisseurs of children's literature will be able to recognize the quality of books, and that generative professional will also be able to recognize when it might be appropriate to include them in instruction. Young, McDuffie, and Ward describe how to support teachers in these types of decisions and suggest that the poorer the quality of a book teachers choose to share with children, the more support teachers will need to give students in learning from that book. We believe this model can be applied to any type of book and especially recommend using it when considering bestselling and celebrity-authored children's books discussed by Lehman.

Pavonetti deals specifically with selecting books for classroom (selected by the teacher) and school (selected by the librarian) libraries and responding to would-be censors who challenge the assignment of a particular book for instruction or the inclusion of a book in the library. Teachers and librarians will potentially face all of these kinds of decisions, and they need to be generative in their responses. We believe that generativity is largely dependent on trust, as mentioned by Martinez and Roser in their opening chapter; teachers and librarians must provide environments and instruction that allow them to trust in the children with whom they work to know their preferences and abilities as readers, and that trust begins with the adults who guide these children to trust their own abilities as capable, generative professionals.

Albright relied heavily in her chapter on the resolutions created by NCTE in supporting teachers to work within the strictures of mandates while also working to change those mandates that do not recognize the value of literature. In addition to the theoretical (and practical) supports for teaching from a literature-based perspective cited throughout this book, and policy statements such as those created by NCTE, teachers and librarians must be familiar with research about the benefits of children's literature in the classroom, because they may be asked to cite research for their professional decisions. While numerous classroom-based studies of children's literature in both K–8 and college classrooms have been published, a good place to start in helping prospective and practicing educators become familiar with this body of work is with the reviews of research found in the various handbooks that have proliferated over the past 15 years. Reviews of research about children's literature can be found in the *Handbook of Early Childhood Literacy* (Hall, Larson, & Marsh, 2003); *Handbook of Research on Teaching the English Language Arts* (Flood, Lapp, Squire, & Jensen, 2003); and the *Handbook of Research on Teaching Literacy through the Communicative and Visual Arts* (Flood, Heath, & Lapp, 2005); and we are particularly excited about the forthcoming *Handbook of Research on Children's and Young Adult Literature* that will be the first work of its kind to synthesize research in children's literature from the fields of education, English, and library science.

Three research-based reports published in the last decade by the National Endowment for the Arts (2004, 2007, 2009) have informed and will likely continue to inform the policies related to children's literature established by NCTE and other professional organizations. Among many others, the research of Stephen Krashen provides compelling evidence for promoting self-selected, independent reading of children's literature in elementary and middle school classrooms. An overview of his work with links to specific studies may be found on his website at www.sdkrashen.com.

Lingering Questions

As we reflect on the issues addressed in the Master Class and throughout this book, we are left with lingering questions related to some of the chapters. We recognize that essentially all of the topics, but especially those related to technology and to children's literature as bestsellers, are "moving targets" that may have changed greatly by the time this book is in print. Here are some of our specific concerns.

Martinez and Roser noted a lack of field work on the syllabi they examined. We believe the sooner prospective teachers and librarians can be "in the field" reading aloud and sharing books with children, the better, and these beliefs are supported by Hoewisch (2000). We are, therefore, concerned that field experience does not seem to be a major focus of a number of college children's literature courses. We are also alarmed by the lack of multicultural books required on syllabi examined by Martinez and Roser. This could be an issue of awareness, because the children's literature instructors we know are deeply committed to promoting social justice and appreciate for diversity; however, it is possible that instructors have not analyzed their own syllabi and course requirements to determine whether their beliefs are being actualized by the assignments they make.

Freeman, in her chapter, mentioned a survey that suggested that 73 percent of youth surveyed do, in fact, read for pleasure daily. While this is a hopeful statistic, we wonder how the number of students breaks down across ethnicity or socioeconomic status. In other words, are 73 percent of American youth from *any* ethnic, linguistic, cultural, gender, or socioeconomic background reading for pleasure daily, or does this statistic tend to be more representative of some groups than others? We know that this survey applied to reading that students were choosing to do, on their own, outside of school, but we also wonder what particular school policies, teachers, and librarians might be doing to encourage this reading behavior. These are areas ripe for further inquiry.

Giorgis provided exceptional guidance for learning more about visual literacy, providing a model for just the type of connoisseurship we are advocating. We wonder how many children's literature professors have as much specialized knowledge on this topic. We also wonder how many are able to devote ample time to this topic in a single introductory course on children's literature since, in some places, "The Art of the Picture Book" is a separate course. Continually developing our own knowledge of subjects such as visual literacy is the basis for the Master Class that was designed for children's literature professors. In addition to the numerous resources provided by Giorgis, we would also like to recommend two books that can be resources for both adults and children: *Artist to Artist: 23 Major Illustrators Talk to Children about Their Art* (Gauch, Briggs, Palmer, & Steurer, 2007), and *A Caldecott Celebration: Seven Artists and Their Paths to the Caldecott Medal* (Marcus, 2008). A professional resource for teachers and librarians would be the Spring 2005 themed issue of the *Journal of Children's Literature* on "Special Collections of Children's Literature, Book Illustrations, and Picture Book Art." We also recommend perusing the websites of the Mazza Museum for International Art from Picture Books and the Eric Carle Museum of Picture Book Art.

Bedford's chapter on children's books with lesbian, gay, bisexual, transgender, and questioning/queer characters dealt with perhaps the most controversial subject at the present time. We continue to ask ourselves how—and if—we would share these books in classrooms if there were strong parental, administrative, or community objections, despite our strong belief that these books need to be shared with the readers for whom they are intended. We wonder how we can better support teachers and librarians in bringing controversial but vital literature into their classrooms. We ask how we ourselves might respond to the vehement objections of college students like those raised in a class discussion led by Jill Hermann-Wilmarth (2010) and look to this recent article for help in answering these questions.

We acknowledged in our introduction that few of us are experts in international children's literature. Short provided excellent strategies that we are eager to try in our own teaching, and we will investigate the resources she recommended. We do wonder, however, how to acquire a large number of the different types of international books she defined, particularly those not written in nor translated into English. We also question how many of us have the funding to build an adequate collection of these expensive but valuable titles.

These are just some of the questions that we are still pondering. We know that readers will have their own questions about the preceding chapters, and we hope that those questions will lead to lively and productive conversations with colleagues and perhaps even with children. We invite any interested readers to attend the Master Class in Teaching Children's Literature at the National Council of Teachers of English Annual Convention. In the meantime, we offer some suggestions to help teachers and librarians self-assess their own literature-based teaching and set goals for their own professional growth.

Assessing Our Own Work

In proposing a model to help teachers at any level of their careers to self-assess the inclusion of children's literature in their classrooms, we turn to the work of theorists who have developed similar models to help teachers transform their curriculum and instruction to be thoroughly multicultural (e.g., Banks, 1994; McIntosh, 1983; Savage & Armstrong, 2008). All of these theorists begin by urging teachers to reflect on their awareness of the subject at hand and how they incorporate that knowledge into the decisions they make as professionals related to curriculum, instruction, environment, and other aspects of daily life. To apply these models to teaching with children's literature at the core, we return to those recommendations proposed by Daniel Hade and Rudine Sims Bishop at the 1997 Master Class (Pierce, 1998).

We recommend that teachers ask themselves the following questions related to two areas—building a classroom library and offering instructional invitations—because both of these tasks are ongoing and may require, as well as lead to, further professional development. Questions related to Dan Hade's four "paths" for children's literature include the following:

- How many books in my classroom library inspire awe, wonder, mystery, and delight?
- How many books in my classroom library allow readers to confront issues of pain, suffering, and fear?
- How many books in my classroom library promote pretend play and the development of imagination?
- How many books in my classroom library help develop compassion in readers and prompt action for social justice?

These same questions could then be asked again, addressing how often and in what ways a teacher offers instructional invitations to students surrounding books from each of these four paths.

The next step of this self-assessment requires teachers to analyze their own children's literature collections. For some, the analysis of kinds of books they already own may be brief, especially if they are preservice or beginning teachers; for teachers who have extensive collections, that analysis will take longer. For those with smaller collections, however, more time will be spent in identifying gaps and planning purposeful ways to add to their collections. First, we recommend that teachers identify the genres of literature represented in their classroom libraries. Instead of listing all possible genres here, we refer readers to chapters by Freeman, Hancock, Giorgis, Mathis, and Short as starting points for classifying their books according to traditional, new, and hybrid genres discussed by these authors. Next, we suggest that teachers list both the themes and the content areas they teach and analyze how much of their instruction in those areas already includes literature, how the books in their current collections can be effectively added to those areas, and what types of books they need to add to their collections specifically to enhance their thematic teaching and to include literature across all content areas, as recommended by Rudine Sims Bishop (Pierce, 1998).

Finally, we return to Bishop's (1990) theory of literature as both mirror and window to apply to library-building and instructional engagements. We encourage teachers to examine their collections by asking:

- How many and which books allow specific students to see themselves represented (books as mirror)?
- How many and which books allow all students to better understand and appreciate diversity (books as window)?

We then prompt them to ask:

- How many and what types of instructional invitations have I offered students that will allow them to see themselves represented in books?
- How many and what types of instructional invitations have I offered students that will allow them to better understand and appreciate diversity?

Finally, we urge teachers to ask themselves the following:

- How many opportunities have I given students to select their own books for independent reading?
- How much do I trust students to make decisions about books that are right for them as readers and how have I prepared them to do so?
- How much of my own reading life do I share with my students?
- How often and what ways do I present myself as a co-learner alongside students, engaged in literary learning?

Once teachers have assessed themselves in each of these areas and determined where they need to fill in gaps—in their collections, in their knowledge base, in their teaching and learning—then we hope they will identify opportunities for professional development that will lead them to become passionate, generative connoisseurs of children's literature.

Works Cited

Applebaum, P. (2008). *Children's books for grown-up teachers: Reading and writing curriculum theory*. New York: Routledge.

Banks, J. A. (1994). *An introduction to multicultural education*. Boston: Allyn and Bacon.

Bishop, R. S. (1990). Mirrors, windows, and sliding glass doors. *Perspectives: Choosing and Using Books for the Classroom, 6*(3), ix–xi.

English, L. M. (2000). Children's literature for adults: A meaningful paradox. *PAACE Journal of Lifelong Learning, 9,* 13–23.

Flood, J., Heath, S. B., & Lapp, D. (Eds.). (2005). *Handbook of research on teaching literacy through the communicative and visual arts*. Mahwah, NJ: Lawrence Erlbaum.

Flood, J., Lapp, D., Squire, J. R., & Jensen, J. M. (Eds.). (2003). *Handbook of research on teaching the English language arts*. Mahwah, NJ: Lawrence Erlbaum.

Garner, B. (2009). Children's literature goes to college. *The Toolbox: A Teaching and Learning Resource for Instructors, 8*(3), 1–3.

Gauch, P. L., Briggs, D., Palmer, C., & Steurer, K. (Eds.). (2007). *Artist to artist: 23 major illustrators talk to children about their art*. New York: Philomel Books.

Hall, N., Larson, J., & Marsh, J. (Eds.). (2003). *Handbook of early childhood literacy*. Thousand Oaks, CA: Sage.

Hermann-Wilmarth, J. M. (2010). More than book talks: Preservice teacher dialogue after reading gay and lesbian children's literature. *Lanugage Arts, 87,* 188–198.

Hoewisch, A. K. (2000, February). Children's literature in teacher-preparation programs. *Reading Online*. Retrieved from: http://www.readingonline.org/critical/hoewisch/childrenlit.html

Marcus, L. S. (2008). *A Caldecott celebration: Seven artists and their paths to the Caldecott Medal*. New York: Walker.

Martino, A. (2008). Wonder rediscovered in children's books. *Chronicle of Higher Education, 55*(17), B-28.

McIntosh, P. (1983). *Interactive Phases of Curricular Re-Vision: A Feminist Perspective* (Working Paper No. 124). Wellesley, MA: Wellesley College.

National Endowment for the Arts. (2004). *Reading at risk: A survey of literary reading in America* (Research Division Report No. 46). Retrieved from http://www.nea.gov/pub/ReadingAtRisk.pdf

National Endowment for the Arts. (2007). *To read or not to read: A question of national consequence* (Research Report No. 47). Retrieved from http://www.nea.gov/research/ToRead.pdf

National Endowment for the Arts. (2009). *Reading on the rise: A new chapter in American literacy*. Retrieved from http://www.nea.gov/research/ReadingonRise.pdf

Pierce, K. M. (1998). Uses and abuses of children's literature in the classroom: Master class for teaching college level children's literature courses. *Journal of Children's Literature, 24*(1), 103–105.

Savage, T. V., & Armstrong, D. G. (2008). *Effective teaching in elementary social studies*. (6th ed.). Upper Saddle River, NJ: Pearson.

Sebesta, S. (2001). *What do teachers need to know about children's literature?* The New Advocate, 14, 241–249.

Yokota, J., & Cai, M. (2002). Reading corner for children: Social justice and critical literacy. *Language Arts, 79*, 432–437.

Index

Begler, E., 141
Bernier-Grand, C. T., 206
Bestsellers, children's books as, 151–63
  author preferences among,
    developing, 160
  award-winning, 157–58
  celebrity authors, 152–55
  children's choices of, 159–60
  comparing with movie versions,
    161–62
  fantasy, 157
  movie and marketing tie-ins, 155–56
  passion for, 162–63
  reviews of, 162
  series books, 156–57
  with similar themes, 162
  teacher evaluation of, 159–63
  trends in, 152–58
Betts, W. E., 112
Bevens-Mangelson, J., 167
Bickel, C., 81
Bickers, J., 71
Bilingual texts, 97
Birdseye, T., 87
Bishop, R. S., xvii, xx, xxii, 68, 214, 222
Black, H., 23
Blacker, T., 123
Bleich, D., 46
Blume, J., xv
Bolden, T., 42
Bond, E., 133
Book lists, 103–4
Book logs, 191–93
Boracks, N., 34
Borzumato, xxv, 173
Branding, of children's literature, 23–24,
  156
Brannen, S. S., 116
Bredsdorff, B., 138
Brenner, D., xxi
Bridwell, N., 23
Briggs, D., 220
Brinkley, E. H., 194
Brown, A., 120
Brown, M., 23
Browne, A., 53
Budhos, M. T., 102

Bunting, E., 67
Burch, C., 122
Burnett, F. H., xvi

Cai, M., 93, 217
Caldecott Award winners, art of, 68–69
Cameron, A., 133
Cammack, D. W., 43
Canales, V., 102
Carman, P., 25
Carmi, D., 138
Carpenter, T. P., 85
Carroll, L., 9
Carter, A. L., 144
Carter, J. B., 71
Carvell, M., 100
Case, R., 133
Cast, K., 29
Cast, P. C., 29
Castek, J., 167
Celebrity authors, 152–55
Censorship, 182–89
  definition of, 182
  expression of concern, 183
  intellectual freedom and, 193–95
  oral complaint, 193
  protection against challenges, 189
  public attack, 184
  self-censorship and selection, 185–88
  silent, 188–89
  stealth, 188
  written complaint, 183–84
Cepeda, J., 66
Charlip, R., 74
Chick, K., 112
Child_Lit, 168–69
Children's literature
  as bestsellers, 151–63
  commodification of, 23–24, 155–56
  criticisms of, xvii
  disrupting heteronormativity
    through, 110–11
  electronic databases for, 172, 176
  as family business, 35, 36
  genres of, 27–32
  impact of, xv

Editors

L ettie K. Albright is associate professor of literacy at Texas Woman's University, where she teaches undergraduate and graduate courses. Her research and teaching interests center on literature and literacy across the curriculum and adolescent literacy, including middle school teacher read-alouds. She has published in such varied journals as *Journal of Children's Literature, New Advocate, Booklinks, Research in the Teaching of English,* and *Journal of Adolescent and Adult Literacy.* Albright is president of the Children's Literature Assembly of NCTE and serves on the board of the Children's Literature and Reading Special Interest Group of the International Reading Association (IRA).

April Whatley Bedford is professor and interim dean of the College of Education and Human Development at the University of New Orleans,. She received her Ph.D. from Texas A&M University. Bedford has been coeditor of the *Journal of Children's Literature* and has published book chapters and articles in various journals including *Language Arts, Childhood Education,* and *Book Links.* She is a former board member of the Children's Literature Assembly of NCTE, past president of the Children's Literature and Reading Special Interest Group of IRA, recent chair of the Notable Books for a Global Society committee, and chair of the Notable Children's Books in the Language Arts committee.

Contributors

Evelyn B. Freeman is dean and director of The Ohio State University–Mansfield. She also serves as executive dean for Ohio State's regional campuses. Freeman is a professor in the School of Teaching and Learning and teaches courses in children's literature and language arts. She has served as coeditor of the *Journal of Children's Literature* and *Bookbird: A Journal of International Children's Literature*. Freeman has coauthored three books, numerous book chapters and journal articles, and has presented at professional conferences nationally and internationally. In 2007, Freeman received the Distinguished Service Award from the National Council of Teachers of English. She is immediate immediate past president of the Children's Literature Assembly of NCTE.

Cyndi Giorgis is a professor of literature education at the University of Nevada, Las Vegas where she teaches courses in children's and young adult literature. Her research interests include literature, reader response theories, multi-literacies, and literature discussion in the elementary and secondary classrooms. Giorgis has published multiple books and articles. Her professional roles include coeditor of the *Journal of Children's Literature* and board member of the Children's Literature Assembly of NCTE and the Children's Literature and Reading Special Interest Group of IRA. Giorgis was a member of the 1992 Newbery Award Committee and the 2002 Caldecott Award Committee.

Marjorie R. Hancock is a professor emerita in the Department of Elementary Education at Kansas State University. Her career research focused on Louise Rosenblatt's transactional theory of reader response with all national/international publications and presentations highlighting children's literature and response. She is a former president of the Children's Literature Assembly of NCTE and the author of two children's literature-based textbooks—*A Celebration of Literature and Response* and *Language Arts: Extending the Possibilities*.

Barbara A. Lehman is a professor of teaching and learning at The Ohio State University, where she teaches graduate courses in children's literature and literacy at the Mansfield Campus. Her scholarly interests focus on multicultural and global children's literature and child-centered literary criticism. She wrote *Children's Literature and Learning: Literary Study across the Curriculum* and is coauthor with Evelyn Freeman and Patricia Sharer of *Reading Globally, K–8: Connecting Students to the World through Literature*.

Miriam Martinez is a professor of education at the University of Texas at San Antonio, where she teaches reading and children's literature courses. Her research and publications have focused on the nature of children's literary meaning-making, children's responses to literature, and their understanding of various literary genres and formats. With colleagues she has also conducted research on instructional interventions that affect children's responses and on classroom libraries. Martinez is coauthor of *Children's Books in Children's Hands* and is coeditor of *What a Character!: Character Study as a Guide to Literary Meaning Making* and *Book Talk and Beyond*. She received the Arbuthnot Award from the International Reading Association for outstanding university teacher of children's and young adults' literature.

Janelle B. Mathis is an associate professor at the University of North Texas where she teaches courses in children's literature and sociocultural issues of teaching and learning. A member of the Language and Literacy Studies Program, she is currently involved in research on multimodal response to international children's literature in a middle school classroom and using multigenre text sets to enhance critical literacy. She actively serves the Children's Literature Assembly of NCTE, United States Board on Books for Young People, and the Children's Literature and Reading Special Interest Group of the International Reading Association, in addition to other research organizations and committees.

Amy A. McClure is a professor and chair of the Department of Education at Ohio Wesleyan University. She is especially interested in reading, children's literature (particularly poetry and historical fiction), excellence in elementary teaching, and special education. McClure has published six books including two textbooks on teaching children's literature. Her other publications include numerous articles and book chapters on using literature in the teaching of reading. She is the past president of the Children's Literature Assembly, Children's Literature Board of the International Reading Association, and the Ohio International Reading Association.

Linda M. Pavonetti received her doctorate from the University of Houston and currently teaches children's and young adult literature at Oakland University in Rochester, Michigan. She served on the American Library Association's YALSA Informational Freedom Committee and is a member of the Informational Freedom Round Table. She has been active in the Children's Literature Assembly of NCTE for almost 20 years and is a past president of the United States Board on Books for Young People.

Nancy L. Roser is a professor of language and literacy studies, the Flawn Professor of Early Childhood, and Distinguished Teaching Professor at the University of Texas at Austin. A former elementary teacher, she now teaches undergraduate elementary reading and language arts, as well as graduate courses in teaching the English language arts and children's literature. She is past president of the Children's Literature Assembly. Her research interests include close inspection of children's book conversations in classrooms.

Amy Roth McDuffie is an associate professor in the College of Education at Washington State University Tri-Cities. She teaches mathematics education courses for future and practicing teachers, and her research focuses on supporting teachers' professional development in mathematics. She focuses on professional growth toward more student-centered approaches that incorporate current research and theory on how students come to understand mathematics. Roth McDuffie has published many chapters and articles in books and journals.

Kathy G. Short is a professor of language, reading, and culture at the University of Arizona. Her classroom-based research focuses on reader response, curriculum as inquiry, and international children's literature. Her books include *Creating Classrooms for Authors and Inquirers*, *Literature as a Way of Knowing*, *Talking about Books*, and *Stories Matter: The Complexity of Cultural Authenticity in Children's Literature*. She is the director of Worlds of Words (www.wowlit.org), an initiative to build bridges across global cultures through children's literature, and is president of the US national section of IBBY, the International Board of Books for Young People.

Sylvia M. Vardell is a professor at Texas Woman's University where she teaches graduate courses in children's literature. Her research has focused on nonfiction, poetry, and multicultural children's literature and she is the author of *Children's Literature in Action: A Librarian's Guide*, and other books, chapters, and articles, as well as the blog on sharing poetry with kids (PoetryFor

ChildrenatBlogspot). She has served on several NCTE committees, including the Orbis Pictus, Poetry Award, and Notables committees.

Barbara A. Ward is firmly convinced of the importance of quality literature and incorporates children's and young adult literature in her classroom practices. She earned her Ph.D. at the University of New Orleans and is currently an instructor at Washington State University. She has published many journal articles, and her research interests center on culturally responsive pedagogy and teacher training. She is president-elect of the Children's Literature and Reading Special Interest Group of IRA and a member of the Children's Literature Assembly of NCTE.

Terrell A. Young is a professor at Washington State University where he teaches graduate and undergraduate courses in children's literature and literacy. He has published numerous journal articles and books, including *Matching Books and Readers: Helping English Language Learners in Grades K–6*, with Nancy L. Hadaway, and *Happily Ever After: Sharing Folk Literature with Elementary and Middle School Students*. He is a past president of the Children's Literature Assembly of NCTE.

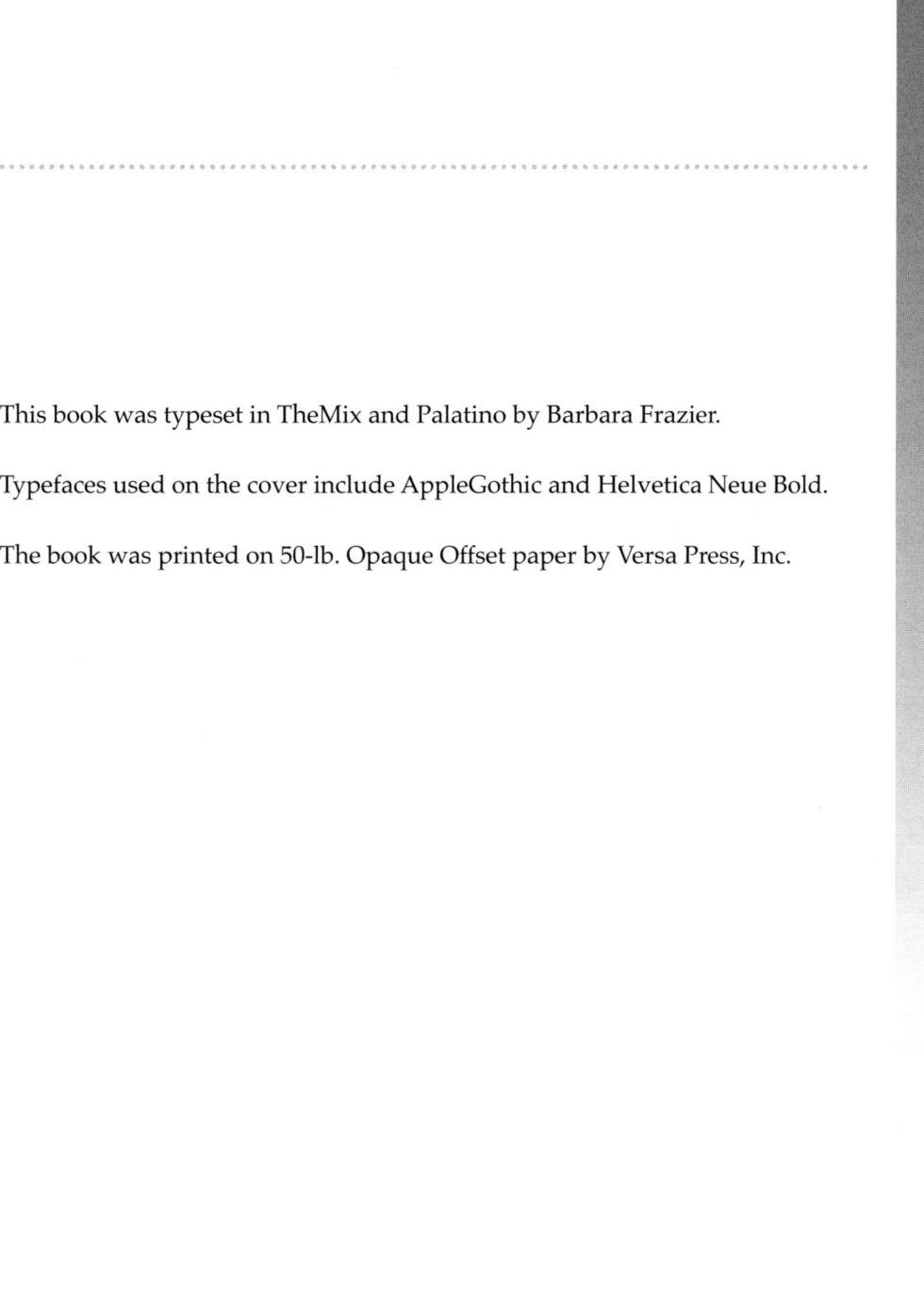

This book was typeset in TheMix and Palatino by Barbara Frazier.

Typefaces used on the cover include AppleGothic and Helvetica Neue Bold.

The book was printed on 50-lb. Opaque Offset paper by Versa Press, Inc.